Secondary educators will cherish this book, as it will promote important conversations in their staff rooms and improved practice in their classrooms. The authors help us reimagine public education with page after page of practical and simultaneously profound ideas. Readers will wish Best Practice High School were just around their corner.

—Shelley Harwayne, Acting Superintendent,
Community School District Two, Manhattan

Anyone who seriously wants to make high schools better should start right here. Organized around the principles of "best practice," Rethinking High School is packed with rich examples of wonderful learning, great teaching, substantive curriculum, democratic organization, and all the other ingredients of a really good school.

—James Beane, Author of *Curriculum Integration: Designing the Core of Democratic Education*

RETHINKING HIGH SCHOOL

The founders, faculty, and some of the students of Best Practice High School:

Left to Right: Alex Chaparro, Joey Collins, Amanda Yeo, Jeanette Malinowski, Deunta Lockett, Marcus Moreno, Zainab Kadzai, Gernell Richardson.

Left to Right, Front: Aaron Howard, Porsha Marcos, Nikia Jones

Back: Teresa Franco, Ruben Bueno, Edgar Rodriguez, Gloria Donoho, Pedro Cano, Elizabeth Hernandez, Edgar Arellano, Patty Salgado.

Left to Right, Front Row: Jenny Cornbleet, Vanessa Breschling, Olga Lamourt, Kathy Daniels, Aiko Boyce, Della Sanford, Beth Meeker, Stephanie Moore

Second Row: Marilyn Bizar, Juanita Tolbert, Melissa Bryant, Arlette Harris, Gwen Downing, Mike Myers, Laura Linhart, Yolanda Simmons

Third Row: Steve Zemelman, Phyllis Curtwright, Tina Peano, Mark Fertel, Theresa Hernandez, Heidi McCaleb, Michelle Dulak, Harvey Daniels

Back Row: Matt Feldman, Tom McDougal, Mike Cannon, Phillip Williams, Carolyn Smith, Peter Thomas, Sonja Kosanovic, Sylvia Gibson, Donnell Epps, Arthur Griffin.

RETHINKING HIGH SCHOOL

Best Practice in Teaching, Learning, and Leadership

Harvey Daniels, Marilyn Bizar, and Steven Zemelman

Center for City Schools

National-Louis University

Chicago, Illinois

Foreword by Deborah Meier

HEINEMANN

Portsmouth, NH

Heinemann
A division of Reed Elsevier Inc.
361 Hanover Street
Portsmouth, NH 03801-3912
www.heinemann.com

Offices and agents throughout the world

Library of Congress Cataloging-in-Publication information is on file.
ISBN: 0-325-00324-6

Editors: Leigh Peake, Bill Varner
Cover photographer: Bob Tanner
Cover design: Catherine Hawkes, Cat and Mouse Design
Manufacturing: Louise Richardson

Printed in the United States of America on acid-free paper

04 03 02   RRD   3 4 5

In memory of
Thomas Phillip Daniels
1938–1999
Founder and Co-Lead Teacher
Best Practice High School

Contents

Foreword

These days, there is more talk about starting one's own school in the public sector than at any other time in history. To us old-timers, this seems odd. In 1974, when we founded Central Park East as a public school in East Harlem, it took a lot of explaining. How could it be ours and also public? How could it have a strong and unique culture by intention and still be part of the system? How could it offer choice to parents and teachers as a public school? Weren't these contradictions in terms?

Today, the idea no longer seems as paradoxical. Public education today is characterized by contradictions and pulled between centralization and decentralization, standardization and innovation, the rhetoric of accountability and the rhetoric of risk taking and autonomy. Finding consensus among the many voices in school reform—about not only what constitutes "best practice," but the cultural norms required if schools are to seek new and more effective ends—is no easy task.

At such a moment, this book is a glorious gift to all educators—teachers, parents, and policymakers alike—for it articulates a clear vision of what comprises a shared consensus of successful secondary school reform over the past few decades, and shows how that consensus can be put into practice. Best of all, it shows us what the advantages are of taking this vision seriously, and also reminds us that putting it into practice is much tougher than just listing it neatly as a credo. *Rethinking High School* is clear, well written, full of the detail that lends credibility and the humility that acknowledges mistakes and problems. In addition to their own stories and ideas, the authors offer a wealth of other examples of successful and innovative high schools that all offer different ways for solving similar problems. There is a desperate need today for more of the stories and ideas found in these pages.

Of course, it's hard not to like people who claim to have followed one's own sage advice. But it's fun to see all the ways in which they didn't follow my advice as well! Their decision not to join the Coalition of Essential Schools strikes me as a mere mistake, a misunderstanding. But many of the ways they diverged from Central Park East practices, I found ingenious and worth copying.

As I read and made pages of notes, I had to remind myself that there is no one way for schools to carry out all the best practices in the world. Each individual school has its own particular context, setting, and history. The four schools I played a significant role in starting never ended up looking alike except in the larger philosophical sense. Central Park East I and Central Park East II soon came to be quite different, as did River East. And twenty-five years later, when I started again at Mission Hill Elementary School in Roxbury, Massachusetts, I found myself urging us to part from all three in some ways. Along the way, I've found that I learn from the work and experience of others. Between the first three schools and the last one—all elementary schools—I spent more than a dozen years in a secondary school and borrowed ideas from it.

It turned out that just as our secondary school learned from the lower grades (we used to say that we were simply extending good kindergarten practice through twelfth grade), so too did I bring to Mission Hill what I learned from a decade of work in a good high school. Mission Hill also borrowed ideas from the prior experiences of its new staff, the ideas of its new parents, and, over time, its students as well. Each school becomes its own entity through the unique combination of the experience and vision of its teachers, kids, administrators, and parents, alongside of lessons learned from other schools. I wish I had this book five years ago!

What these schools, regardless of level or location, share with Best Practice High School are commonly held views about what constitutes the purposes of schooling, the kind of practices consistent with such purposes, and a commitment to take the needed time to work them out together.

No matter how successful, however, the Central Park Easts and Best Practice High Schools of the world can be too easily crushed, as past experience with successful innovative school reform has demonstrated. Our history is strewn with schools that commanded front-page attention for being both novel and successful and yet are barely distinguishable from the rest of the pack a mere ten years later. Too often, their failure is used to reinforce the contrary movement toward more centralization, more standardization, and other so-called reforms that depend not on the wisdom, passion, and experience of the people who actually live and work each day in the school, but on imposed rules and uniformities from above.

We must use the ideas and experiences in this marvelous book as pilots, beacons, and exemplars for our own best practices in our schools and communities. *Rethinking High School* offers us a repertoire of practical possibilities for making the shared consensus come to life in our nation's schools. We all owe a lot to the authors, the teachers, the kids, and the founding fathers and mothers of this school for having the courage to put a credo into practice, and for putting it down on paper so that others may take heart.

—Deborah Meier

Acknowledgments

If jotting notes and stashing away documents constitutes the beginning of a book, then this one commenced in the fall of 1994, shortly after Madeleine Maraldi suggested that we start a new high school. After we stopped laughing and realized that Madeleine wasn't kidding, we were slowly, inexorably drawn into this improbable dream. Maybe we *could* start a new high school, one that made education more authentic, more collaborative, and more challenging for young people. Thus this book begins with the germ of an idea and ends six years later, with our first ninety-two graduates walking across the stage in their sky-blue caps and gowns.

While this book speaks about secondary education generally, it is very much rooted in our experience at Best Practice High School (BPHS). We are profoundly indebted to everyone who helped bring BPHS to life. First among these, of course, are the students—and especially our first class of "pioneers," one hundred thirty-seven kids who came to us on faith and promises in the Fall of 1996. You might ask: What kind of eighth graders would sign up to attend a high school that didn't even exist yet—that didn't have a single stick of furniture, a book in the library, or a graduate on its rolls? What kind of teenager would want to attend a school offering vague pledges of student voice, integrated curriculum, and internships around the city—but one with a really dumb name and no prospects of fielding a football team in the next century? Who'd take a plunge like this?

Well, some really great kids, that's who. Our invitation for young Chicagoans to join us in creating a better kind of high school attracted a disproportionately large share of adventure seekers, budding reformers, and teenagers who valued community over conformity. You'll read about many of these young seekers, most of whom are now in college (Hey! Do your homework!), in the coming pages. Without the courageous, risk-loving Class of 2000, and the wonderful kids who have come after them, there would certainly be no book, and no Best Practice High School, either.

We're equally proud of and indebted to the faculty of BPHS, a remarkable group of professionals who we helped to lure, over four years, from other schools and graduate programs around the city and across the country. We have been on a long journey together, and now there are more than thirty of us. We've had some hard-won achievements, some family squabbles, and some heartbreaking setbacks. We are joined by our mission to create something special for kids, and bonded by our understanding of how phenomenally difficult it is to deliver on that kind of promise. You'll soon meet these teachers, whose brave, intelligent, and loving practice supplies many of the examples of this book.

Kathy and Tom Daniels (no relation to Harvey, except by a twenty-year friendship) were the first faculty members of Best Practice High School, supplying vision as planners and then serving as co-lead teachers once the school opened, carrying full-time teaching loads throughout most of this time. Total dedication to the young people of Chicago has characterized Tom's and Kathy's long careers, including more than thirty years of teaching each, consulting for the Chicago Board of Education, leading the Illinois Writing Project, and finally, starting BPHS. Since Tom's death in the fall of 1999, Kathy has carried on their dream. With students, Kathy is among the warmest, most caring teachers we've ever seen, and she is also one of our city's most uncompromising progressive educators. It's not surprising that students in her classes and her advisory sometimes refer to Kathy as "my second mom." But two minutes after she has hugged a troubled student or led an English class into uproarious laughter, she can be on the phone to the central office negotiating for supplies, combing through the fine points of a budget, or planning far-off events in deep and careful detail. Kathy has a most unique array of talents, without which BPHS could never have started, survived its challenges, or gotten this far.

The three small schools in our "multiplex" share not just a building, but a principal. When we interviewed candidates for this special and delicate role back in 1996, we were mainly looking for a competent building manager who wouldn't make things any harder for evolving schools. We got so much more than we hoped for when Sylvia Gibson accepted the position. Sylvia genuinely embraced the idea of small schools where curriculum and instruction are determined by a collegial faculty, not dictated by the principal or central office. She also understood that whatever her official job description might say, she herself would be held publicly accountable if our schools didn't work—and she would get little of the credit if they did. In fact, when things have gone wrong, people have headed for Sylvia's office. And when successes are announced, people sometimes forget to mention this dynamic, humorous, and wise woman who is strong enough to let teachers lead.

People in urban education sometimes comment that Chicago seems to have more partner organizations than any other American city. How true, and how fortunate for us. Best Practice High School could never have established without the shrewed advocacy of Alex Polikoff and Jeannie Nowaczewski of the Business and Professional People for the Public Interest and the steadfast lobbying of John Ayers and Robin Staines at Leadership for Quality Education. Bill Ayers, Mike Klonsky, and Susan Klonsky at the Small Schools Workshop, and Don Moore and Susan Davenport at Designs for Change helped to create the policy climate in which proposals like Best Practice get the green light.

As the pages of this book will reveal, Deborah Meier, founder of Central Park East High School, took a special interest in our school during its planning stages. She gave us precious guidance, most of which we luckily followed. And the few things we ignored? You don't want to know. And when it came to the design of our curriculum, trying to embody our amorphous dreams of student-centeredness, we relied shamelessly on the ideas, the books, and the persons of James Beane and Barbara Brodhagen, who joined us at school, at our summer institutes, and in a few emergency phone calls, to work through the details of negotiated curriculum.

While BPHS operates on the same basic per-pupil funding as other Chicago schools, we have needed some extra money, first to get started and equipped, and later to create a professional development center where educators from around the city and the country can learn with us. When the plan for our new high school was first developed, Jill Darrow at the Fry Foundation and Nikki Stein at the Polk Bros. Foundation stepped forward immediately with grants. The grants that helped our initial faculty to visit other progressive schools and to develop curriculum, as well as releasing our co-lead teachers half-time for a semester of planning. Elizabeth Periello Rice at the Prince Charitable Trusts paid for our first computer lab and training to make it work, and the Quest Center of the Chicago Teachers Union provided some welcome start-up funding.

Since those beginnings, we've been able to provide ongoing staff development both for our own faculty and other colleagues with support with Pat Ford and Ken Rolling at the Chicago Annenberg Challenge, Fred MacDougal and Randi Starr at the McDougal Family Foundation, Carla Asher at the DeWitt Wallace-Readers Digest Students at the Center Project, Warren Chapman at the Joyce Foundation, Ted Oppenheimer at the Oppenheimer Family Fund, and the J. C. Penney Foundation. Daniel Cheifetz of the Enterprise Development Foundation made the first major gift to our school scholarship fund, while his son Daniel worked one-to-one with students on their website designs.

Another group of crucial partners are the more than eighty internship sites—businesses, museums, hospitals, and elementary schools—that host our four hundred forty students for their weekly service learning internships. These community-minded institutions do benefit from the program—they receive generally eager and curious helpers. But they give even more: time and effort to train, supervise, and evaluate transient rookies who probably don't contribute much to productivity or profits. However, site coordinators tell us, they are compensated by getting to know fine young people. These kid-oriented agencies are listed on page 156 of the book, where, in Chapter 7, we discuss structures for making high school more authentic.

Inside the Chicago Public Schools, we've had some vital supporters. Chief Executive Officer Paul Vallas made the decision to authorize our school and handed us a beautiful, rehabbed building at 2040 West Adams. We are proud to be one of the schools he points to when people ask him for new answers to old questions about high school. Olivia Watkins, Special Projects Officer, has worked with us from the start, carrying our message into forums both friendly and skeptical. Hazel Steward, our Region Superintendent, has taken pride in our achievements, even though we sometimes broke the mold or confounded expectations.

People always ask what the three of us are doing at Best Practice High School. Aren't we supposed to be professors at National-Louis University? Then why do we spend more time at BPHS then we do on our own campus? Well, that's because our Dean, Linda Tafel, assigned us to do this work. She believes it is the responsibility of teacher education institutions like ours to be fully immersed in school reform, and not just as spectators, critics, or documentors. Now serving as Provost, Linda assures us that our college's founder, Elizabeth Harrison, who started the nation's first professional training school for kindergarten teachers in 1886, is up there smiling as we carry on our college's steadfast commitment to urban education.

And speaking of leadership, who'd expect a university president to take a consistent personal interest in a small public high school in the inner city? Curtis McCray, whose presidency at National-Louis University began just as BPHS was gearing up, has been a loud, generous, and effective supporter of the school from day one. Among many kindnesses, we thank Curt for bringing down the house of our first graduation. He recognized that the huge audience, on its Sunday-best behavior, was suppressing a lot of celebratory energy. So instead of offering pedantic presidential remarks (not his style in any case), Curt simply invited everyone to cheer and scream at the top of their lungs—which they delightedly did.

Lately, much of our work—including support for Best Practice High School—has been focused through a new branch of our university, the Center for City Schools. The Center serves as an umbrella for a dozen interrelated, foundation-funded projects that support teachers and parents in restructuring schools around Chicago and the Midwest. At the Center, Clarke Schneider and Kim Sagami keep the wheels turning and the accounts balanced as our assorted staffers spin our ideas, events, and documents. And down in the Grants and Contracts Office—the engine room of funded projects—the indefatigable Chris Sorenson helps us to administer the funds that make all these projects run.

Under the Center's umbrella, we've had the privilege of gathering a family of brilliant, committed teacher-consultants who work with Best Practice High School and many other schools in our staff-development projects. This team has included some amazing facilitators, including Barbara Morris, Pete Leki, Pat Bearden, Toni Murff, Marianne Flanagan, Lynnette Emmons, Linda Bailey, Julie Flynn, Mirlene Cadichon, Mark Rodriguez, and Bobbi Stuart. While all of these people have contributed to BPHS, it is the miraculous Yolanda Simmons who has been assigned there most consistently, becoming a treasured resource to both kids and teachers.

We have borrowed these amazing people from different branches of the Chicago public schools (classrooms, parent councils, computer labs) and watched with delight as they have entered hundreds of colleagues' classrooms, sharing their expertise with tact, energy, and concern. It's when we're working with all these dedicated professionals that we feel most confident—sometimes downright euphoric—about the prospects for reform in America's schools. We've seen schools change in deep and enduring ways when outstanding teachers like these are empowered to lead.

One constant in the professional lives of our consulting team, as well as the whole BPHS faculty, is attending the Walloon Institute each summer. There, in a beautiful retreat atmosphere, we spend a week with other teachers, parents, and principals from around the country, all of whom are trying to bring best practice teaching and learning to life in their schools. We don't know whether it's the provocative speakers, the respite from back-home pressures, the late-night dormitory debates, or the lumberjack buffets, but we always come back from Walloon smarter, stronger, and more committed than ever to progressive principles. Our thanks go to the forty-member staff who make Walloon possible each summer.

Since we have written several previous books for Heinemann, we knew we would be working with smart, dedicated, and caring editors on this project. But we didn't expect that Leigh Peake, Bill Varner, Michael Cirone, and Mike Gibbons would all visit BPHS, some several times, walk the halls, sit in classes, hang with the kids, celebrate our victories, and agonize with us over bad days and sick colleagues. As our Heinemann friends pitched in with suggestions, help, and commiseration, we felt we had not just selected a publisher but added to the BPHS family. And these guys know a few of the family secrets, too.

Because the three of us have been working together so closely for so long, finishing each other's sentences and claiming credit for each other's ideas, many people have started to think of us as three bodies with one brain. Actually, we occasionally operate as separate people, and we would like to thank those who know us best outside the trio.

Harvey observes that one of the best ways to learn about education is to have some children of your own and then watch what happens. His children, Nick and Marny, have provided quite a demonstration over their twenty-two and sixteen years. Traveling through schools that mostly embodied the best of best practice, they have grown into two creative, passionate, independent, and completely different young people. Elaine Daniels, in addition to mothering these now-grown children, teaches, advises, and supervises student teachers, and always manages to be Harvey's friendliest and most insightful reader.

Marilyn would like to thank her husband, Michael Koch, for his support and for his interest in her work. Although not in the field of education, he can now make a pretty good argument for the benefits of small schools. Marilyn has learned a great deal about the highs and lows of the high school experience by watching the young adults in her life, Josh, Michael, Stacy, Jeffrey, Liza, Dina, Laurie, and Mark. She is grateful for the opportunity to watch her first grandson, Noah, grow, learn, and eventually go to high school.

Steven thanks Susan for sharing her own dedication and boundless energy as a teacher, consultant in the corporate world, and life partner. And his sons, Mark and Daniel, as they've held steadfast to their principles to create fascinating careers in art, dance, and music. They've taken risks and created meaningful lives in ways we never could have anticipated.

Chapter 1
Best Practice by Design

Reform comes to high school—at last.

About six years ago, we did something crazy. The three of us started planning a new public high school. With some dear friends and colleagues, some smart elementary principals, and a few politically adept community groups, we drafted a proposal for our dream high school. Two years later, something even crazier happened. The Chicago Board of Education said, "OK. Go ahead." The superintendent even came by to officially hand over a beautiful 1902 neoclassical building. He said a lot of hopeful words, and as he left he also said: "By the way, this better work." We were stunned.

As a matter of fact, we are still stunned. But we have just graduated our first class—93 kids launched off to college, work, and the military from a school that didn't even exist when they were eighth graders. Because it is so new, we're not quite ready to say that our school "works." But it is starting to work in some important ways, thanks mostly to a unique group of young people, our pioneers and guinea pigs, a group of teenagers who wanted something different.

Our school's name says a lot, and sometimes it says the wrong things: Best Practice High School. When we picked the name, we weren't really looking beyond the proposal-writing stage; we were just trying to infuse our long-shot application with credibility, one page at a time. Since Steve and Harvey had coauthored a book called *Best Practice: New Standards for Teaching and Learning in America's Schools* (1998), it seemed sensible to mention it in the proposal, early and often. Too bad we didn't stop and think about how dumb a basketball uniform would look emblazoned with this name. Too bad we never foresaw our students having to explain the odd moniker to their friends who went to regular-sounding schools. And really too bad that people would someday assume we meant that our school *was* the best. What we meant to mean was that this school would be guided by the principles of "best practice," as embodied in our country's emerging curriculum standards—a lofty goal that would take many years to reach.

Today, with a dedicated crew of 440 students, thirty staff, and some wonderful families and community partners, we continue to try to invent a high school that works better for kids. Every day, we are holding our own feet to the fire—and our feet get plenty hot. As our cofounder Tom Daniels always said: "This is the hardest work we have ever done." As he also said: "We are flying this plane while we are building it." And some days it feels as if all we have built is a wing and a prayer. We have a long way to go, and we will be at this job for many years to come.

REFORMING AMERICA'S HIGH SCHOOLS

These days, it seems everyone is complaining about America's high schools. Politicians, parents, blue-ribbon commissions, and editorial writers—every citizen seems to have strong opinions about high school, and few of them are flattering. But then, complaining has always been an ingredient of the high school scene. It is practically part of the teenage job description to continually remind grown-ups that school is boring, teachers are unfair, and the food in the cafeteria is bad. And sadly, these kid complaints have been entirely valid in too many high schools, for too many years.

But now the complaining is much louder and more ominous, and it's coming from every direction. The emerging indictment of high schools in today's media is both familiar and ubiquitous: achievement test scores are disappointing, dropout rates are soaring, misbehavior is rampant, racial disparities in achievement persist, and the widening gap between the official curriculum and the actual workings of our society is both costly and worrisome. The recent epidemic of school shootings has sent chills down the spine of every parent in America. And on top of all these troubles, many high schools are bursting at the seams with kids, as a new baby boom works its way through the school system.

Of course, for every worrisome problem afflicting high schools, there are upbeat interpretations and hopeful signs. Violence may be increasing on the streets, but most schools remain islands of safety in an increasingly dangerous world. While American teenagers may score poorly on international comparisons in science and mathematics, the Nobel prizes somehow keep rolling in, and U.S. dominance in technological innovation appears unchallenged. Adolescent drug use and crime are down, college attendance rates are up, and community involvement by teens is at an all-time high. Yes, those students who drop out of high school do face crushing disadvantages, but fewer are actually leaving—graduation rates have been creeping steadily upward throughout this century.

Whatever the validity of all these complaints and exculpations, an undeniable turning point has been reached. Attention has been focused. After nearly two decades of school reform aimed mainly at the elementary level, it is now the high schools' turn. Everyone involved seems hungry for a change— teenagers, parents, teachers, school administrators, board members, communities, colleges, and employers. All the stakeholders in secondary education seem ready to retire the assembly-line high school, forged on factory floors nearly a century ago, and now at least a generation out of date.

Already, pioneering high schools across the county have started experimenting with new programs, schedules, courses, models, and structures. Some faculties are developing rich, problem-based, interdisciplinary courses that break down discipline barriers and integrate English, history, science, math, languages, music, and the arts. Others are "detracking" ability-grouped classes and moving toward more inclusive, democratic classrooms that embrace students with different thinking styles, cultural traditions, and learning needs. Some schools are striving to replace skewed and unfair standardized tests with more sensitive, local performance assessments. And in still other schools, teachers are being offered more voice in governance, more control over their own professional development, and more opportunities to collaborate with colleagues and develop innovative programs.

Teams of educators, parents, and concerned citizens are experimenting with a wide variety of strategies to reinvent America's high schools. Some groups are trying to revitalize the curriculum and improve instruction within existing school structures. Others are trying to make oversized high schools feel and work smaller, dividing them into thematic units, programs, or houses. Still others are inventing brand-new schools—charter schools, independent schools, new public or private schools. This is a fertile, exciting time—and change is long overdue.

STARTING A NEW HIGH SCHOOL

The three of us have been involved in public schools as teachers, parents, staff developers, and teacher educators since the early 1960s (and as students ourselves, during the late Cretaceous Period). When Chicago's ambitious, nationally watched school-reform movement was kicked off by state legislation in

1988, we were drawn into the maelstrom and have been swirling there ever since. With support from several local foundations, we built a network of fourteen elementary schools where, along with a growing team of skilled teacher-consultants, we offered workshops, summer institutes, and lots of in-classroom consulting on writing, reading, and curriculum integration. As our projects grew and new funders signed on, we established the Center for City Schools at National-Louis University as the headquarters for our efforts.

Around 1995, some of our network principals—especially Madeleine Maraldi from Washington Irving School—started asking us to create a new high school. They were worried about their eighth graders, who seemed to have no real alternative to enrolling at huge, impersonal, and often gang-dominated high schools, where many would be unknown, get lost, and eventually drop out. Knowing some of these kids from their classrooms, and having seen regular city high schools up close, we shared the principals' concerns. So did Tom and Kathy Daniels, old friends of ours (but not relatives of Harvey's), fellow Illinois Writing Project leaders and celebrated English teachers at Farragut High School. Tom and Kathy had been trying to create pockets of progressive teaching inside of big, tough high schools for twenty-five years, by leading workshops for colleagues, writing curriculum for the Board of Education, and supporting change through the local AFT chapter.

Just for fun, just to keep Madeleine happy, the five of us began playing with the idea. Like anyone who has ever taught school, we had all secretly entertained the fantasy of taking a few favorite colleagues off to a special place where, freed from red tape and evil administrators, we'd create an educational nirvana. Of course, we never acted on this universal teacher fantasy—it just comforted us when things got really stressful at school. After all, there hadn't been a new high school created in Chicago for twenty years, and the only really innovative one, Metropolitan High School, had just been disbanded. But still, what if we did it? What would a "best practice" high school look like?

As the vision grew, somewhere along the way we stopped fantasizing and started planning. Our emerging idea was to create a new, small, public high school, not a charter school, but a teacher-led "regular" school where the national standards of state-of-the-art instruction would guide the whole program. We would enroll a random assortment of Chicago's young people, not a hand-picked cohort of proven high scorers. There were already several elite high schools "creaming" the system, producing predictably stellar test scores. Instead, we wanted to show that progressive methods—call it best practice, or standards-based instruction, or just good teaching—would work with kids from ordinary neighborhoods and elementary schools just as they do in magnet schools, wealthy suburbs, or the elite private schools perched in the high-rent districts.

Once we had developed a plan and a budget, we were in for a long wait. The proposal languished inside the CPS bureaucracy for a year. Finally, on November 22, 1995, a fax arrived from newly appointed CEO Paul Vallas: "The Chicago Public Schools (CPS) is pleased to offer the Best Practice High School a space in Cregier to begin planning and recruitment activities in February 1996 and classes in September 1996!" Apparently, we were going to have a school. And we really liked the CEO's exclamation point. But the fax also went on to warn: "As a new small high school opening its doors at a time when public high schools are under intense pressure to improve, Best Practice will be watched particularly closely." This was getting very real.

Our first task was to find 140 freshmen who'd like to attend a high school they'd never heard of. In Chicago, all eighth graders may apply to any of the seventy-four high schools across the city, some of which (like our school-to-be) have open enrollment, while others have selective admissions. From the schools' point of view, this means you have to compete for students in order to survive. We looked at the calendar: the recruiting season was already well underway. Yikes! On our first day of existence, we had already fallen behind all the other high schools in town.

We realized that we needed a brochure, quickly. So we borrowed some mature-looking eighth graders from Washington Irving School and photographed them in front of the nearby United Center, figuring that our proximity to the site of Michael Jordan's exploits might be a selling point. Our vague but sincere brochure promised:

> When students have finished four years at BPHS, they will be accomplished readers, writers, and thinkers. They will be skillful at setting goals, managing time, and organizing and assessing their own efforts. They will be ready to make important choices about their future: to make strong college applications and do well in the schools they choose; to seek good jobs and perform them well; and to pursue any other training they need to meet their life goals.

We pledged in "A Note to Parents" that the school would be caring and safe, prayed that we could make good on the latter promise, and printed up a thousand copies.

Then the five cofounders fanned out around the city, visiting the fourteen elementary schools in our "Best Practice Network," now the prospective feeder system for the new high school. We talked to groups of eighth graders, some of whom already knew us as helpers in their own classrooms, and shared the plan for a new high school. We explained that BPHS would include internships around the city every week, that the curriculum would be integrated, that we would be continuing some of the collaborative learning activities already happening in their middle school classes.

We also answered some tough questions: No, we wouldn't have a football team. No, there wouldn't be instrumental music. No, there wasn't a pool for swimming. Yes, there would be some "little kids " running around the building we were sharing with two elementary schools. As students peppered us with specific and thoughtful questions, we were constantly reminded of all the things we hadn't yet figured out—or even thought of. Our most recurrent answer in these Q and A sessions was, "We don't know—but if you come to BPHS, you can help us figure it out."

By the end of this crash recruitment drive, 137 kids had agreed to become part of our first class. Were they truly a random assortment of Chicago teens? Based on standardized test scores and racial demographics, yes. But personality-wise, the distribution was probably skewed toward adventure and risk taking. After all, these kids had chosen to attend a nonexistent school, one that needed to be created from scratch. These were our precious pioneers (of course we never called them this to their faces), the young people who would invent this school with us, create its culture, establish its traditions, and forge its character.

Here are a few of those young people, with a few words about how we met them and what they were doing when we said good-bye four years later.

When **Maricela Zapian** first enrolled as a freshman, her advisor, Tom Daniels, was concerned about her shyness and lack of confidence as a student. Four years later, she stood at the podium in front of a thousand people—parents, families, faculty, and students—to address the crowd as BPHS's first valedictorian. "We must continue to do what this school has taught us," Maricela said, "to go beyond the books and the guidelines and find ourselves and our destiny." After interning with a computer consultant during her freshman and sophomore years, Marcie is now seeking her own destiny at the University of Illinois at Chicago, where she is a pre-engineering student.

In 1995, **Candace Walker** was gravely wounded in an attack that took her mother's life. Lynnette Emmons, Candace's eighth-grade teacher at Nettelhorst School, encouraged Candace to attend BPHS, where she'd be both safe and prized, and where her many emerging talents would be nurtured.

Over her time with us, Candace was a leader, a scholar, and a conscience. She's goaded us to give blood, mediated disputes between fellow students, and won a shelf of awards and recognitions. Today, she is a premed student at Northwestern University.

Jamal Leki came from Waters School on the north side, where his father was chair of the Local School Council, and a dedicated school reformer himself. Jamal was academically talented and highly creative, a divergent thinker, a skeptic who saw clearly through the flaws in his teachers' efforts. BPHS wasn't resourceful or flexible enough to meet Jamal's needs, and he left us early, to study music and Japanese at a local community college and to earn his high school diploma through a GED. Today, Jamal is playing a lot of piano and has embarked on a self-guided exploration of classical music.

Carlton Jackson and **Ed Redd** were actually pretty easy to recruit—they were both attending Nia School, an Afrocentric, entrepreneurship-oriented middle school that was already occupying the building that BPHS would share. We simply had to convince Ed and CJ to move "upstairs." In high school, Ed was an immediate basketball star and emerging mathematical whiz. After taking a special summer course in accounting and working at a part-time job designing math computer games, Ed was a catch for Marquette University in Milwaukee. Carlton's steadfast interest in art was stranded through his high school career, and his series of internships in video production earned him part-time jobs with the Museum of Broadcast Communications and the Community Television Network. Carlton is now enrolled at Chicago State University and hopes to eventually study at Grambling State University.

Lilia Moreno came with a group of her friends from Ruiz Elementary School, twenty blocks south of Best Practice. After a year, her friends transferred to another school, but Lilia hung on with us, becoming a dedicated and solid student. Nothing was going to make Lilia miss a step toward her dream of going to college—including marriage, pregnancy, and the raising of the beautiful Natalie, whom our faculty and office staff doted upon extravagantly. Today Lilia is at National-Louis University, studying to be a respiratory therapist.

John Yates came to us from Jenner school. John was a quiet boy, an average student, with plenty of friends, a wide and ready smile. We used John's picture on the cover of our second-year brochure—his extraordinarily handsome, youthful face seemed to be the perfect reflection of our school's vitality and energy. Over a February weekend in 1998, John was killed in a neighborhood shooting.

These and one hundred thirty-two other young people joined us on our opening day, August 23, 1996, in the sweltering auditorium of our new school, as we embarked on the adventure of creating a new school together. Four years later, on June 5, 2000, ninety-two of these young people received their diplomas. Eleven of the original freshman had fallen back to junior status, having failed to earn enough credits to graduate. Twenty-two transferred to other high schools. Twelve dropped out of school altogether, some working full-time and others running with gangs. Since 1996, we've seen four marriages, seven babies, three deaths.

Other outcomes were similarly complex and mixed. On standardized tests, our students outperformed expectations in some important areas. Despite our nonselective enrollment policy, State of Illinois science examinations placed us eighth out of seventy-four high schools in the city. In social studies, we ranked twelfth, with 88 percent of our kids meeting or exceeding state goals. Throughout the first four years, our reading and math scores on the Test of Academic Proficiency (TAP) consistently ranked in the top third citywide, though this still meant our kids were well below national averages. During the 1999–2000 school year, our TAP reading scores rose 47 percent, and math went up 37 percent. Of our senior class, two-thirds went directly to college, 10 percent into the military, and several into full-time jobs. There was also a small group of "undecided" students, who gave the faculty and the counselors real concern as graduation approached.

Looking back to the original planning of the school, we realize that we had no idea what we were getting into. Rereading our dewy-eyed original proposal, with its vision of a perfect, seamless implementation of our dream, our planning process seems about as sophisticated as one of those old Mickey Rooney and Judy Garland movies: "Hey! Let's get a barn and put on a school!" We have since been humbled by the staggering difficulty of creating a high school that works better for kids. We have been educated by the hard knocks of attempting change inside a big, complex school district. It is tough to focus on curriculum innovation when you are constantly fighting bureaucratic rearguard actions just to get basic supplies and services. It's hard to sustain educational momentum while worrying about your students' safety in the streets. And, while trying to do something new, you always have to resist the seductive siren song of predictability, of old habits, of going back to the "regular" way. As we've steered down this bumpy, winding road of starting a new school, we feel that we have hit every single pothole. Indeed, our original and only half-ironic working title for this book was "How *Not* to Start a High School: The Hundred Biggest Mistakes We Made and How You Can Avoid Them."

So what have we learned? Our lessons are woven through every chapter of this book. Some things we think we have done pretty well, and we may even encourage you to follow our example. At other times, though, we've made mistakes, sometimes big ones. Indeed, some of our warts have grown warts. We'll try our best to steer you away from our mistakes toward better models and smarter experts.

But there's the one thing we have learned that we can share right at the outset. We are now much, much slower to judge or criticize anyone else who works in a high school. As three college professors who enjoy the luxury of assembling fulfilling lives for ourselves out of a mixture of teaching, writing, research, and consulting, we stand in awe of people who get up every day, get in their cars, and go teach five classes of teenagers, one hundred fifty complicated souls, a day, twenty or thirty years in a row, who keep believing, trusting, and laughing. Teaching adolescents is not a job for the faint of heart. This is among the hardest work in the world, and these teachers, these veterans, the ones who have stayed in touch with their idealism, who have kept reading and learning themselves, who never give up on a struggling student, these are some of the finest people in the world.

But even the best of these teachers are mostly trapped in a system that is not designed well for kids—or for teachers either. That is the problem this book tries to address. Over the next eleven chapters, we are asking: What are the structures, the procedures, the design features, that can create high schools that work for young people? How can we devise warm and caring places that support teenagers' risk taking, that provide the scaffolding for constructing identities, that offer just the right balance of security and challenge to stretch young minds?

ASKING THE RIGHT QUESTIONS

Decades of critiques have left us with a pretty good idea of what's wrong with our high schools. We know what traditions need to be questioned, which procedures and practices we should reexamine, what old habits might need to be broken. And while every teacher, school, district, and community will need to find its own answers, there are common questions that we must all address.

This book aims to support that rethinking process, to help guide the inquiry of people who want to make high schools better—the schools where they teach, or administer, or serve on the school board, or send their own sons and daughters to be educated. Among our readers will surely be many concerned individual teachers trying to make a difference in their classrooms. But we also hope that the book will be used by teams of people who are trying to think systematically about high school change: teacher groups, school boards, parent committees, curriculum study groups, academic departments, or teams of school people and external partners. We want to help groups like these to plan their own changes, including:

- reforming an existing high school
- starting new programs within a larger school
- breaking a big school into smaller ones
- creating a new public, charter, or independent high school
- just starting to think about what these choices might mean in your school or district.

For the people engaged in this difficult and urgently important work, this book aims to assist your reflection, discussion, and planning.

The book is organized around eleven key ingredients of good high schools. We think that anyone who is thinking about improving secondary education, whether in their own individual classroom or across a whole district, must eventually address these eleven issues, assertions, or principles.

1. *Size.* The high school is small—or feels small.
2. *Climate.* Every student is known, appreciated, and included in a diverse, collaborative community.
3. *Voice and leadership.* Both students and teachers exercise choice and make decisions in all elements of school life.
4. *Teaching.* Teachers collaborate with students to explore and employ a growing repertoire of instructional strategies.
5. *Curriculum.* With their teachers, young people engage in challenging inquiry into topics that matter.
6. *Community experiences.* Young people are engaged in the life of the community and the world of work.
7. *Scheduling.* The school day and calendar provide flexible and variable blocks of learning time.

8. *Technology and materials.* Contemporary technology and rich materials support students as thinkers, researchers, and authors.

9. *Assessment.* Teachers help students to monitor, evaluate, and guide their own thinking.

10. *Professional development.* Teachers are students of instruction, with many opportunities to learn and grow.

11. *Relationships.* The school works closely with parents, community organizations, and educational institutions.

Where did this list come from? These eleven topics and their accompanying assertions come from several sources. First, we looked at the national curriculum standards developed over the past two decades by twenty subject-area organizations and national research centers. These authoritative reports define the nature of excellent teaching and powerful learning across the curriculum. Next, we reviewed the educational research, asking, What is known about "what works" in secondary education? What are the mainstream, consensus findings about the structures, procedures, and conditions that support the growth and learning of teenagers? We also studied a variety of pathfinding, high-performing schools all around the country, trying to understand how they provide "value added" for students. In their stories of invention, struggle, and change, we have found not just new ways of doing high school, but guidance about what questions need to be asked.

Finally, we've drawn on our firsthand experience at Best Practice High School. Over the past several years, while designing, opening, and running a new school, we have grappled very directly with these eleven issues, working to shape a personal and localized response to each one. So, while we are happy to tell our own stories, we are *not* offering our school as a model to be emulated. We are very young, and we don't have the right answers for anyone else—or even ourselves half the time, since we are constantly tinkering with our own program.

So this book is built around eleven assertions, and in the following chapters we will take them one at a time. For each, we'll first show how the issue— size, curriculum, community participation—affects students, often with a real-life story from BPHS. Then we will review the relevant research, trying to answer the question, What do we know about this ingredient of secondary education? What works and what doesn't? We will introduce key people who have developed models, pioneered variations, or investigated results. We will visit different schools and programs where this particular ingredient has been adapted, translated, or modified in different ways. We'll also talk about how we have addressed each element at our own high school, both during the planning and now in the living-it-out stage. Toward the end of each chapter, in a section called Finding Your Next Steps, we offer some specific and concrete ways for readers to engage with the ideas in that section.

Another important part of this book is its accompanying website, rethinkinghighschool.com: Any time you see this web icon in the left-hand margin, it means that the website has additional material that expands or extends that section of the book. There, you'll find samples of student work, more details about specific projects, or step-by-step plans for programs or lessons. But we want the website to be more than an electronic appendix. We hope it will be a place where people engaged in rethinking high schools can connect for conversation, sharing, and support. We invite readers from around the country to post their own high school renewal plans, curriculum units, programs, designs, stories, statistics, or samples of student work. The site is set up to facilitate discussion among colleagues and to connect educators to the best resources for restructuring secondary schools. Doing this work on the web, elaborating on a book, and trying to support a movement at the same time is an experiment for all of us. But revitalizing America's high schools in the spirit of progressive practice will be a long and complex undertaking. We are going to need all the ideas, friends, and solace we can get. So please join us on-line.

While this book is partly the story of one school, we think it can also serve as a broader guide for people inquiring into the nature of high school reform. While we do recommend some destinations in the following pages, we won't tell you which route to take to get there. It is one thing to say that a high school should be or feel small. But how? There are dozens of ways to make schools feel smaller to students, and no single one of them is right. That's a choice that has to be made in every locality, every classroom and school, by the people who are closest to the kids. So we don't claim to have the specific answer for any one school, but we do offer to help you find your own answer in the research, in the stories, and in the school profiles in this book.

DEFINING BEST PRACTICE IN SECONDARY EDUCATION

How do we know what "best educational practices" look like in the high school setting? What models do we have to follow? Which pathfinders have been out there experimenting and testing new ideas? Luckily for us all, while some national school reformers have been preoccupied with indicting and blaming, others have focused more on what works for high school kids. Our national curriculum research centers, twenty subject-matter professional associations, scores of capable individual researchers, and thousands of on-the-line classroom teachers have been struggling to define clearly "best educational practice" in every important content area.

As a result, we now have national curriculum standards, meta-analysis of instructional research, reports from pilot classrooms, and landmark sets of professional recommendations in every teaching field. Some of these reports were produced with funding from the U.S. Department of Education, while others were financed by professional organizations. Taken together, this family of authoritative documents provides a strong consensus definition of state-of-the-art teaching in every critical field. We have summarized these documents in our earlier book, *Best Practice: New Standards for Teaching and Learning in America's Schools* by Steve, Harvey, and colleague Arthur Hyde.

One might expect that when experts and practitioners from such disparate fields as art, science, mathematics, writing, and social science sit down to define their own field's best practices, the results would be some very different visions of the ideal classroom, contradictory ways of organizing subject matter, and divergent models of what good teachers do. But, in fact, such polarities do *not* characterize these reports. Whether the recommendations come from the National Council of Teachers of Mathematics, the American Association for the Advancement of Science, the National Writing Project, the National Council for the Social Studies, the National Council of Teachers of English, or the International Reading Association, the fundamental insights into teaching and learning are remarkably congruent. Indeed, on many key issues, the recommendations from these diverse organizations are unanimous.

Of course each of these groups has some very particular, finely detailed suggestions for its own practitioners. But there is also a clear and deep consensus across these documents. Behind the thousands of subject-specific recommendations, the reports consistently prescribe a similar kind of learning environment. Regardless of discipline or grade level, the national curriculum standards recurrently call for classrooms that are:

Student-centered. Schooling should start with young people's real interests; all across the curriculum, investigating students' own questions should take precedence over studying arbitrarily and distantly selected content.

Experiential. Active, hands-on, concrete experience is the most powerful and natural form of learning. Students should be immersed in the most direct possible experience of the content of every subject.

Holistic. Young people learn best when they encounter whole ideas, events, and materials in purposeful contexts, not by studying subparts isolated from actual use.

Authentic. Real, rich, complex ideas and materials are at the heart of the curriculum. Lessons or textbooks that water down, control, or oversimplify content ultimately disempower students.

Expressive. To fully engage ideas, construct meaning, and remember information, students must regularly employ the whole range of communicative media—speech, writing, drawing, poetry, dance, drama, music, movement, and the visual arts.

Reflective. Balancing the immersion in experience and expression must be opportunities for learners to look back, to reflect, to debrief, to abstract from their experiences what they have felt and thought and learned.

Social. Learning is always socially constructed and often interactional; teachers need to create classroom interactions that "scaffold" learning.

Collaborative. Cooperative group activities tap the social power of learning better than competitive and individualistic approaches.

Democratic. The classroom is a model community; students learn what they live as citizens of the school.

Cognitive. The most powerful learning comes when children develop true understanding of concepts through higher-order thinking associated with various fields of inquiry and through self-monitoring of their thinking.

Developmental. Human beings grow through a series of definable but not rigid stages, and schooling should fit its activities to the developmental level of students.

Constructivist. Learners do not just receive content; in a very real sense, they re-create and reinvent every cognitive system they encounter, including language, literacy, and mathematics.

Challenging. Students learn best when faced with genuine challenges, choices, and responsibility in their own learning.

Our national curriculum standards, no matter how you summarize them, still seem a bit abstract. But these abstractions can and do coalesce in powerful, amazing classrooms. University of Wisconsin researcher Fred Newmann has shown that when "best practice" teaching is the standard, achievement is higher—much higher. In a study conducted in Chicago, Newmann found that students who were offered what he labeled an "authentic" curriculum, similar to the one mandated by the national curriculum standards, achieved at levels two to three times higher than students in traditional, skill-oriented classrooms with low "authenticity" (1998). In both writing and mathematics, students learned far more when teachers invited them to go deeply into subject matter, engage in deep conversation about the topics at hand, and make explicit connections between classroom subject matter and their lives outside of school. But, people wondered: What about standardized test scores? Newmann's study had used specially constructed tests of content knowledge to determine how well kids had learned. But what about the mandated city and state assessments? How would kids with high-challenge teaching perform on the do-or-die assessments, the ones that really count? Two years later, working with Tony Bryk and Junko Nagaoka, Newmann investigated just that correlation. The result? Students doing authentic and challenging work in their classrooms scored significantly higher on both the Iowa Test of Basic Skills and the Illinois Goals Assessment Program, across grade levels and regardless of socioeconomic status (2000). Newmann's research came as a shock to many educators in Chicago, since it implied that, for all the talk of higher standards and "raising the bar," most students were still not being significantly challenged or intellectually supported.

SUCCESSFUL SECONDARY REFORM MODELS

While inertia and resistance have characterized much of the high school world in recent years, several important national institutions have bucked the hand-wringing trend: the middle school model, the Coalition of Essential Schools, and the newly emerging small schools movement.

In the early 1970s, the idea began to take root that young people between ten and fourteen needed a special and different kind of schooling. This new view of early adolescence eventually sparked the reorganization of more than 10,000 junior high schools into places designed to work better for kids. Among the key tenets of genuine middle schools are students grouped into small "houses," a personalized learning environment, intensive teacher teaming, curriculum integration, daily advisory, and genuine student responsibility and choice in the everyday experience of school.

When it is implemented faithfully, middle-level education has much to teach high schools, and in planning BPHS, as well as in our previous writings

(1998), we have tried to borrow, transplant, and adapt everything we could. We are especially indebted to our colleague James Beane, whose books form the intellectual core of the middle school movement (1991, 1995a, 1995b, 1997). Jim's practical model of negotiated curriculum has shown educators all over the nation exactly how to develop worthwhile and challenging curriculum from kids' own questions about themselves and their world. Fortunately for those of us who work in school systems saddled with curriculum mandates, state tests, and district benchmarks, Jim also showed us how to "backmap" our student-driven units, proving to all the inspectors and authorities how it's possible to teach required lists of content and skills while giving students a real voice along the way.

At the high school level, the Coalition of Essential Schools has been the nation's leading model of comprehensive renewal, and a vital partner in our own thinking. Started in 1980 by Ted Sizer, author of several important books on secondary school reform (1992, 1994, 1996), the Coalition has now grown to include more than 1,000 schools across the country. Indeed, the CES has gotten so big that it recently had to restructure its organization, decentralizing into two dozen regional centers that provide coaching and technical assistance to nearby member schools.

The Coalition was built around key principles:

- The central goal of schooling is intellectual development.
- Students should study a few essential areas deeply.
- High expectations should be held for everyone.
- Learning environments should be personalized.
- Students should be constructing meaning rather than being filled up with information.
- Teachers should act as coaches and guides.
- The key outcome is not test scores but what students can actually do.
- Families should be central to school life.
- Faculty should teach kids first and subjects second.
- Schools should operate as model democracies.
- Schools with these goals may cost more or need to omit some of the wide-ranging functions performed by modern high schools.

The overlap between the Coalition principles and the recommendations of the national curriculum standards, of course, is noteworthy and immediately apparent.

Among other achievements, the Coalition has seeded some of America's most important model schools. One of the first of these, arguably the single most influential model high school in the country, is Central Park East Secondary School (CPESS) in New York, a charter member of the Coalition and a prototype of its principles in action. The history of the school is told in former principal Deborah Meier's book *The Power of Their Ideas: Lessons for America from a Small School in Harlem* (1996), one of the most important guides to the deep principles and the practical realities of starting and running a truly different kind of high school.

When we were planning to create our own high school, we visited countless sites around the country, but we kept coming back to CPESS, and we ended up shamelessly imitating many of its ideas, structures, and procedures. While we felt a little guilty about aping another school so slavishly, we were also comforted by the fact that CPESS has been experimenting, growing, and refining its program for more than twenty-five years. When you are running a school just over four years old, contemplating how far you still have to go, it is reassuring to know how long it takes to become great.

As harmonious as we felt with Coalition values, the vision we had for our own high school was different in a few important respects, so we didn't seek membership in the Coalition, officially adopt its key principles, or copy every structure we saw at CPESS. We were uncomfortable with the Coalition's description of the "student as worker." While we understood the point of the mantra—that kids should be active meaning makers, not recipients of information—we liked the idea of "students as citizens" better. While the Coalition's focus on smallness and personalization resonated with us, we felt that decentralized forms of instruction were just as important as smaller class sizes and teacher loads. And as much as we admired the Coalition's signature graduation-by-exhibition model, the seniors we met in some schools seemed overwhelmed with completing their monumental portfolios, many times involving ten or twelve large projects, some of which seemed mechanical and uninspiring. We hoped to devise a senior experience that was more narrowly focused on students' interests. We also had some different ideas about how the teachers would govern themselves, which we discuss in Chapter 4. Looking back on these judgments five years later, we do still differ philosophically and operationally with CPESS on a few matters—while on others we clearly might have been better off to borrow even more of their hard-earned ideas.

The loosely organized "small schools movement," which we'll discuss at length in Chapter 2, has spawned the growth of smaller, more personalized high schools (and elementary schools) around the country, and has begun to document significant changes in student achievement in these special learning environments. Students do better both academically and personally in schools (including clearly defined schools-within-schools) that are small—fewer than 500 students. But limited enrollment isn't the only ingredient of truly successful small schools. According to the Small Schools Workshop, a Chicago-based national clearinghouse, the best small schools have a clear mission or theme, open admissions, deep parent involvement, and strong professional community among teachers. The evidence that smallness works is mounting so dramatically that recent federal funding for high school reform is being targeted at efforts to help oversized high schools feel smaller and work smaller for students. In some ways, the small schools movement seems to be at the same level of development today that middle schools were perhaps twenty years back— at the beginning of an effort that, over the long term, shows genuine promise of changing the paradigm of high schools across the country.

There are many other groups, movements, and documents that have helped shape this emerging consensus. As far back as 1990, a highly influential U.S. Labor Department report titled *The Secretary's Commission on Achieving the Necessary Skills (SCANS)* outlined what high school graduates should know and be able to do as effective citizens, workers, and parents. In a surprise to many who work inside public education, the report listed eight key outcomes, only one of which involved the "basic academic skills" taught and tested by the standard U.S. curriculum. Just as important to life success, according to SCANS, were skills like working effectively on a team, managing time and resources, using technology, and operating in a multicultural society. The SCANS report dovetailed powerfully with the research of Fred Newmann and his colleagues, who documented the need for schoolwork to become more authentic, genuine, and applicable to real-world problems and activities.

Breaking Ranks, a 1996 report from the National Association of Secondary School Principals, looked as though school administrators had been studying the SCANS report right along with the national curriculum standards. The principals sounded six themes of change: personalization, coherency, time, technology, professional development, and leadership. The report acknowledged that American high schools had a long history of clinging to outmoded and counterproductive practices, and called for high schools to "be much more student-centered and above all much more personalized in programs, support, services, and intellectual rigor." Coming from principals, who work inside the system, these recommendations carried special weight—and their congruence with the view of other reformers helped to sharpen the emerging picture of a better kind of high school.

The United States Department of Education (USDE) has recently begun promoting its own broad vision of high school reform, called the New American High Schools (NAHS—the same name is also being used by the quite different initiative of the National Center for Education and the Economy, a private group). The NAHS is primarily a recognition program that locates and honors schools that are working well and offers them as models to be studied and adapted by others. The designated NAHS schools are demographically divergent: they include small and large schools, rural and urban locations, and both open admissions and selective entry policies. The diversity is intentional. As a 1999 USDE report explains, "Although each New American High School is committed to rigorous academic standards that prepare all students for college and careers, each uses different methods for reaching this goal. Each school has undertaken the challenge of reform in its own way."

SCHOOL REFORM COMES TO HIGH SCHOOL—AT LAST

The fractious debate over "just how bad are our high schools?" has now been raging for over fifteen years. There have been plenty of bright spots in secondary education, as we noted earlier in this chapter. But the bigger picture is undeniably troubling. Most high schools have shown little or no progress during the recent reform era, especially compared with the improvements in the lower grades. In Chicago, where the percentage of elementary schools on probation has dropped from 20 percent to 7 percent in recent years, more than half of our seventy-four high schools remain on academic probation, because fewer than 20 percent of their students can read at national norms. This pattern is reflected across the country. Even elite high schools, those with significant numbers of high-performing students, often cater to a few star students at the expense of the wider student body, leaving "regular" kids unknown, unchallenged, and psychologically discarded.

Indeed, most American high schools still look pretty much the way they did when the milestone *A Nation at Risk* report was released in 1983 and, for that matter, how they looked in 1923. Even acknowledging that promising innovations are afoot here and there, and factoring in a healthy skepticism about perennial gloom-and-doom scenarios, the conclusion is inescapable: American high schools are far from becoming the vibrant incubators of intelligence, creativity, and citizenship that reform envisioned.

As institutions, high schools are profoundly, frustratingly intractable. They seem to shrug off all criticism, squirm out from under all indictments, and repel all change. In order to document any significant improvement in

American high schools at all, we are forced to look back across many decades. From this longer perspective, we can identify some patterns of permanent growth: at the start of this century, females were just starting to be grudgingly included in public high school programs, and ritualized corporal punishment was still a routine part of school life. Now, with the turn of the millennium, girls are apparently here to stay, and caning is on the wane. But what a slow system!

Change in high schools seems to unfold in geologic time, more resembling plate tectonics than social engineering. Indeed, geology may be the proper metaphor for talking about high school reform in America. We know, for example, that the earth's continental plates do not move at a steady, gradual pace, but rather in sudden fits and starts—short bursts of change followed by long periods of stasis. Well, we've had about eighty years of stasis in American high schools; and we could really use an earthquake.

Of course, all this resistance to change is neither accidental nor perverse. In a sense, schools are *designed* to be conservative institutions. One of the main functions of education is to transmit the core traditions of a culture to its children. With this as one of their missions, we shouldn't really expect public schools to be hotbeds of social experimentation or cutting-edge innovation. On the other hand, high schools are also supposed to equip students to function as adults in the "real world" outside their doors. Depending upon the moment in history, high schools may be more or less closely attuned to that world. Back in the 1920s, when high schools were systematically redesigned to mimic factory models of organization, they were arguably preparing kids for the manufacturing-oriented economy of that era.

But today, American high schools seem more out of synch with society than at any other time in our national history. High schools aren't just lagging a bit behind the times—they have become an anachronism. In spite of a few mid-course corrections, they remain wedded to the archaic, eighty-year-old manufacturing model, where the students substitute for widgets flowing down an assembly line. Our high schools are better suited to making Model Ts than programming computers, more attuned to 1920 than to Y2K. Even the field from which the factory model was borrowed—assembly line manufacturing—has long since moved on to more effective patterns of organization.

Our outdated high school model also carries with it the harsh and retrograde social attitudes of the factories in which it grew: the authoritarianism, the class stratification, the treatment of human beings as machines, and the pillaging of resources. Clearly, these are not the values we should embrace in the schools of the new millennium. Instead of training docile workers for smokestack industries, we should be mentoring young citizens. As George Wood has so eloquently put it:

> High school is democracy's finishing school—the last shared experience that all Americans will enjoy, the place where the skills and dispositions that citizens in a democracy need should be secured and nurtured in all of our youth. Our children leave high school as fully enfranchised citizens, not only able to take a job or go to college, but also to vote, to engage in discussion over public issues, to buy the house next door, to become our neighbors. To live up to this task, the place we call high school should . . . teach each student, through example, what it means to be part of a democratic community. (38)

Since the three of us are parents as well as educators, we also look at the crisis in American high schools in personal terms. As we have raised seven high school graduates among us (with one still in the pipeline), we have repeatedly been reminded, viscerally reminded, of the way high school *feels*. Some of our children were welcomed and reasonably well served by their schools, others had mixed or indifferent experiences, and some were ignored, misunderstood, or injured.

When we put our family experiences together with our professional concerns, we feel that the most urgent problem with American high schools is not their long-term statistics or their ranking in international tests, but how they are treating millions of real, live kids *today*. High school is personal. It stands at the center of the complicated and challenging stage of life that is adolescence. How young people are treated in these places during these years has profound impact on their present as well as their future.

High schools are the places where our society officially gathers its young people during adolescence. As an institution, high school can either make this time better—more supportive, more helpful, more constructive—or it can make it worse. Far too often, high school makes things worse. Young people who are yearning for connection are silenced and marched through compulsory exercises, programmed into endless, disconnected days of involuntary activities, and overseen by adults who cannot know them and do not have the opportunity to care. Thus, in the seams and on the fringes of this unhelpful institution, young people are left to struggle on their own, often heroically, to find links with the larger world and to forge identities.

Any consideration of secondary education in America must address the recent outbreak of student shootings in our schools. In the wake of these chilling events, critics have laid the blame on ineffective parents, or dysfunctional communities, or video games, or unchecked bullying, or on the schools themselves. Indeed, a 2000 report on school violence by the FBI named overall school climate as one factor that can prevent or increase the risk of school shootings. The FBI warned against "a static, unyielding and insensitive" school culture, inequitable discipline rules, and a "pecking order" in which some groups of students are considered more prestigious than others (Dorning 2000). But as James Garbarino points out in *Lost Boys* (1999), his searing book about youth violence, when all the analyzing and blaming are done, one inescapable fact remains: for a variety of reasons, most American high schools are likely to enroll some young people who are dangerously close to the edge. And the experience they have in school can either pull them back or push them over.

To summarize: From the unromantic standpoint of efficiency and economics, America's high schools are badly out of tune with the times. Ethically and politically, they are a telling contradiction of our national ideals and espousals of democracy. From the kid's-eye view, looked at as a place where a young person might grow and develop, they are usually boring, frequently a waste of time—and sometimes a danger. We are brought to the sad but inevitable conclusion: America's high schools are failing all of our kids some of the time and some of our kids all the time.

But we can do better. And in many places around the country, we are. Teachers, kids, principals, parents, community members, and local employers are joining together to make their high schools better for young people—more challenging, more authentic, and more collaborative.

In popular culture, adolescence is routinely depicted as a wholly negative time, a stretch of misery, a struggle and a curse. Those of us who work with teenagers every day reject this toxic stereotype. Of course, these years can be hard, damn hard, even heartbreaking at times. But adolescence is also suffused with amazing, joyful, exhilarating possibilities: deep friendship, powerful emotion, reaching toward the new, trying on and discarding possible identities, coming into possession of your powers as a physical body and a thinking person. And let's not forget music and laughter and dancing and, maybe, falling in love a time or two.

Today, too many of these exciting, crucial, transforming, and joyful moments of adolescent life happen outside of school—or in spite of school. Is that how we want it?

Chapter 2
Size

The high school is small—or feels small.

It's 8:15 on a Thursday morning, and the three of us are hurrying to an early meeting at Best Practice High School. It has been a tough week; a million problems, nothing seems to be working right. For about the six hundredth time, we're wondering why we ever started this school in the first place. We park the car and trudge up Adams Street toward the entrance, joining the stream of students strolling from the bus stop on Damen. As it happens, we fall in step about twenty-five feet behind Candace Walker, a junior student who was home sick yesterday, absent for one day. She doesn't notice us as we walk quietly along, preoccupied with our own worries.

As Candace climbs the front steps, we hear two kids say, "Hi," and ask her where she was on Wednesday. She goes through the door and past James, the security guard, who greets her by name with a smile. Still walking behind Candace, we start paying attention. Along the first-floor corridor, social studies teacher Peter Thomas passes going the other way saying, "Ah, you're back." Going up the stairwell, first one kid and then another greets her. One asks, "Where were you yesterday?" Another warns, "You missed a test in math, girl." Twenty feet further on, lead teacher Kathy Daniels stops and asks Candace if she's feeling better. We are still following quietly behind, counting the check-ins. Within two minutes, between the front steps and the third floor, Candace has been greeted, acknowledged, welcomed by nine different people, both teachers and kids.

Marilyn has coined a phrase to describe events like this one. She says, "Even when it's not working, it's working." We have come to realize that there are certain structural features of high schools that can work for kids, that can make the environment supportive—by design. Lesson plans may fail, teachers may have bad days, standardized tests may distort the curriculum, and a thousand other efforts may flounder. But if the school is designed correctly, there will be some underlying, built-in elements that work for kids every day, no matter what. People will know each other. Teachers will have small daily advisories where they connect with the same kids for four years. The staff will be teamed so that they follow small cohorts of kids, and scheduled with common planning time so they can share these students' struggles and successes. And whenever we think about these special design features, the word *small* keeps coming up, again and again.

THINKING ABOUT SCHOOL SIZE

When we do workshops on high school restructuring with teachers or parents, we sometimes start off with this simple puzzle: "Why do elephants have big ears?" We invite people to get into small groups and pool their knowledge, trying to come up with theories about the purpose of those distinctive elephantine accessories.

Once people get past the usual jokes about flying like Dumbo or swatting insects, they often start theorizing that the prime function of elephants' ears is *cooling*. Indeed, these handy devices are filled with small blood vessels that, as their owners fan them back and forth, act as quite efficient radiators for the large amount of heat created by the animal's metabolism. As this body-cooling theory emerges, we throw in another question: "Why don't *mice* (or squirrels or guinea pigs) have big ears, too?" This tends to slow things down a bit.

As groups work on the problem, we hand out stacks of wooden blocks—just the regular one-inch toy-store variety with alphabet letters. We encourage participants to assemble model "animals" of different sizes using their blocks. Thus, a single cube might represent a mouse, while a 6 × 6 × 6 cube (containing 216 blocks) could stand for an elephant.

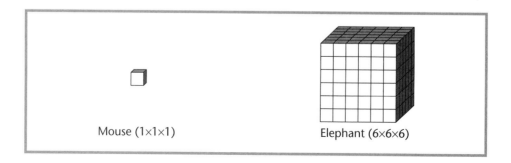

Mouse (1×1×1) Elephant (6×6×6)

The blocks (or "manipulatives," as we'd call them in first-grade math) help people to look three-dimensionally at the relationship between surface area and volume. They demonstrate the physical fact that as size increases, the ratio of surface area to volume decreases. For example, consider the calculations for the simplified "mouse" and "elephant" in our diagram.

"Mouse"	"Elephant"
Surface area: $1 \times 1 \times 6$ sides = 6	Surface area: $6 \times 6 \times 6$ sides = 216
Volume: $1 \times 1 \times 1 = 1$	Volume: $6 \times 6 \times 6 = 216$
Ratio of surface area to volume: 6:1	Ratio of surface area to volume: 1:1

These findings suggest that if an animal has a high ratio of surface area to volume, body cooling can be accomplished through radiation from the skin—a simple and straightforward adaptation. But as the volume rises relative to available skin surface, some other structure or process must aid in cooling. Just visualize the thick mass of hot tissue simmering inside a huge critter like an elephant, and you realize the need for those big mobile radiators mounted on their heads. Of course, there are lots of other solutions to the cooling problem—some anatomical, some metabolic, some behavioral. Hippos, shaped a lot like elephants but with tiny ears, deal with heat by wallowing in cool mud. Dogs, who can't perspire, drool to cool. And so on.

So, what does this exercise say about school? The point is that *as things get bigger, they become different in kind*—and this goes for human institutions like schools just as much as it does for animals in the wild. As our schools get bigger, how do they get different? In great big high schools, how do kids and teachers cope? Do we (metaphorically) drool? Wallow? Grow organs?

In the animal kingdom, increases in size bring problems with cooling. In the school world, increases in size bring problems with almost *everything*. When high schools have enrollments in the thousands, they sprout all kinds of specialized organs and behaviors to cope with their massive size—bell schedules, attendance offices, up and down staircases, ability grouping, detention rooms, multilevel tracking systems, random locker searches, hallways full of noneducators with walkie-talkies who herd and spy on students, and physically separate "administration buildings," where the leaders of the school work entirely without student contact.

In addition to the structures spawned by adults, young people also invent ways of making big schools feel smaller, the most notorious of which is "cliques." Almost any large high school's student body is divided into several unofficial but very powerful subgroups, each with a name, a characteristic look, a fixed ranking on the social scale, and very little mobility of membership between them. At one enormous suburban high school we know well, a group of students readily named the main cliques: nerds, jocks, preps, hippies, artsies, druggies, punks, straight-edge, neonazis, and gays. While adults often bemoan the existence of these cliques, even berate students from forming them, they can also be looked at as an attempt by young people to create some kind of community in the midst of overwhelming bigness. Sadly, it may feel better to be labeled as a punk and restricted to that category than to be adrift in a school of 2,000 kids without any attachment, any home.

Many of our high schools have now grown so big that the local eighth graders are literally afraid to go there. Every September, at family dining-room tables all across America, new freshmen report to their parents how they got lost in their huge new school, dragging a forty-pound backpack up and down cavernous stairwells and across acres of hallways, with three minutes to get to a class a quarter-mile away.

Of course, bigness also has its compensations. Sometimes, larger high schools can offer a wider range of courses, with the possibility of engaging more students' interests or developing their talents. They can also draw on larger student talent pools to field more competitive football teams and stage more professional musical shows. Since their larger faculties have a wider range of interests and skills, big schools can sponsor a greater array of after-school, extracurricular activities, offering outlets for diverse student interests.

However, the fact that big schools can offer these benefits does not guarantee that they do. Sometimes, big high schools don't so much offer different courses, but rather different *levels* of the same few courses, most prescribed by state or local mandates or by college entrance requirements. The course catalog may look thick, but when an actual student sits down to choose her courses for the next year, there's often little real choice at all, except, will it be Spanish or French, and how hard do I want each course to be?

Offering three or four or five levels of the same course doesn't exactly make a curriculum "broad." And such course leveling certainly doesn't respond to student interests—what it mainly does is promote student-against-student competition, while making teachers' classroom instruction a little easier by providing homogeneous classes. From the student's-eye view, different ability tracks aren't choices at all. Indeed, which would you rather pick from—five different difficulty levels of sophomore English or, say, Shakespeare's tragedies, writing poetry, modern nonfiction, journalism, and mystery literature?

Of course, a sizable fraction of students are well served by large high schools, even huge, gigantic high schools. Generally, those kids in the top rank of academic talent and social ease don't just negotiate a big school; they thrive in it. As one of our colleagues puts it: "These kids happen to high school, rather than having high school happen to them." They can quickly figure out the rules, learn how to "listen fast" to lecture-style teaching, memorize effectively, get good grades, display their talents, and attract the attention of faculty who will mentor them. Not surprisingly, the parents of these selected kids become fierce advocates of the school and its "excellent program," and they watch their privileged progeny graduate near the top of the class. The problem is that everybody else, the other hundreds or thousands of kids who were never invited to join the "excellent program," drift through high school unengaged, overlooked, and underserved. At best, this neglected majority of kids will simply survive high school, developing their talents elsewhere or later in life. A few will become angry and resentful, unconsciously realizing that they deserve better. At the very worst, for kids who are already troubled and struggling outside of school, being treated like a discard in a huge, uncaring high school can be another factor that feeds rage and violence.

RESEARCH ON SMALL SCHOOLS

Research has been rapidly accumulating that, as far as high school is concerned, size does matter—and smaller is better. So what makes small high schools good? Maybe we should start by asking the privileged parents who spend upwards of $20,000 a year to send their children to the nation's elite private schools. What are these families paying for at Andover, Choate, St. Albans, the Sidwell Friends, or the Blake Schools? Here in our hometown of Chicago, what do parents prize about Francis Parker, the University of Chicago Laboratory School, or the Latin School? Among other things, they are almost always getting a small school, with a guarantee that each student will be known, included, attended to, kept track of, challenged, cared about, and maybe even loved.

The educational value of small schools—private or public—has been documented in a long and impressive body of academic research (Hill, Foster, and Gendler 1990; Hallinan 1994). A number of recent studies have shown that small school size is related to improvements in student test scores and grades (Klonsky 1995, 1998; Raywid 1995; Meier 1995, 1996). The Coalition of Essential Schools, which has always held small, personalized learning environments as one of its key tenets, has repeatedly documented improvements in student test scores and the completion of college-level courses (Coalition of Essential Schools 1995a, 1995b). Crain et al. (1997) concluded that small learning environments could account for a variety of important outcomes, including a better school climate, less class cutting, less drinking, and more college credits earned.

Chicago's nationally watched reform process has provided a laboratory for studying the connection between school size and student achievement. Since the 1988 reform legislation was passed, the Consortium on Chicago School Research at the University of Chicago has done independent studies, and one of their most striking findings has been that small schools have been able to take far better advantage of school reform than larger ones. In the Consortium's 1993 report, Lee, Bryk, and Smith showed that school size was a key factor in explaining variation in student achievement and engagement. A later study showed that school size had positive effects on such measures as student attendance rates, frequency of disciplinary actions, school loyalty, satisfaction with school, and self-esteem (Klonsky 1995).

Summarizing the literature on school size, Visher, Emanuel, and Teitelbaum (1999) conclude:

> Investigations of the effects of school size on a range of outcomes have been one of the longest and best-established traditions in the field of education research. Researchers and educators have studied this issue extensively, using data ranging from large nationally representative surveys to small qualitative case studies of schools of varying sizes. Rigorous statistical analysis has been applied in attempting to isolate the effect of school size from other variables. . . . The majority has found that size matters for outcomes such as academic achievement, graduation and dropout rates, and successful school-to-work transitions. With a few exceptions, most studies have shown that small environments lead to improved outcomes. (23)

Another research summary, this one compiled by the Small Schools Workshop in Chicago, confirms the special value of small schools for students who have not been well served by traditional high school structures.

■ Female and nonwhite students, in particular, do better in smaller schools.

- Students with special needs, including so-called "at risk," "exceptional," "disadvantaged," and "gifted" students, are better served by smaller school units.

- Small school size greatly improves attendance rates and lowers dropout rates.

- In the small-school environment, security improves and violence decreases, as does student alcohol and drug abuse.

Indeed, as Ayers, Klonsky, and Lyon conclude in their 2000 book *A Simple Justice: The Challenge of Small Schools*, providing small schools for disadvantaged students might be looked on not as a matter of educational innovation but of civil rights.

All these good outcomes are not a simple result of smallness alone. Small school size is one of several design features that combine to create a distinctive and principled learning environment. Researchers have found that smallness seems to work as a facilitating factor for other desirable practices (Lee and Smith 1995), such as personalizing the school climate, raising teachers' expectations of students, enhancing teacher collaboration, detracking leveled classes, forging external partnerships, and establishing collective responsibility for student achievement—all of which can contribute to elevated student achievement. One of the most important and best documented "indirect" effects of small school size is "professional community" among teachers (Newmann 1995). In small schools teachers typically have more time, opportunities, and procedures for meeting with each other, planning cooperatively, and tracking the progress of individual students. It is features like these that combine to help students achieve better in small schools than traditional settings.

BEST PRACTICE HIGH SCHOOL: STARTING SMALL

From the moment our friend Madeleine Maraldi challenged us to start a new high school, even when we were just humoring her about actually doing it, we knew it had to be small. Madeleine was the principal of Washington Irving, one of fourteen elementary schools where we had been doing staff development for several years, and she was pressing us to create a progressive alternative for some eighth-grade graduates. As we warmed to this improbable idea, we immediately realized that we had better start small, beginning with a group of freshmen and growing one year at a time. At that point, we hadn't yet studied the burgeoning body of research on the academic and social benefits of small schools. It was just our gut-level assumption that big-ness is a primary design flaw of traditional high schools. Above all, we wanted our school to be a personal place, where every single kid was known and cared about, where nobody could fall through the cracks.

But how small is small, when you are starting a new high school? We'd heard about many Coalition of Essential Schools around the country and New Visions schools in New York that had begun with groups of fewer than a hun-dred and had carefully grown over several years. Many opened with enroll-ments around seventy-five, using three teachers with multiple certifications who could handle the whole curriculum and teach the whole day. Obviously, schools this small dramatically address one of the most dysfunctional struc-tures of traditional high schools, where teachers work with 150 kids a day. With so many people filing through your classroom every day, how can you possibly know all of them well, give them personal attention and care?

When we were starting BPHS, we were lucky enough to get some personal help from the smartest high school educator we know, Deborah Meier, the founder and former principal of Central Park East Secondary School (CPESS). Deborah had thought a lot about school size. First of all, she reminded us that small high schools are no great invention, no newfangled experiment. In fact, she said, every big high school in America *already* has a small school hidden inside it—an unofficial but highly developed and powerful institution. Usu-ally, this small school consists of the 200 or 300 students who star on the sports teams, excel in academics, and lead extracurricular activities. What these kids get that other students don't get is extra time with adults—extra mentoring, modeling, and coaching. They get this special treatment while spending countless after-school hours in rehearsals, on practice fields, or in cars headed for distant games or debate tournaments. They develop relation-ships with teachers that are more personal, richer, and more lasting than most students ever enjoy. And these special kids' parents, not surprisingly, tend to become big boosters of the school, even though they may not quite recognize how different their child's experience is from most. Deborah's critique went far beyond our own inchoate suspicions that big high schools tended to favor their "top" kids; she showed us that the problem was structural, it was *designed* into the system.

So how do students get "admitted" to the unannounced small-school pro-gram in every big public high school? By being high achievers, by being unusually personable, by being fluent with adults—or some combination of the above. And though Deborah didn't put it this way, our own experience as parents suggests another "admission" criterion: showing an early talent in some conspicuously adult-pleasing activity. Kids who do something adults admire and approve of—like playing the violin—have a much better chance of being drafted into the small school than, say, those who show an early talent for punk rock drumming.

Deborah's point was that small schools are already implicitly recognized throughout American secondary education as a good way to nurture young people to use their minds well and to become valued and valuable citizens. She just thought that *every* kid should be in a small school, instead of just a secretly selected fraction. This could happen if people started new small schools, as Deborah had done, and as we were now doing—or by breaking bigger schools up into smaller, identifiable units.

Sitting at the breakfast table at Steve's house, Deborah was very firm about what "small" high schools meant. Any more than 400 kids was too many. She said that when CPESS surpassed this number, things started to feel as if they were falling apart, that people would sometimes forget kids' names and stories. She talked about how CPESS had recently drifted over its own self-imposed limit and how they were trying to shrink back to their original number.

Having visited her school twice and witnessed its powerfully cohesive and caring atmosphere, we were surprised by her self-criticism. While our planning team had always wanted a small school, we still wondered: only 400? Some of the Chicago staffing regulations made it advantageous for us to go closer to 500. Would there really be any difference? We were coming from a world where schools with thousands of kids was considered normal, so this 400 limit sounded somewhat arbitrary, even a little dogmatic.

We pondered the numbers. Since we were going to be a regular Chicago public school, and not a charter school exempt from Board and union rules, we needed to look closely at CPS staffing formulas. According to the rules, if we admitted a freshman class of about 140 kids, we could get five teachers—one English, one social studies, one math, one science, and one elective teacher—just enough to create a legal freshman curriculum and cover the mandated subjects. A nice loophole in Board guidelines, which never anticipated any intentionally small high schools, was that we would get a full-time librarian regardless of our enrollment. We also found that if we had ten or more special ed kids (which we were committed to anyway), we'd get a full-time special education teacher. Finally, depending on how many of our kids were classified as low income, we'd receive just enough Chapter I money to hire two additional staff members. Lead teacher Tom Daniels would use one slot as our computer teacher, and we would need a coordinator for our school-to-work internship program. Down the road were some other goodies. Though we'd never get more than a fraction of a social worker and nurse, their time with us would grow with our enrollment. We'd also get one counselor when we hit 200 students, during our second year, and another counselor two years after that.

One hundred forty seemed like our magic opening number, though multiplying it by four pushed our eventual enrollment well over Deborah's red line. Still, given that the K–8 network urging us to launch this adventure had fourteen schools, the mathematics was compelling: if we admitted ten kids from each school, that would give us the freshman class we needed. We could set up a lottery: if a school sent us ten kids, we'd take all ten; if they sent fifteen, we'd select ten at random; if they sent us only five, we'd put the extra five back in the pool and take more kids from other schools. It made things simpler that we didn't want a selective admissions process—we just wanted a good assortment of the kids in the network schools. Ultimately, this formula worked perfectly our first year—"perfectly" in the sense that only 137 kids applied, and we took every single one.

FINDING A FACULTY

We also needed to assemble a small community of teachers. We'd begun with Tom and Kathy Daniels, who'd taught English around the city for twenty-five years each, leading workshops for colleagues, writing curriculum for the Board, and spearheading the Illinois Writing Project. Along with Steve, Marilyn, and Harvey as university planning partners, they'd dreamed up the plans, coauthored the proposal, and lobbied a host of officials at the central office. Then we waited. Despite the efforts of dozens of friends both inside and outside the Board of Education, silence reigned. One long year and one superintendent later, our languishing proposal was suddenly green-lighted. Now it was time to actually find some colleagues.

Since we figured that most of our first year's staff would be experienced teachers transferring in from some of Chicago's seventy-three other high schools, our main advertising consisted of an announcement in the district's weekly bulletin. We described the school's progressive, integrated-curriculum model and listed some open-ended teaching positions. The plan was to read résumés first and then screen possible candidates on the phone. We'd invite the most promising ones for an interview with the whole team and then visit the classroom of anyone who seemed like a possible fit. We ran the search on a "rolling admissions" basis. The five of us selected the sixth staff member, who happened to be librarian Jackie Chappel, and then we added her to our search team. Then the six of us screened, interviewed, and observed candidates for the next job. As each faculty member was hired, he or she joined the search committee of the whole and had a voice in the selection of all succeeding teachers. This meant an increasingly cumbersome process and growing scheduling headaches, but everyone had a real chance to pick their colleagues.

One of the joys of beginning a new small school is that instead of hiring people to staff a program, you can create a program around special people. We knew that our students would have to take three years of laboratory science, but until we met Arthur Griffin, we'd never even heard of the Physics First approach. When Arthur sat down with us and explained the vision, described his hands-on, collaborative approach to physics, and told us about his work with Nobel laureate Leon Lederman, we raced to see his classroom on the south side. It didn't hurt that Arthur had grown up in our school's neighborhood, that his father was a prominent minister in the community, that he played piano and organ, and was a choir director. Within a few days of our meeting Arthur, Best Practice became one of two Physics First schools in Chicago—a decision that would lead, three years later, to some of the highest science test scores in the city.

Aiko Boyce was a similar story. The CPS curriculum guidelines said freshmen needed a fifth subject, which could be a foreign language, home economics, music, business, or a variety of other courses. Then Aiko showed up, an award-winning art teacher from a north side high school, talking about ways of using art to integrate the curriculum, explaining how computers were changing the world of art, showing us examples of her students' gorgeous artwork in a variety of media, and looking for a chance to grow herself. Suddenly it became clear that art should be our fifth freshman subject, and it has been the glue holding together many of our best integrated units ever since. Aiko also turned out to be the school's unofficial documentarian and record keeper; whenever we need photographs or videos or just a clear recollection of some past school event, we know where to go.

We could have offered several different social studies courses to freshmen, but Tom and Kathy persuaded their longtime colleague Peter Thomas from Farragut High School to apply for a job. Peter had a rare and deep background in geography, with a specialty in urban geography and an encyclopedic knowledge of the city of Chicago—perfect for a school committed to making the community part of the curriculum. Mathematics was a must, and we liked what we saw in Mark Fertel's humorous and energetic algebra and geometry classes. The bonus was that we also got a chess coach, a computer whiz, scheduling expert, a future lead teacher, and a much-needed linear thinker on a faculty overbalanced with left-brainers. We knew we'd never locate a CPS teacher with prior experience running a comprehensive school-to-work internship program. But then we found Shelley Freeman, an elementary art teacher who had already been placing her own students as docents in a local museum. Within a few months, Shelley had parlayed her service learning experience and citywide personal contacts into 137 weekly placements.

Our growing search committee was a little skeptical when Sonja Kosanovic applied for our special education slot from Ruiz Elementary. How could someone who had worked only with little kids possibly meet the needs of the full-size LD students in our prospective freshman class? At the interview, Sonja confidently explained how she would set up a one-woman, full-inclusion special education program. She calmly committed herself to learn physics, a subject she had never taken, if that was what the kids would be studying. When we visited Sonja's resource room at Ruiz and saw her working with skill and delicacy with great big junior high kids, we knew she would make the jump to high school just fine. With the addition of Pat Gregory, a wonderful physical education teacher who focused as much on team building and community as on traditional sports, our first-year faculty was complete. Finally, to run our office, we recruited mother hen and vocabulary master Gwen Downing and our efficient chenchita clerk Olga Lamourt.

STRUCTURING THE STUDENT BODY

Once our freshmen class was assembled, the faculty had to decide how to program them. The size of our initial enrollment and our eventual growth to about 440 were fixed by the proposal approved by the CPS, but how should we structure our student body? We could split the students into two teams or "houses" of about seventy kids each, reducing every teacher's student load by half and making the school feel even smaller. University partners Steve, Marilyn, and Harvey argued for houses, pointing to the successful models we'd visited elsewhere. This approach would pose some teacher certification problems, though these probably could be worked out. But the teachers really wanted to teach all 137 kids. Two arguments carried the day: one was that the teachers didn't feel comfortable enough with the "house" structure, didn't feel prepared to operate something so different from their past experience. And secondly, people were simply looking forward to working with all the kids we'd recruited for our school. They were excited by the planning process, had bonded to each other, and didn't like the idea of splitting the brand-new school in half before it even began. They figured that since the school itself would be small, since all nine teachers would be working with every kid, and since we were committed to daily advisories, there would be plenty of personalization built in.

Further, since we planned to use a block schedule, teachers wouldn't actually see all 137 kids every day, but about half that number—and none on Wednesdays, when kids would be out at their internships. While our schedule later went through some unforeseen gyrations that we'll describe in Chapter 8, this prediction did generally come true. And above all, the teachers were committed to teaching in ways that made the school and its classrooms feel small. We felt we had enough kinds of "small" built into the plan.

Since our breakfast with Deborah Meier five years ago, we have grown in four steps to 440 kids, and we can testify that Deborah was right, there is a limit. While on August 23, 1996, our 137 freshmen did seem like a horde, they quickly settled into a very manageable and personable group. Adding the second class felt like a relatively minor adjustment. We'd hired a strong corps of new teachers, and we were pleased to see how the sophomores showed the ropes to the newcomers. When we added the third class, growing to 330, the building suddenly seemed full. There were lots of size and space issues to deal with, and while the program still seemed to work well in grade-level teams, whole-school cohesion seemed weaker. The next year, when we added our final class, even though we purposely took a smaller group, we suddenly felt overwhelmed with kids—there were bodies everywhere.

At 440 students, we are really pushing the limit of smallness. The halls are so jammed and noisy between classes that it is impossible to hear or to think. It's harder to notice, as we used to do so effortlessly, who's present and who's missing on a given day. Where our clerk, Olga, used to call home about every absent student during our first two years, she simply cannot do it with 440 kids, and there's no funding to assign this task to someone else. While every student is still known intimately by one faculty advisor, and known very well by all the members of their grade-level team, there may be other adults in the building who know them only by face or name. This is especially true with incoming students in the fall; it takes a while for the teachers who work on the junior or senior team to get to know the new freshmen. So we're not quite a big school, but we are teetering on the brink. Four hundred does seem to be the practical maximum for a high school that wants to be small.

Deborah gave us one other way to monitor the size of our high school: when the faculty can no longer sit around a table and meet face to face, she said, the school has gotten too big. Well, you should see all the tables we now have to push together every Monday afternoon to meet Deborah's criterion! When everyone shows up, there are thirty-four of us: twenty-one classroom teachers, a lead teacher, a lead/computer teacher, an internship coordinator, a librarian, two counselors, a building principal and assistant principal, three university partners, and two office staff members. We can still do it, still deal with issues as a whole—but perhaps only because we started four years ago with only twelve of us, and have adapted as we kept widening the circle. And we've increasingly found faculty closeness and collaboration in smaller groups, especially in our grade-level teams of five and six.

THE COSTS OF SMALLNESS

In Chicago, all eighth-grade graduates can apply to attend any of the city's high schools, and fewer than half ultimately attend their neighborhood high school. While a handful of vaunted high schools with selective entrance requirements are inundated with applicants, the other schools—including BPHS—have to find their own students. So every fall, we visit a number of elementary buildings and high school fairs to talk with eighth graders. And when we meet them, we have to be honest about what our school has—and what it doesn't have. We talk to them about the advantages of smallness, of being known, of our family spirit, of the chances to connect with other kids from all corners of the city, of our care that no one ever falls "through the cracks."

But more than once we've had to tell an eager young man, "If you really want to play varsity football, you'd better go somewhere else," or say to an outstanding musician, "Sorry, but we don't have a marching band." As a small school, there are some things we cannot do—and that big schools do better. But when we "lose" a kid like this, we feel comforted by the thought that if she already has a clear-cut interest, talent, or direction, she will probably find a niche in a bigger high school. Maybe she'll even be inducted into that secret "small school" Deborah Meier talked about. And after all, if a young person has found an interest that could help launch her life and livelihood—whether it is in athletics, music, or astronomy—we're happy to see her go where she will be both noticed and challenged.

Compared to the larger city schools, not to mention the rich suburban schools nearby, we have a pretty meager assortment of after-school activities. Yes, many of our teachers do stay to give extra help to students; we keep the computer lab open for kids who want to stay late; we have some sports teams that practice and play in second-tier conferences (basketball for both boys and girls, volleyball, softball, and sporadic others, based on student interests); and we do have student council and other meetings. We compensate somewhat by offering special activities every Wednesday, during "choice time," a two-hour period when students can select from a dozen constantly changing topics, including art, chess, poetry, wrestling, cartooning, women's issues—or use the time to get special help from teachers in a variety of subjects. But still, we have no jazz band, no radio station, no improvisation club, no debate team. Because we are small, because our kids come from all over the city and many have a long trek home on the CTA (Chicago Transit Authority), because some have after-school jobs, and because resources and faculty energies are finite, we don't do much after school.

But some of us have also been parents at those rich suburban schools, and we've had some questions about the staggering variety of after-school clubs and activities offered in those places every day. Sometimes it seems as if the big suburban schools are saying, "Well, from 8:00 A.M. to 3:00 P.M., our program is pretty boring and regimented. We admit that we'll give you little choice or engagement, and that hardly any of the adults in this building will know or care who you are. But if you can hang on until 3:00, we have really great clubs. After school, you can follow your interests, work with other kids, and get personal contact with interested and interesting adults."

At Best Practice, we are saying something different. We admit that our small school doesn't have very many clubs. But between 8:30 A.M. and 3:00 P.M., we're going to do our damnedest to know you, to care for you, to challenge you—and not to waste your time. At our school, involvement is not an after-school activity.

A SENSE OF PLACE

As we were gathering the kids and teachers who would create BPHS, we were also thinking about space. We needed a place that would be right for a small school and that didn't mean just providing the necessary square footage or the right number of classrooms. We dreamed of something special, a place with character and texture, where we could build a home. We knew that wherever we ended up, we would be creating the environment right along with our first crew of students. We'd be able to look these kids in the eye and say, "We're going to build this school together. How do *you* want to it to be?"

After the frustrating and lengthy search that we describe in Chapter 12, we were offered a chance to share a beautiful 1902-vintage school building with two small elementary schools. One of the most exhilarating events in our history was when our embryonic faculty toured the building with the Board's architects, to give input on the remodeling plans. When we would ask, "Could you tear down this wall?" or "Could there be a bathroom over there?" they would simply say, "Sure," and make a note on a clipboard. We were drunk with power. We were doing something most teachers never get to do: planning the physical shape of our own school. Of course, five years later we realize that, in our intoxication, we made tons of mistakes.

Best Practice High School occupies half of the second floor and all of the third floor of our graceful gray building, while two elementary schools share the first floor and pieces of the second. Having this special place is important to our sense of identity and community. The building is handsome and historic, with its dark woodwork and iron railings well preserved. We like being on the upper floors, well above the street. Many of our classrooms have dramatic views of the skyline of downtown Chicago; the library has a twenty-foot-wide half-circular window that looks out over the city at treetop level. Turning west, we gaze over an unfinished work of urban renewal, where abandoned houses stand next to brand-new townhomes. Out the back door is the United Center, home of the Chicago Bulls and Blackhawks, just kitty-corner across the parking lot. When any Chicagoan asks where our school is, it only takes one sentence to guide them there. Taxi drivers never get lost trying to find us. We are in a distinctive, prominent, central, noteworthy, historic location. We like that.

Inside the building, we find that physical separation from the other schools is very important, though not all boundaries are clearly defined. The predictable problems of sharing a building tend to break out in the common spaces—the lunchroom, the auditorium, the front hall, the stairwell, the middle of the second floor. There's always friction in negotiating the use of one gym for 900 kids. Sometimes our students are too loud going down to lunch, and they bother the children in first-floor classrooms. Sometimes the little kids come through and litter our floors, just when we are having guests come to visit. Then those younger kids are occasionally exposed to premature sex education lessons when our high school couples pause for a grope in the stairwell. There's always plenty to talk about when the lead teachers of the three schools get together—and luckily for us, building principal Sylvia Gibson is a superb mediator.

Sometimes we like to think that these issues of turf and territory are distinctively Chicagoan, since we take perverse pride in our city's reputation for hardball local politics. But on reflection, we realize that space and place are important to all human beings, probably dating back to the days when our prehistoric ancestors battled over caves and the winners painted on the walls.

One piece of advice we would offer to anyone who is planning to create a new small school, or especially to launch a new program within a larger, existing school: find a special, identifiable, separate, and psychologically defensible space, whether that means marking it, walling it off, or building it.

Today, with 440 kids, we have finally outgrown our space in this beautiful place. We've had to split some big classrooms into two smaller, very cramped enclosures. We've walled off one hallway to make another room, relocated the school office into a ridiculously small space, and are now thinking about converting our beloved faculty workroom to a classroom. But as tight as our space needs get, there's one solution we have never even considered: having teachers share classrooms.

It isn't surprising that sharing rooms is standard procedure in most high schools. Simple efficiency says that if a teacher's load is five classes and a school day has seven periods, it's crazy to leave a classroom "fallow" for two periods a day, just so the teacher can have her own personal space. As any number-crunching school business officer could explain, a high school can operate with about one-third fewer classrooms if teachers share and if all classrooms are used every period.

This unassailable logic, of course, leads to high schools where teachers have no sense of home, no opportunity to create small subenvironments equipped for their discipline and infused with their own personality. Instead, both teachers and students shuffle between neutral, interchangeable, institutional settings, lacking both warmth and interest. To us at BPHS, it's impossible to think of teaching well without owning a space. Beth Meeker wouldn't be the same teacher without the comfy couches that sit by the window, under the ten-foot-tall "tree of life," which dangles its branches over her young readers and writers. And as Laura Linhart has gradually covered every square foot of Room 209 with lovely Spanish and Mexican artifacts, pictures, posters, and flags, she has made herself a better teacher—and immersed her kids ever more deeply in the language they are learning.

When teachers share rooms, the sacrifice involves more than aesthetic or morale problems. Teachers who want to employ "best practice" methods, using lots of hands-on materials, primary sources, simulations, experiments, work portfolios, and classroom libraries, must somehow drag all this stuff around their building. We remember following our friend Kath Bergin around Glenbard West High School during a year when each of her classes met in a different room. Kath had found herself a large cart and devised a system for storing on it everything she needed for "best practice on wheels." The cart weighed about eighty pounds. Not only did Kath have to push her vehicle down the hall six times a day through hordes of class-changing kids, she also had to get an elevator key and ride up and down four times, since her classes were on different floors. Twice a day, at lunch and during her planning period, she'd push her cart back to the English department office and reload.

Let's face it. Very few teachers—heck, very few normal human beings—have Kath's dogged dedication. Most of us would just give up and do it the easy way. Let each kid carry around their own textbook and leave it at that. So this simple, seemingly businesslike practice of not giving teachers their own classrooms actually has its own hidden costs. At worst, it degrades school climate and undermines good instruction. At BPHS, we seem to understand this in our bones. We've spent many hours talking about our urgent, sometimes critical space crunch. But no one has even mentioned the possibility of sharing classrooms. We'll handle it some other way.

HOW BIG SCHOOLS CAN GET SMALL

Many American high schools—or at least the buildings that house them—will remain physically large for the foreseeable future. The majority of our teenagers will remain packed into high schools that are too big by any standard, with 1,000, or 2,000, or even 4,000 pupils not being uncommon. The typical school board and its taxpayers are not going to shutter Central High and construct an assortment of boutique minischools around town, no matter what the educational research might say about the downsides of bigness or the advantages of smallness. So the question for large high schools, which means thousands of buildings, their faculties, and communities, is, How can we make school feel smaller and work smaller for our students? How can we tap the power of small inside four really big walls?

First of all, we do have a head start: about 48 percent of America's high school buildings are already small, enrolling fewer than five hundred students. These obviously include a large number of rural areas and small towns, as well as many private and parochial schools. These "naturally small" schools enroll about 25 percent of America's high school kids, while the other 75 percent attend larger city and suburban schools. Indeed, many of the country's very largest high schools are now in the suburbs, not the cities where populations are declining and dropout rates are still troublesome. We can learn a lot from rural schools, schools that have never been big, and that know a thing or two about personalization and community. They can also tell us what is lost when rural high schools are consolidated into bigger, regional comprehensive schools—a trend that worries many rural educators.

Back in those suburban and urban areas where bigger schools are the norm, school leaders have been experimenting with a variety of "smallification" structures. And some big cities, including New York and Chicago, have officially embraced the small-schools movement. There are many different ways to create small schools, many different models suited to different situations. Among the choices:

Free-standing small schools: small schools with their own facilities and administration

Schools within schools: one or more small schools that develop within a larger, "host" school

Multiplex: one building that houses several small schools

Scatterplex: two or more small schools at different sites that share a principal

Charter schools: independent, often small, public schools, designed and operated by educators, parents, community leaders, educational entrepreneurs, and others.

And of course, there are any number of hybrid structures, combining elements from two or more of these types.

Any of these models can yield a school that is caring, tight-knit, and cohesive, but limiting the enrollment is not enough. Several other key ingredients must also be in place. According to the Small Schools Workshop, a genuinely effective small school must have:

- a maximum population of 250–300 students (400–450 in a high school) in a heterogeneous mix that represents the local school community

- a nonexclusive admissions policy

- a consistent educational experience for students over an extended period of time (more than one year)

- a coherent focus and philosophy of education, and a curriculum that is integrated around that focus

- a cohesive group of teachers that collaborate and discuss the needs of their students

- a sense of shared leadership and investment among those in the small school
- involvement of families in the school community.

These criteria provide an excellent checklist for teachers, parents, or others seeking to establish a small school or a school-within-a-school, to ensure that the program they create will be effective and enduring.

When we talk about making big schools smaller, the question inevitably arises, What can one teacher do? What if you are working in a big, traditional high school where there are no reform initiatives under way? What if there are no task forces, study groups, interdisciplinary teams, or pilot programs aimed at making the school seem smaller to students? What can you do in your own classroom to make high school more personalized, more coherent, more caring for the 150 kids you see every day?

Chapter 6 of this book, which describes "best practice" teaching, offers many answers to this question. There are certain patterns of instruction—teacher-student conferences, book clubs, reading and writing workshops, inquiry teams, thematic units, digital portfolios, and more—that can make the classroom more personalized, more engaging, more student-centered. Unlike traditional textbook-lecture-and-test approaches, teaching methods like these help kids feel known and heard, give them a chance to make choices, take responsibility, connect with others, generate products with craftsmanship and care, gain recognition, and develop a voice. By teaching in this way, one lone teacher can make school seem smaller—one class, one period, one student at a time.

No one should doubt the significance of this contribution. What individual teachers do in their classrooms matters tremendously—especially from the student's point of view, from the perspective of concerned parents, or even filtered through our own memories of how high school seemed to us. We know that having one special teacher with one interesting class, one fifty-minute bright spot each day, can make the difference between giving up on school and hanging on.

What individual teachers do is also the starting point of any deep and durable school reform. After our thirty years each in education, we have learned that school change works only when it grows up from the classroom and is simultaneously supported from the top down. If there are no brave teachers doing innovative instruction and creating engaged classrooms, what will we build our improvement efforts upon? Bribes for higher tests scores? Inspirational auditorium lectures? Threats and videotapes? Who will spread the good ideas, demonstrate the alternatives, provide the models? Indeed, all the broad structural and design reforms we can think of only make new ways of teaching and learning possible—but they do not guarantee anything. Only individual teachers, working with their students face to face, can bring life to these hopes and enact these changes.

But most teachers are not so completely alone. What happens in places where teachers and administrators and parents start collaborating, talking about how to make a big school feel smaller? Well, designing a new small school from the ground up is hard enough. But it's nothing compared to dividing an existing school into smaller units. That's because you have to shake off the original school's whole history and institutional inertia, to think beyond the thousands of old habits that have quietly seeped into everyone's DNA. In a brand-new, small school like BPHS, you have to figure out new ways of doing everything—but when you split off from an existing larger school, you have to *unlearn* old habits, challenge ingrained patterns, remember that there are other ways. Split-off schools may also encounter various kinds of opposition or competition from the original "mother" school or other, new small schools. But despite all these challenges, studies from across the country show positive outcomes for schools created from originally larger schools. The research also suggests that small schools newly carved out of larger schools need an especially clear identity, strong boundaries, and a high level of autonomy to maximize their benefits to students (Crain et al. 1997).

One way of creating smaller learning environments is for large high schools to encourage enterprising groups of teachers to design new, small schools or programs to serve voluntary groups of kids and families who elect a certain kind of choice. If these teachers and students are given planning time, space, resources, and enough autonomy, they can create personalized learning environments for their students, help reduce the perceived size of the remaining school, and provide pathfinding models for other programs that colleagues can start later on.

That's what happened at Addison Trail High School, in Chicago's western suburbs. In 1992, English teacher Katy Smith and social studies teacher Ralph Feese began team-teaching an American Studies program that gave them two-period time blocks to work with consistent groups of students. Gradually they learned, as Katy explains, how to do "more and more to integrate our disciplines; to add enrichment activities that tie in music, architecture, and the visual and performing arts; to team teach rather than parallel teach; and to involve our students in group processes" (Smith, 1993). These two teachers carved out a piece of the daily schedule and brought together a group of students to create a smaller, more personalized, innovative program within a larger, traditional "comprehensive" high school of 1,700 students.

Katy and Ralph used this structure to guide students in democratically choosing themes and topics for the class to explore. They learned how to help students work in cooperative groups on study projects that the groups then presented to the rest of the class. They came to understand new roles for themselves as facilitators and guides, rather than daily lecturers. This interdisciplinary block-scheduled program has now grown to include two-thirds of the school's freshman class and has added science to English and social studies. The school is exploring ways to take the next step and make this three-discipline, integrated learning program part of the curriculum for all freshmen.

Addison Trail is an example of a big, fairly traditional school putting its institutional toe in the water of change, liking the feeling, and then diving in. By starting very small, unleashing the enthusiasm and professionalism of some innovative teachers, the school discovered some new ways to operate. Now, more teachers are getting to know their students better, working in a much more focused way on the kids' intellectual and social well-being, and exercising professional autonomy and cooperation. Students have a say in what and how they are learning and become more enthusiastic about their studies. And, of course, the successful model that Katy and Ralph and their colleagues created has now become part of the school's repertoire—it is a choice that other teachers may pick up when they are ready. This is what we mean when we say a bigger school can work gradually toward "feeling small."

Another, more radical approach is breaking a whole big school down into several smaller schools, each with distinct mission, space, and staff. This strategy was followed at Chicago Vocational High School, once one of the city's most academically troubled schools and still among its largest, with 2,500 students packed into a sprawling, three-block-long building. Starting in 1990, under the leadership of principal Betty Dispensa-Greene, CVS divided itself into eight vocationally based small schools, with enrollments ranging between 100 and 500 students each. Students were invited to choose their preferred career theme—business, automotive, transportation, health care—and then began to receive their whole high school program inside the chosen small school.

Each subschool's faculty includes not just the appropriate trade teachers, but a team of academic teachers—English, social studies, science, mathematics, the arts—matched to the enrollment of the school. Some teachers need to split their time between two schools, but as much as possible, Greene tries not to split personnel, in order to keep faculty clearly identified with particular schools. One advantage Greene had to start with was that the vocationally oriented building was already divided into different sections equipped for each trade. This made it easy to have an identifiable space for each of the new small schools. Of course, the eight schools aren't completely separate. Every day there is sharing of lunchrooms, the auditorium, and physical education facilities.

Anyone familiar with school politics, especially in big inner-city systems, will probably cringe to think of the staffing battles that would inevitably arise when a school was being split into eight faculties. When Greene started pushing to reorganize CVS, she tried to give teachers a choice of which school to work in. But as she herself tells the story, the final assignment of teachers to schools was a mixture of volunteerism and coercion, which in the early years led to some staff departures. Today, the faculty is mostly composed of teachers who believe in the small-school model, and CVS is one of the most-visited educational innovations in the city. Since the small-school experiment began in the early 1990s, student tests scores and attendance have gone up, disciplinary actions have decreased, and parent involvement and satisfaction have grown.

Given that America has invested heavily in large high school buildings, people often question whether the movement toward small schools can realistically be called a "significant" ingredient in reform. For one answer we can look to the city of New York. After a commitment to nurture "new visions" for nearly two decades, the city now has 15 percent its students enrolled in schools that are intentionally small—meaning newly created small schools or subdivided (and reinvented) older ones. So is 15 percent of the enrollment a significant contribution to school reform or not? Here's another way to think about the question: 15 percent of New York City's public school enrollment is about 160,000 children and teenagers—more than all the school children in San Diego, or Denver, or Boston, or Detroit. That's a lot of young people enjoying the advantages of safer schools, better grades, and higher graduation rates.

FEAR OF SMALL: A CAUTIONARY TALE

Splitting up big high schools or spinning off satellite programs can be highly political endeavors. If some teachers or a community group wants to reduce the "felt size" of a large school by creating an alternative program or smaller school-within-a-school, they may find themselves immediately attacked by fierce and well-organized big-school defenders.

Huh? Why would someone stand up for huge, anonymous high schools and work against smaller alternatives for kids? Perhaps because some of the apparent advantages of big high schools actually only benefit a tiny fraction of students, such as the kids who captain football teams or star in musicals, and the parents who get the attached bragging rights. That's why a ferocious defense of bigness can be mounted by those who benefit from the status quo. The families for whom the big school works, talking the language of "quality" and "excellence," can swiftly close ranks to defend their own kids' advantages.

We recently watched this dynamic play itself out in an elite local district. When the high school's enrollments started to rise toward a predicted peak of 4,000, it became clear that the district would have to recommission its mothballed second building. The extra school wouldn't be needed for its full capacity, but just to bleed off about 1,000 students. A group of eager faculty floated the idea of starting a small "school of choice" on the site, to offer a different, more personalized program to students who elected it. There were even hints at a more integrated curriculum, though the savvy teachers promoting the small school were careful not to scare off potential supporters with any wild-eyed innovations. Many parents—especially those whose children hadn't found a place for themselves at the huge, competitive school—responded to this initiative with delight and hope.

The small-school proposal was immediately and publicly attacked. Opponents argued that dividing into two schools would "water down the quality" of sports and performing arts programs. What if the best quarterback or flute player or debater chose the small school? Then the big school might not win the state championship, the music competition, or the debate tournament, as it felt entitled to by years of conference dominance.

The parents supporting the small school had naïvely reasoned that having two schools would mean more opportunities for participation for more kids. Instead of one soccer team with twenty-four varsity slots, for example, there could be two teams with forty-eight kids having the chance to play and earn a letter. Maybe the small-school team wouldn't win the conference championship; maybe it would even have to join a less competitive league. But from an educational point of view, from the kid's-eye view, two schools seemed to make sense. After all, don't we want the largest possible number of students to be deeply engaged in their school life?

Well, no, according to the letters column in the local paper and chitchat in the checkout line at the grocery store. Many people in the community—at least the loudest ones—wanted a competitive, not an inclusive, high school system. Some of these were simply spectators at high school events who wanted, for their own entertainment, to see the most professional possible performances. Others were alumni who didn't want to see their alma mater's ceaseless saga of conquest interrupted, its trophy cases left unfilled. Quieter but profoundly influential objections came from a few teachers inside the school itself, who seemed to feel their own reputations were linked to the acclaim accorded their students' performances and products. Then there were the "gifted parents," families of some top-achieving kids, who defended tough competition linked with limited opportunities for success as a crucible for forging teenage character. They seemed to feel that their own children's achievements were enhanced by the number of classmates they had beaten out to capture the valedictorian slot, the lead in the play, the starting goalie job, or the yearbook editorship.

Meanwhile, the school administration, being pummeled daily by such defenders of quality and perhaps unnerved by the potentially runaway small-school proposal, issued an improbable statement rebutting the "wider opportunity" theory. Not only would two schools not offer more opportunities for students, the administrators explained; it might actually mean less opportunities for everyone at both schools. This catch-22 reprise hinted darkly at possible funding limits and shortfalls (this at a school spending more that $15,000 a year per student). Needless to say, this official wet blanket confused and silenced the small-school supporters long enough for an alternative freshman-only school plan to be approved for the empty campus.

The point of this story: some of us may see competition as a negative and corrosive element in American high schools, but many of the key stakeholders in a community may approve of competition, even embrace it in its most ruthless and gratuitous forms. Therefore, people who are planning structural changes to address issues of size need to prepare carefully and build a strong base of support before they publicly launch a proposal of this type. Small-school options need to stress voluntary enrollment and win-win possibilities, and not the abolition or erosion of a school's current program.

Smallness advocates don't need to conquer, or even win over, those who are committed to traditional programs. They just need to ensure that there are choices for everyone and that the alternatives are voluntary. Nor should they worry about attracting students to the options they create. In every high school community there are plenty of neglected kids and silenced parents, belittled by tracking, grading, and ranking systems, classified as the "middle" or "bottom" clients of the school. These young people and their families deserve the choice of progressive, small-school initiatives, and plenty of them will eagerly sign up if given the choice.

A FINAL WORD

We know how lucky we have been at Best Practice High School. We started fresh, from scratch. We picked our own colleagues and even our principal. Our students have picked us—they come to our school by choice. We designed our own space. We have many special partners and innovative programs. All these assets are important to whatever success we may achieve. But the first of our strengths, the design feature that always works, that saves us when we fall short, that provides a safety net for kids, is that we are small. As Marilyn always says: even when it's not working, it's working.

The day of the Columbine student shootings in Colorado was a heartbreaking test of faith for our school. One of the very first changes we had made in our building back in 1996 was to remove the sinister-looking metal detector that stood at the front door, a relic of days when our building housed a tough, gang-dominated high school. We were going to run our school on trust, not suspicion and coercion. We even believed that the metal detector signaled to kids that we expected them to be dangerous, to carry weapons, to break rules and cause trouble. Since that decision, we'd enjoyed three years without any problems with weapons or student violence beyond a few hallway fistfights. Now, as the news of Columbine sank in, the thought kept recurring: there, but for the grace of God, goes our school, any school.

We felt deep empathy for the Columbine teachers and administrators officials who were criticized by the media for not foreseeing and preventing the tragedy. While we took pride in our small school, the way we tried to know every kid and to see problems coming, to be in touch with families, to have all the right structures in place—we realized that we could still miss one. Being small improves the odds but doesn't remove all risk. A disturbed and clever kid can always slip through the cracks. As we adults debated ways of responding to the shootings, the students started to tell us that they didn't feel safe. They were afraid that someone would come into our building and repeat the Columbine massacre. They didn't fear their classmates, we were heartened to hear. It was outsiders they were afraid of, some deranged stranger who might invade our community and do us harm. So, with the greatest regret, on April 28, 1999, we reinstalled the metal detector at the front door of Best Practice High School, right at the top of the white marble stairs. It's still there.

FINDING YOUR NEXT STEPS

Reflect: A good beginning point for thinking about any kind of high school reform is to recollect and review your own high school experiences—no matter how recent or how ancient. After all, any school renewal ideas any of us generates will inevitably be influenced, at least unconsciously, by what high school meant to us. So, to surface your own images, assumptions, and feelings, please think back on the high school you attended. Approximately what was the enrollment of your high school? How many students were in your graduating class? What was the average class size at your high school? How did the size of the school affect your experience there? Did you feel known and recognized by adults? By other kids? List as many adults as you can who knew you well at your high school. How did each one get to know you? If you were going to list some advantages of your high school's size, what would they be? What disadvantages would you note?

Investigate: At a high school that you are interested in studying or improving, conduct some research to find out what students and their families think about school size. "Shadow" a few of the students for one day each, observing how each kid is known and acknowledged in the course of the school day. Is the experience one of anonymity and loneliness, or of recognition and involvement? What are the differences between the included kids and the others? Develop a written survey or conduct face-to-face interviews asking students and parents about the school's size/enrollment, and their perceptions about how that size affects the day-to-day experience. You might ask: What do you think would be the optimum size for a high school? Why? What kinds of smallness seem most powerful? A small total enrollment? Small class sizes? Reduced daily student loads for teachers? The results from such surveys may surface the concerns of kids and families who feel lost in large schools but blame themselves and are reluctant to criticize the school.

Read: *The Power of Their Ideas: Lessons for America from a Small School in Harlem,* by Deborah Meier, tells the inspiring and sometimes gritty story of the formation and development of Central Park East Secondary School. Meier covers all the ingredients of good high schools, but she always keeps coming back to issues of size and personalization. *A Simple Justice: The Challenge of Small Schools*, by William Ayers, Michael Klonsky, and Gabrielle Lyon, offers two dozen stories of small-school innovation from across the country, in the voices of the movement's key leaders. You can also visit the companion website (www.smallschoolsworkshop.org) to review the latest research, get connected with the community of small-school educators around the country, or seek technical assistance for improving your own school.

Experiment: If you are working at a high school that is ready to start getting smaller, begin organizing to launch one of these strategies:

- *Invite* self-chosen teams of three teachers from different disciplines to propose and pilot an integrated program for part of the day, perhaps using seventy-five kids, three back-to-back periods, and three adjacent classrooms.
- *Invite* the development of a thematic small school within the school, planned by volunteer faculty, students, and parents.
- *Devise* a freshman program that provides a small-school experience for incoming students.
- *Reduce* student loads for an experimental group of staff members, by substituting a period of individual student conferences for one or more classes.
- *Develop* a comprehensive, four-year daily advisory program.

Chapter 3
Climate

Every student is known, appreciated, and included in a diverse, collaborative community.

When people visit BPHS, they often comment about the climate, the atmosphere of the school. They describe the feeling as energetic, homey, and purposeful.

If you arrive during classes, the school seems orderly and peaceful. The halls are empty of kids, and as you walk down the corridor glancing in classrooms, you're more likely to see kids working together in groups than hear a teacher lecturing. The kids generally seem relaxed, engaged, responsible, and playful. When classes start to change, watch out. As the halls gradually flood with kids, you'll find yourself like a rock in a rushing stream—a really loud rushing stream. In this deafening traffic, you'll see a lot of good-natured roughhousing and equally many hugs.

Visitors are struck by our diversity, by the way our black and Hispanic kids seem to get along so well, to work together. Indeed, we have never had a single ethnic meltdown; never had an incident when groups fractured along ethnic lines or turned against each other. This has been a special comfort to many of our founding faculty, who came from schools where racially sparked cafeteria fights were a daily occurrence. But people also notice that, outside of class, the Hispanic kids still tend to hang out together, as do the African American students. If this kind of group identification and loyalty is a problem (and we have debated this), we haven't entirely solved it yet.

Perhaps our generally positive climate results from the combination of all the programs we've consciously used to build community: detracking, daily advisory, inclusion, engaged classrooms, good relationships with parents, and peer mediation to back things up when disputes arise. Certainly it also has to do with the luck and magic and chemistry of the teachers and kids who've chosen to be here instead of somewhere else.

All we know is that when we are discouraged or unhappy, what we do is this: we go and stand in the middle of the third floor hallway during any class change and just let the kids wash over us. It's like getting a healing injection of energy, hope, and humor, and it works every time.

Sadly, high schools are not usually like this. People throughout the country are recognizing that as places where our kids grow up, all is not well with high schools. As we write this book, near the first anniversary of the Columbine tragedy, newspapers and magazines are filled with the national dialogue. In the *Chicago Tribune*, for example, psychologist Louis Kraus drew the connection between that tragedy and the climate in schools: "It got us all talking about what we will tolerate in terms of bullying, prejudice and scapegoating. People here are more apt to call now and say, 'We have the same demographics as Columbine. We're a community at risk' " (in Leroux 2000).

As for teenage violence itself, our own region is typical of the nation. The Illinois Council for the Prevention of Violence reported that in a recent survey of 4,305 freshmen in thirty-eight randomly selected Illinois high schools, one-third of the females and two-thirds of the males had been in a physical fight during the previous twelve months. A study by the Community Mental Health Council in Chicago, of 203 African American freshmen in one Chicago public high school, revealed that

- 45 percent had seen someone killed
- 66 percent had seen a shooting
- 38 percent had seen someone stabbed
- 49 percent, mostly boys, had been shot at.

While we are gratified that, according to law enforcement officials, the incidence of such tragedies has declined slightly, overt violence is just one symptom of a harsh atmosphere.

Even when acts of violence are not involved, high school can be a disturbingly uncivil place. A recent portrait by Adrian Nicole LeBlanc of outcast boys in a small-town high school shows kids taunted and bullied every day (1999). One study, LeBlanc tells us, reveals that the average high school student hears twenty-five antigay slurs per day. How can kids do well and concentrate on learning in such an atmosphere?

Yet much as we need sheer safety, prisonlike controls only further degrade school climate, signaling adults' distrust of teenagers and failing to get at the roots of the problem. As one social worker at a high school for depressed teens put it, "There'll be less violence when we make school a more support-ive place. . . . In a climate where inclusiveness and cooperation is woven into the fabric of daily life, there's less of a chance of a Columbine happening" (in Leroux 2000, 15). The mandates of the Chicago Board of Education and our own students' and their families' concerns for safety have forced Best Practice to reinstall the metal detector that we'd removed from our entrance when the building was being rehabbed. Nevertheless, we abhor the mistrust and regi-mentation that its beeps signal to our kids.

It's not that high school has changed all that much over the years. After all, the school many of us remember from our own experience was probably a big, impersonal place with cliques we could never belong to, mostly lecture classes, and an atmosphere in which only the most competitive kids were rec-ognized. You rushed through the crowded halls during passing periods between fifty-minute classes that had nothing to do with one another. This conveyor-belt factory model was never particularly functional. Only now, the stressors are greater—schools larger than ever, more pressures to perform on both teachers and kids, less adult attention and guidance for the kids, more violence in the surrounding culture. We can't continue to settle for this.

WHAT MAKES A SUPPORTIVE SCHOOL CLIMATE

No single activity or project can change the tone throughout a school. Rather, schools must take a wide range of steps to build respect, civility, acceptance, and, ultimately, a true community atmosphere. We quickly learned how big a job this would be the first day Best Practice High School opened. We had no equipment, books, computers, chalk, or paper—nothing but several hundred blue plastic chairs, 137 kids, nine teachers, three university partners, and lots of enthusiasm. The building was unavailable throughout August because the mayor magnanimously lent it to the news organizations covering the Demo-cratic national convention across the street. Never mind that a school had to be created from scratch. Painters were still plying their brushes on Labor Day.

The students spent most of that first day in advisory getting acquainted, amid dizzying paint fumes and 90° heat. Later, in the auditorium, they wrote exit slips reflecting on their introduction to this new school. The one we remember most simply asked, "Why are all the teachers so chipper?"

This kid's slightly sarcastic question actually says a lot about the ingredi-ents of a supportive school climate. First, it starts with the teachers—if they don't feel it, the kids won't. Only if teachers feel supported, excited, empowered, will kids begin to catch the wave. However, students won't automatically buy in just because the teachers are chipper and think they've got a better way. True, after nine years of schooling, kids have experienced plenty of boredom, isolation, and hurt from the constant competition. But that's a familiar world, and anything different seems alien. Better the devil you know.

Then there are the cultural influences that work in a variety of divisive ways—the rules of the street that say you must fight to maintain face; the spirit of competition that turns fellow students into opponents grasping at limited opportunities; the prejudices of race, class, and gender always lurking just below the surface. And some dysfunctional structures are created and enforced by the kids themselves, reflecting the worst elements of the surrounding culture: cliques, in- and out-groups, hazing, labeling.

So building a healthier, safer, more positive and welcoming school climate requires efforts of many different sorts—all sending the same message over and over, day after day, year after year—making sure that everything reinforces the message: "You have a voice here. You matter to all of us and to each other. We are getting to know each one of you well as an individual. We want you to work hard and succeed, and we're going to do everything we can to help you. We must find ways to work together and ways to resolve the inevitable differences and conflicts that human beings experience. We are one school, not a collection of cliques. This is a family."

Activities and strategies for making this message a reality must go on at every level if a high school is to be a place kids want to come to and be successful, and so these are the various efforts that we'll describe in the rest of this chapter:

- *in social relationships:* organizing peer mediation to settle disputes; promptly and thoughtfully addressing incidents of discrimination, whether against individuals or groups; scheduling activities that allow students of different backgrounds and social styles to get to know and understand one another

- *in the schedule:* a daily advisory period during which students deal with governance issues and social relationships, and teachers keep in touch with individuals' personal as well as academic problems and successes

- *in the placement of students:* a nontracked program, with the inclusion of special education students in regular classrooms; teachers use strategies for decentralizing classrooms so that everyone is challenged, rather than lectures inevitably aimed at only one achievement level

- *in classroom curriculum and instruction*: inquiry on topics that young people care about and that address the very issues of community; collaborative activities in which students learn to work together and get to know each other; activities in which students take leadership roles to help learning happen
- *in school governance*: giving both students and teachers a significant voice in key decision making, like teacher hiring and curriculum choices
- *in other relationships*: with parents, community members, external partners, visitors, enacting the same habits of respect, warmth, and inclusion that are modeled within the school.

WHAT THE RESEARCH SAYS

Later in this chapter and in several others we'll address each of the strategies we've listed. But first, let's talk about why climate is so important and review some of the research on how climate makes a difference in students' achievement.

So often, educators divide school into the "cognitive" and the "affective," which ensures that the latter is given second place. In the larger world, however, the division isn't so clear. The Department of Labor's SCANS *(Secretary of Labor's Commission on Achieving the Necessary Skills)* report, which we referred to in Chapter 1, emphasizes interpersonal, self-management, and leadership skills that can't be learned simply in a traditional hear-the-lecture-read-the-chapter-take-the-test classroom, where students sit silently, disconnected from one another.

But whatever the work world holds for kids' futures, we cannot ignore their immediate focus on social and personal relationships. Every parent of a teenager knows this. Peer pressure is not just a negative force but a fact of teenage life. And it can be positive: students learn from one another how to think and debate, how to develop good work habits, and whether they are worth the effort. Although we often demand that school employ every minute "productively" for learning content, group-dynamics specialists tell us that every group needs "maintenance" as well as time-on-task. Only through social relationships built over time will a school have underlying networks of trust among students for solving difficult conflicts and misunderstandings when they arise.

While we certainly cannot claim that improving a high school's climate will prevent all teenage violence, we must learn what part school can play in either helping reduce violence or increasing the social pressures that lead to it. In *Lost Boys: Why Our Sons Turn Violent and How We Can Save Them*, psychologist Jim Garbarino lists the factors involved in youth violence and how we can help ameliorate them. From epidemiology, Garbarino draws a key concept, the "tipping point." This is the stage at which a variety of worsening conditions finally add up to cause an outbreak of a disease or other breakdown. School, in other words, may not be the direct cause of particular violent acts, but it can contribute either to degrade surroundings, or to help bring a vulnerable child back from the brink.

"Threats accumulate; support ameliorates," Garbarino concludes. This "offers hope to those responsible for policy and programming on behalf of youth. It tells us that life need not be risk-free for development to proceed successfully. And one way to succeed with kids is to inject compensatory opportunity factors into the equation of their life" (Garbarino 1999, 75–76). Attention and love from at least one person frequently help turn a violent child around. Often, it is attention from someone unable "to change the situation but nonetheless able to feed the child's soul enough tidbits of love to sustain it during its hibernation, its long winter of discontent" (36–37). We can structure schools so that more and more of the people in it—teachers, staff, students themselves—are placed in positions that allow them to give such important help to kids.

Some may say that school was not designed for this and can't possibly make up for the community's many failings. But we educators are responsible adults, and school is often one of the few functioning organizations in a struggling neighborhood. If we don't do what we can, who will? And if we better organize schools for the social health and well-being of the students, we'll have a greater number of successful kids, even on the standardized tests. Perhaps our most troubled students are like canaries in the coal mine, telling us whether the environment is safe or toxic. If they have more opportunities to thrive, it's likely that the atmosphere throughout the entire school is positive.

Research indicates that climate does, in fact, make a difference. A recent study by the Consortium on Chicago School Research asked whether "social support" and "academic press" affected student performance in Chicago public schools. It looked at whether teachers took an interest in students and related subjects to the students' own lives and whether students treated each other with respect and learned to work cooperatively. The findings: those experiencing high social support advanced .74 grade-level equivalent more in reading, during one year of school, than those without that support. The improvement in gain for math was even stronger, with kids who received high social support doing .86 grade-level equivalent better than their less-supported peers. Students experiencing high levels of social support *and* high levels of academic press surpassed those experiencing just one form of encouragement (Lee et al. 1999).

The research on peer mediation and conflict-resolution programs reflects how just one element in the school setting can influence students' lives and work for the better. In the first empirical study on a school mediation program (1992), researchers observed positive effects on discipline, with fewer disruptive or violent problems occurring; and, not surprisingly, the student mediators' self-image and social attitudes improved. In the largest study to date, the National Center for Children in Poverty reports that among five thousand children in fifteen New York City schools, those exposed to an average of twenty-five lessons per year in a high-quality conflict-resolution program showed significantly slower growth in number of hostile and aggressive actions, *and* their reading and math scores on standardized achievement tests increased significantly, compared to students in the same schools who did not experience the lessons (Aber et al. 1999). At a more general level, a comprehensive survey of American adolescent health reported in 1997 that the more loved children felt, and the more comfortable they were in school, the less likely they were to engage in problematic behaviors (Resnick et al. 1997).

Let's now outline some of the key programs and structures that we've adopted at Best Practice High School to create a caring climate, one that nourishes and enriches the lives of the students.

PEER MEDIATION AND OTHER STRATEGIES FOR STRENGTHENING SOCIAL RELATIONSHIPS

Nicholas (mediator): We want to thank you for coming to peer mediation. As you know, this is voluntary.

Steve (second mediator): I'm Steve and this is Nicholas. And you are . . . ?

Itanzia (disputant): I'm Itanzia.

Jeanette (second disputant): I'm Jeanette.

Steve: We need each of you to agree to several rules. First, this is confidential. Do you both agree?

Itanzia and Jeanette: Yes.

Steve: No interrupting while the other is talking, and no put-downs. Do you agree?

Itanzia: OK.

Jeanette: All right.

Steve: Each of you must try to be truthful and agree that you want to settle this argument. Do you agree?

Jeanette: Yeah.

Itanzia: I guess so.

Nicholas: Itanzia, would you like to tell us the problem?

Itanzia: She tryin' to take my boyfriend because I made the team and she
didn't!

Steve: Jeanette, you tell us your side of the story.

Jeanette: Well, it's not even like that, that I'm trying to steal her boyfriend.
It's not like I want him anyway.

Itanzia: In the letter I found, that she wrote, about how she love him and
all this!

Nicholas: OK, could you tell us how that made you feel?

Itanzia: Mad! Angry, upset, want to beat her up! . . .

Four experienced peer mediators are role-playing the resolution of a dispute for the rest of their team at Best Practice High School. After dozens of
such problems they know just how to portray fellow teenagers with an attitude. When our school first opened, we imagined that a smaller setting where
teachers knew all the kids would automatically be safer and more peaceful.
Wrong. Some of our kids grew up with the customs of the street, learning only
one way to preserve themselves. So we were horrified when a few physical
fights broke out in the halls during those first few months. How could this be
happening? What could we do about it? The school would need to actively
promote a more civil life. We happened upon Judith Ferrara's thorough and
lively book *Peer Mediation: Finding a Way to Care*, and we knew immediately
what we had to do.

Peer mediation is usually sorely misunderstood by those unacquainted
with it. Almost every news reporter who describes our program calls it a student "court" where good students mete out punishments to the troublemak-
ers. But it's far more powerful and educational than that. Instead, student
mediators learn to elicit disputants' views of the events, issues, and feelings
about a conflict and help them identify their own solutions to it. Mediation is
voluntary and confidential. Even teacher-sponsors are not permitted to listen
in, though an adult is always close by to ensure safety. The mediators reflect
the full range of the school's social groupings so they aren't perceived as elite
goody-goodies. And they are extensively trained to be good listeners, to
respond neutrally, and to facilitate the disputants' own initiatives instead of
proposing solutions themselves.

Peer mediation is one of the essential first ingredients for a positive school climate, because conflict simmers just below the surface in most high schools. Students often keep it out of sight of the adults, while the grown-ups either avoid dealing with it or try to suppress it with rules and punishments. In seemingly safe suburban schools, it quietly distracts some kids. In urban settings, it can cause students to skip classes or even drop out of school, just to avoid getting hurt. All too often, punishments meted out by assistant principals only encourage students to intercept the notices mailed home or to save their fights for after school, when they are more likely to end in serious violence. Yet the Conflict Resolution Education Network estimates that of the 86,000 public schools in the United States, about 8,500, or fewer than 10 percent, have conflict-resolution programs of some kind. In our experience, the percentage is far lower for high schools.

A successful peer-mediation program requires a carefully designed organizational structure. Mediators must include students from many different groups, not just the star performers in the school. They must be thoroughly trained—Best Practice uses a two-day training program based on a manual obtained from the National Resource Center for Youth Mediation. Mediation request forms must be readily available throughout the school, and quickly funneled to a faculty sponsor who can locate the disputants and a pair of mediators for a timely mediation session. At first, at Best Practice, mediators served duty during lunch and advisory every day. But we found that to avoid confrontations between periods or after school, mediation sessions must occur more promptly. And so mediators take turns being on call, absenting themselves from classes when needed. With a large enough team, no one mediator experiences major disruption in his or her schedule. Such fine tuning of the program constantly continues.

Because the solutions worked out in mediation are about settling the conflict rather than punishing perpetrators, disagreements tend to stay settled, instead of spiraling into later retaliation. Mediation enacts respect for the students who come to settle their conflicts (even when, as is often the case, the mediators view the issues as petty or trivial). And the behaviors required on both sides of the mediation table involve lifelong skills that kids will need in order to be successful family members, community leaders, managers, and workers. Thus, peer mediation gradually helps a school to develop more civil, respectful behavior. Even teachers at Best Practice have begun to employ their own modified version of the process for conflicts among themselves. It's not lost on anyone at the school that those taking responsibility for students are the students. And of course the mediators learn the most, as they become skilled, sophisticated questioners and facilitators. The high point of the year occurs when the experienced mediators interview new candidates for the job and then, as teachers, conduct two days of training for the new recruits.

Some Peer Mediation Basics

A mediator is . . .

- a good listener
- a fair person who takes no sides
- a fact finder
- trustworthy
- caring and supportive
- a person who helps people feel safe to talk.

A mediator is not . . .

- a judge who decides who's right and who's wrong
- a person who gives orders or advice or proposes solutions to a problem
- a person who talks about others.

Mediation must be . . .

- voluntary
- confidential
- neutral.

Disputants must agree to . . .

- try to solve the problem
- allow the other person to speak without interrupting
- avoid name-calling or put-downs
- be as honest as possible.

Skills a mediator must learn . . .

- active listening
- asking questions in a neutral way
- remaining neutral, nonjudgmental
- restating and clarifying issues

- creating a comfortable setting for mediation
- working as a team.

—*Adapted from* Student Mediation in Secondary Schools, Training and Implementation Guide, *National Resource Center for Youth Mediation, 1995.*

Changes in a school do not happen overnight, however, and are unlikely to result from peer mediation alone. Resistance to this constructive strategy is deep in our society. The court system presents a much more oppositional and punishment-oriented approach to settling issues. Many teenagers do not trust the mediation process and view it as a weak alternative to physical fighting, particularly if survival outside of school in a difficult neighborhood calls for maintaining a tough "face." Our mediators must conduct repeated campaigns to educate students and teachers about the program. They struggle to retain their own sense of purpose in an atmosphere where their way is sometimes belittled. We have to keep reminding them that many students are secretly relieved to have an alternative for settling a small conflict or disentangling a deeper misunderstanding before it lurches out of control.

Teachers, administrators, and students in a good high school must therefore constantly look for other ways to reduce labeling, misunderstanding, and discrimination. At Best Practice, we're now searching for a high-quality conflict-resolution curriculum to use in advisories. And in the classroom, teachers watch for opportunities to explore issues of discrimination and community in literature and social studies, linking content with the social concerns in our own school.

DAILY ADVISORY

I feel that the teachers know me very well. And the outcome because of this is good—you feel more comfortable, more relaxed, almost like real good friends or even family.

Everybody knows each other and looks out for each other. It's had a good impact because you can rely on your peers.

*My teachers know me well and yes it affects me because they try to know **too** much about me and I don't like it.*

—Students at Best Practice

A great deal can be learned about improving high schools by paying attention to middle school reformers. Advisory, or "home base," or "prime time," has been a widely adopted feature of middle schools, and even large school systems such as Chicago's are applying it to high school. Yet many teachers remember previous incarnations of this strategy deteriorating into a brief ten-minute period for taking attendance and delivering flyers or report cards to be carried home. How can high schools make this an effective part of a stronger climate for kids?

First, let's be clear about what we mean by an advisory program. Middle school experts have defined it very explicitly:

> One adult and a small group of students have an opportunity to interact on a scheduled basis in order to provide a caring environment for academic guidance and support, everyday administrative details, recognition, and activities to promote citizenship. (National Middle School Association, 1)

Some important characteristics of advisory

- *Time:* Advisory should meet frequently, three to five days per week, for at least half an hour.
- *Size:* Groups should be small—no more than fifteen to twenty—so students and teacher can get to know one another well.
- *Continuity:* In many high school programs, students have the same advisor for four years. Some schools, however, have advisors who teach the same grade level as their advisees, which provides the trade-off that the advisor is better acquainted with the students' academic program.
- *Key duties:* The advisor is the student's and family's first contact at the school, to solve problems or meet special needs. And the advisor's purpose is to support the whole individual, rather than to teach subject matter.
- *Focus:* A plan or program ensures that advisory is not limited to students merely hanging out or completing bureaucratic business.
- *Teacher autonomy:* There's room for each advisory to reflect the personality and interests of the teacher and the students.

Middle school expert Nancy Doda stresses that teachers must have the opportunity to seriously plan advisory based on the needs they perceive among their students, rather than simply receive from the district office a fat manual of activities that teenagers will never be comfortable with. If teachers don't buy into the program or fear that it is too "touchy-feely" for their teaching style, it will never truly take hold. As with so many efforts to strengthen high school, if the teachers don't become active, decision-making members of the community, students are unlikely to gain that role either.

As Doda observes, there are trade-offs between teachers advising the same grade level they teach (so they'll know the curriculum) or staying with the same students for four years (so they'll know the kids better). Assigning advisories to specialist staff—librarians, special education teachers, counselors—helps to keep the groups small. And focusing some experiences on celebrations, community service, special guests, and outings provides informal opportunities for students to grow, often in unintended ways (Doda 1991).

Fenway High School in Boston offers one model for using advisory periods effectively. Within its three smaller "houses," Fenway schedules one-hour advisory periods three days per week, with twenty to twenty-five students per grade-level group. Most of the advisories are conducted by two teachers each, which allows for creative teaming. Sometimes, for example, an advisory will divide by gender in order to talk about sensitive social issues. Freshman advisories focus on team building and diversity training, the sophomores on work in the community, the juniors on service projects and preparations for applying to the school's "senior institute." Seniors participate in six-week school-to-work internships and work on plans for college, other training, or jobs.

House coordinator Suzanne Panico says that advisory enables each student to be well known by at least one adult, who offers counseling on both social and academic issues. In many advisories, one day per week is devoted to a group social activity; another day features individual teacher-student conferences while the balance of the group gets homework done; and the third day focuses on a specific topic, such as career options or conflict resolution. Discussions on issues in the school or the larger community are often initiated by kids or teachers. Recalling the intense conversations that took place after the Columbine shootings, Panico says that most students believed such indiscriminate killing couldn't happen at Fenway because students all knew each other too well. They realistically agreed, however, that individual feuds still had the potential to boil over.

Some teachers find it easy to conduct advisory activities, Panico explains, while others feel less prepared for the task. Pairing strong teachers with less experienced ones helps. Advisory teachers get help from other staff members, with counselors visiting to lead sessions on diversity or mental health. This not only aids students, but models for the teachers how to conduct advisory activities themselves.

At Best Practice High School, our thirty-minute daily advisory period utilizes all regular teachers plus support staff, so that groups are typically no more than about fifteen. In most cases, students keep the same advisory teacher for all four years of their high school career. Advisory is a first line of communication with parents, and a place where at least one teacher keeps track of the overall progress and needs of each individual student. Kids and teachers discuss a wide range of concerns—how students treat each other, how cultural groups relate, gender issues, how individuals are doing in their classes, how to study, how to think about the future. Sometimes these issues are explored directly, through structured discussions, and sometimes indirectly, through social activities and, as kids say, just hanging out. In addition, advisory has become the home for our portfolio process. In this supportive environment, students share and respond to each others' collections of work.

Math teacher Vanessa Breschling tells the story of a Best Practice sophomore in her advisory:

Alicia arrived as a freshman with a chip on her shoulder, questioning everything. "Why do we have to pay school fees? Why do we have advisory?" She got into fights and cursed out teachers, and her parents were called in for numerous conferences. "I thought she hated school," admits Vanessa. "She tried out for basketball, and after the first half she walked off the floor saying, 'These girls don't know how to play.'"

One day Vanessa asked her advisory kids to jot on note cards "Things you like about Best Practice" on one side, "Things you want changed" on the other. Alicia spoke up, "If there was anything I didn't like about BPHS, I wouldn't be here!" And she proceeded to list only the positives: the classes, the attention from her teachers, the sports she was in. Half a dozen other kids followed her lead. "I started seeing her in a new light," Vanessa observes. "She's becoming a leader."

Back on the basketball team, Alicia has become a star. Other kids respect her. This winter she earned straight A's for the quarter. The fights have stopped. For her internship, she asked to stay at school and work as Vanessa's assistant—and she works hard, Vanessa says. How did this happen? "I think it was the safety here, and the attention, which is what advisory is about. I don't do lots of organized activities in advisory. They just don't come from my heart. I do like to bring in challenging games like Mastermind and Mancala. And I talk with the kids a lot, conversations at each table, individual conferences. If Alicia doesn't show up for basket-ball practice, I find out and talk to her. I'm the one tracking her progress.

At Best Practice, our advisories vary greatly from teacher to teacher, with a few common activities. Everyone uses one advisory period per week to promote reading in books and magazines of students' own choice from classroom libraries. On Thursdays, students write in their journals about their weekly service learning internships. Seniors are helped with career planning and college applications. There's always room for individual initiative. For example, building principal Sylvia Gibson conducts her own advisory-time literature circle discussions with a small group of girls who have been acting out. Art teacher Aiko Boyce guided her advisory in making artificial roses for cancer patients. When one teacher expressed discouragement that her freshman students were uninterested in sending get-well cards, Aiko recommended from her own rich experience: buy one big card and have the kids jot messages and sign it. Or ask one or two art-oriented students to make up a large poster-sized card that the others sign. Kids learn to take initiative and show care for one another in small steps, she reassured us.

Advisory at Best Practice is not yet as clearly focused as we'd like. Some of the goals on the list given earlier are being met more fully than others. For example, faculty are presently investigating conflict-resolution programs, since none is yet in place, and our peer-mediation program can address only immediate crises. Nevertheless, when fifteen students and one teacher spend time together daily across four years, relationships grow and develop, and our small school grows still closer together. As Marilyn says, even when it's not working, it's working.

INCLUSION

Freshman algebra, sixth period. Math teacher Tom McDougal explains the steps in multiplying polynomials and then assigns several problems for students to try it out. Special education teacher Sonja Kosanovic sits at one of the tables between Kiesha and Nikia, as they try their hand at the problems, reminding them of various steps as they go. Kiesha behaves like a mother hen herself, monitoring and prodding the others at the table—"Are you doing this problem? . . . Better get started. . . . You got the answer yet?"

At Best Practice, Sonja and fellow special education teacher Michelle Dulak spend the majority of their time directly in English, math, and science classes, alongside the special education students, helping them with tasks and assignments, quietly providing additional explanations as work proceeds. The students' schedules place them mostly together in a given period, for the subjects in which they have identified needs, so that the special education teachers can get to all the key subjects themselves. With our normal schedule, in which each class meets for two fifty-minute periods and one hundred-minute period each week, the special education teachers visit each core class about twice weekly.

If you observe for a while in the algebra class, you will notice that Ms. Kosanovic not only coaches her own charges, but also responds to others who have questions. Labeling is avoided, and students in the school see the special education teacher as just another adult giving help to anyone who needs it. Three days per week, the special ed students attend a one-hour after-school resource room and homework session. Both teachers circle round the room helping individuals, using the homework as an opportunity to teach coping skills and learning strategies.

Sonja and Michelle stress that the key to this system is close communication with the regular classroom teachers. Between the two of them they talk with every teacher in the school once a week, scheduling fifteen-minute meetings during preparation periods. The other teachers appreciate these meetings because Sonja and Michelle brainstorm alternative ways to present material and assess student learning, which of course helps all the students learn more effectively. As one teacher stated appreciatively, these valued consultants and coteachers have great teaching ideas and are especially able to evaluate a lesson from the learner's point of view.

The special ed teachers focus, too, on helping their students to "self-advocate," that is, to actively request changes in assessment strategy or any other variation in the learning process that they may need. As they learn to understand their own needs and to seek accommodations, the students become less passive. One mother declared that the program had completely changed her daughter, turning her into an outgoing, positive, and successful student. Everyone on the staff recognizes that this system has successfully supported the special ed students without calling undue attention to them.

As Sonja and Michelle muse on the challenges that other schools would face in converting to such a system, they remark on the sharp difference between running one's own self-contained classroom and serving primarily as a support to others. "You can't have too big an ego," Sonja observes. If you have your own separate class, you have more control to ensure that instruction is multimodal and user-friendly. On the other hand, as the program becomes more established, the level of instruction and help for all students increases in the rest of the classrooms. They caution, however, that the transition isn't easy for the special education kids themselves. These students usually come to high school having experienced many years of learning in separate classes, and change is challenging, so support must be provided for them to make the adjustment.

DETRACKING

The full inclusion of special education students is one system that enhances community in our school. The other half of the process in the formal school program is to eliminate tracking. Tracking is the American high school's nearly ubiquitous practice of dividing students into levels of perceived "ability" and placing them by these levels in different classrooms for each subject. Some high schools employ three levels—"basic," "regular," and "honors"— while others divide each grade into four, five, or even six levels. Then add on "special education" at one end and "advanced placement" at the other. While the classes for these levels may bear the same names, the curriculum in, say, American history is often quite different. "Basic" students simply aren't exposed to the same possibilities for learning as the "honors" kids. Parents in most districts can request that their children be moved up or down a level, but in practice, once students are placed in a track, they are likely to stay there for their entire high school career.

To place students in lower academic tracks signals that it is acceptable to look down on others. Students who divide into cliques are often simply mirroring the divisions initiated by adults. While some educators want to continue debating the issue, research delivers conclusive statistics on tracking: students in low-ability tracks receive lower-quality instruction, covering less content, with more rote drill, and teachers more preoccupied with classroom management (Seceda 1992). Tracking consigns the lower ranks to a lesser level of learning from which most never escape. The worst news is the racial inequity that tracking brings. As studies by Oakes et al. (1990) show,

> during the elementary grades, the science and mathematics experiences of children from low-income families, African-American and Hispanic children, children who attend school in central cities, and children who have been clustered in "low-ability class" differ in small but important ways from those of their more advantaged and white peers. By the time the students

reach secondary school, their science and mathematics experiences are strikingly different.

Detracking, by contrast, confers important benefits—as long as teachers learn how to support students of all levels within a heterogeneous classroom. Improvement occurs, not only in student relationships, but even in test scores. One review of longitudinal research data found that high-scoring eighth graders in tracked schools did not do better later on than similar students in untracked schools (Braddock and Slavin 1993). Another study of multiability classes in a Philadelphia school found that students of all levels showed significant gains in reading scores, with the high-scoring students improving the most (MacIver, Plank, and Balfance unpub.).

The main argument schools give for tracking is that it's easier to teach when all the students in the room are at a given level—and this does seem logical if the teacher mostly lectures. However, a good teacher who attends more to individual students quickly finds that even when the kids are tracked, those in a single level still have differing needs, so the convenience of tracking is largely illusory. Meanwhile, the best and most experienced teachers usually avoid teaching the lower levels if they possibly can. So students at those levels rarely receive the quality of education that their higher-ranked comrades do.

Once the levels are in place, powerful political forces combine to keep them there. Parents of honors students fear their kids won't learn as much and won't get into the best colleges if they attend classes with basic students. Grading scales are "cooked" to reward upper-track kids and punish the lower ones. And since educators communicate so little with the public about what good teaching is, the parents can't imagine any other way but tracking. They have no concept of how a teacher could individualize and help all the children within one diverse classroom.

When we were first planning Best Practice High School, one of our bedrock assumptions was that tracking is a pernicious, deeply misguided strategy that undermines both learning and community in schools. We agreed with Anne Wheelock's seminal 1992 book, *Crossing the Tracks: How "Untracking" Can Save America's Schools*:

> Tracking does not result in the equal and equitable distribution of effective schooling among all students. Instead, on the one hand, it allocates the most valuable school experiences—including challenging and meaningful curricula, top-quality instruction, and high teacher expectations—to students who already have the greatest academic, economic, and social advantages. On the

other hand, those who face the greatest struggles in school—and in life in general—receive a more impoverished curriculum based on lower assessments of their learning capacity. . . . Furthermore, the sorting of students into groups of "haves" and "have-nots" contradicts the American educational credo that schools are democratic communities of learners whose purpose is to offer equal educational opportunity to all. (6)

But to successfully teach detracked classes, teachers need to be able to help students of varied learning styles and achievement levels, all together in the same room at once. Traditional lecture classes won't work because they must be pitched at just one level. Instead, teachers must learn to use "classroom workshop" structures, to individualize learning, to organize reading discussion groups for inquiry projects, and to balance among these (see Chapter 5, "Teaching"). In reviewing successful detracking programs around the country, Anne Wheelock and Leon Lynne quote one school administrator as he reflects on what is now being called "differentiated" curriculum: "The teacher should be able to decide who needs enrichment, who needs acceleration, when to use cooperative learning, when to use peer-to-peer tutoring." And this savvy curriculum director says of flexible grouping for particular needs, "That must be a constantly changing group. . . . You don't put fifteen kids aside at the beginning of the year as the geniuses. We want to see constant changes in groupings, based on constant teacher assessment of the needs of all students" (Wheelock and Lynne 1997, 8).

Wheelock lists six elements that must be addressed to successfully move away from ability grouping:

- developing a culture of detracking—helping students and teachers to believe that having everyone work together in a school is valuable and can support learning

- involving parents—helping particularly the parents of already successful students to understand that detracking will advance all students in the school and not lower teaching and learning levels for their kids—otherwise, parent opposition can destroy the effort

- providing professional development for teachers—introducing strategies and curriculum for working with diverse students in the classroom, and facilitating the planning needed to reorganize the school

- phasing in change gradually, so that changes are supported and problems are addressed

- rethinking other aspects of the program, such as ways to deliver extra help for those students who need it without using pull-out activities that implicitly label the "pullees"

- obtaining district and state support.

Wheelock and Lynne emphasize that moving a school to an untracked program requires extensive staff development, including summer workshops on a range of instructional strategies, planning time during the school day, peer coaching, and observations of strategies being used in other classrooms. In many settings, schools work with university partners to obtain ongoing in-classroom support instead of the one-shot in-service sessions that too often masquerade as district support for change (Wheelock and Lynne 1997).

At Best Practice High School, we're sorry to say we don't have much of a story to tell on this topic. We simply started without tracks, and nobody seems to miss them. We've heard no complaints from parents. The teachers all routinely conduct classes using workshop and small-group activities, conferencing regularly with individual students. Some kids work harder and achieve more than others, though the teachers continue to encourage everyone. A number of students have requested the option to do extra work and receive honors credit for it, but they are adamant that they don't want to be placed in a separate class. Through their electives, juniors and seniors pursue a few topics of their choice at more challenging levels. The students who do well are getting into good colleges and universities, and 67 percent of our first senior class was accepted to college somewhere. What can we say? It works.

CLIMATE IN THE CLASSROOM

While we devote two later chapters of this book to teaching and curriculum, we must also emphasize here how central these are in creating a positive school climate. After all, the curriculum and how it is enacted with students are the core of schooling, and if they do not help students feel heard and respected, and promote strong relationships among them, then all the other efforts to do so will seem like frills.

Supporting community in the classroom does not mean dumbing down learning. It simply makes good sense to teach algebra, for example, by respecting students' needs and concerns: by showing them how mathematics plays an important role in modern life; by demonstrating the value of the subject and connecting it with real-life problems; by providing choices among aspects of the subject to explore more deeply; and by asking kids to take responsibility for working with and helping their fellow students.

What are ways that good teachers use curriculum to enhance climate in their classrooms? They include:

- introducing topics that connect with students' lives—defining classroom rules when studying the U.S. Constitution; writing about students' own cultures for composition; reading literature that connects with their concerns (whether it's contemporary or classical), by authors from a variety of cultural backgrounds; applying science topics to social, political, and health issues; using math to analyze surveys on behavior and beliefs of people in the school and the neighborhood

- providing choices among topics for deeper investigation and helping students to choose meaningfully to maximize the likelihood for engagement and success; even in more abstract sciences, like physics, helping students take ownership of the material and feel as if it "belongs" to them, not just to the teachers

- spending at least some time on topics that integrate curriculum, helping students appreciate how all their learning is linked, rather than reflecting only the parochial interests of separate school departments.

These ideas are not revolutionary, but they aren't used nearly as widely as they could be.

And what are strategies for good instruction that support a positive climate as teachers cover this curriculum? They include:

- conducting discussions so that ideas from all students get heard and respected

- organizing students both to work together on some topics and to make choices and express themselves individually on others

- frequently rotating student groups and partners so that students get to know and work with all their classmates

- diagnosing students' needs and structuring classroom time so the teacher helps with these needs, through individual and small-group conferencing

- giving all students opportunities to become expert on aspects of a topic and to serve as instructors for the rest of the class.

We'll leave most of our concrete examples of such strategies to the more extended chapters on these topics. But here's just one revealing story. The setting: teachers working in interdisciplinary teams at a Chicago suburban high school, guiding student-chosen inquiry projects, as the students worked in pairs on presentations for the end of the quarter. John, a fairly strong student who pretended to be cool and uninterested in his studies, paired up with Mike, who was immature, had a short attention span, rarely turned in work, and served many detentions for his behavior problems.

The program integrated science, English, and social studies, and the two boys conducted a comparison of skateboarding and in-line skating, using principles of mechanics. To the teachers' surprise and delight, John and Mike introduced their presentation with a humorous skit and covered all required elements clearly and expertly. The boys' still more enthusiastic second-quarter presentation explored science ethics questions on cloning, complete with props and costumes. The teachers even noticed that other students had adopted the format that these two had developed. The collaborative structure elicited a level of work Mike had not achieved before and allowed John's strengths, which he'd been unwilling to share publicly, to rub off on others.

It's clear: teachers cannot leave students sitting silently in rows listening to lectures and expect that some special program, in some other room at some other time, taught by some other teachers, will create a climate that makes kids eager to come to school every day. However, good teachers recognize that the same energizing strategies that help students work together, appreciate and understand one another, and invest in their learning and the school are also strategies that promote critical thinking, strengthen communication abilities, and provide skills needed for life in the adult world.

SCHOOL GOVERNANCE

What a hard book this is to organize! Almost every feature of high schools that we discuss contributes to the others and yet also calls for a chapter on its own. Student participation in governance is one of those, and so we'll discuss it briefly here, tell just one story about our struggles with it, and leave the rest for the next chapter. But we can't ignore its role in creating a strong school climate.

It's one thing to talk about creating "ownership" among students and to tell the kids the school "belongs" to them, but another to really enact this principle. It's simply not central to the history of the American high school. On the contrary, the rebellious and self-focused side of normal teen development might lead many to doubt that major student decision making is a prudent option. Yet kids also tend to live up to our expectations of them. To give them serious responsibility demonstrates serious respect. We mean more than asking the student council to run more service projects or asking students to establish classroom behavior rules, valuable as those activities may be. Rather, how can students be made part of the real decision-making structure of a school?

We learned about this at a Best Practice High School faculty meeting a couple of springs ago when a delegation of students asked to speak. They'd heard that we were beginning the search for the new teachers as our school expanded one grade level each year. We'd told the kids they had a voice in their own education. So, they asked, shouldn't they be involved in the hiring process?

We were embarrassed by our own hypocrisy and immediately agreed. The kids formed an interviewing committee, so that each teacher candidate would meet first with the students before sitting down with the staff. The committee's input becomes part of the decision-making process. Not only are the kids' observations insightful, but it is especially valuable to see the candidates' reactions as they emerge from the student interview to join the adults. Teachers with a student-centered orientation walk in stimulated, smiling. Those less committed to our approach show the ambivalence on their faces before they even speak.

The student committee members are forced to think about some disconcerting realities, too. In one case, they strongly preferred a white candidate over a person of color and were shocked to learn of the Board of Education's affirmative action requirements. The faculty considered the candidates essentially equal and preferred the minority person to keep the school "in compliance." The kids were unbelieving. Hadn't we been teaching that skin color shouldn't matter? In the end, Board rules prevailed. The students were not happy with our answers, but the dialogue was a valuable one.

Nevertheless, the Best Practice faculty are not satisfied with the limited level of student involvement in decision making. This is so foreign to schools that it will take considerable effort for this school, or any other, to expand its role. For example, our school does not have, at this writing, a regular process of student "town meetings" to address community issues. A student representative should be reporting on student concerns at every faculty meeting. There's much more to be done.

RELATING TO PARENTS AND COMMUNITY

Teenagers may say they don't want their parents around. And parents have limited time, with so many working full-time jobs. Yet the presence and voices of parents in schools send a strong message about what is important in a community and what adult supports are available when kids need them. We'll talk more about the possibilities for parent and community partnerships in Chapter 12, but we mustn't forget their particular contribution to a strong and positive school climate.

What does meaningful parent involvement in a high school look like? It certainly can't be like elementary school, where parents may visit classrooms to help with art projects or read stories to groups of kids. In many high schools, parents join sports booster organizations and serve on community advisory committees. But they also need to be involved more directly with students. There are many possibilities:

- parents sharing formally or informally about their careers
- workshops in which parents share their own particular skills and abilities—in music, the arts, fitness, sports, etc.
- student-led parent conferences, where kids guide their parents through portfolios and displays of their work, explaining concepts they've learned in each subject
- committees that bring together parents, students, teachers, and administrators to plan new or improved programs at the school
- parent involvement in special projects. At Best Practice parents helped the assistant principal conduct a semester-long entrepreneurship program for students that met during choice time on Wednesdays and culminated in a trip to an out-of-town conference on the topic.

We'll save the balance of our stories and ideas about parent and community involvement for Chapter 12. But educators know all too well that students' behavior in school mirrors the character of the society around them. Rather than complain about the failings and weaknesses of that society, schools can take action to focus the best energies of the community on the students, helping them realize that the institution they are part of is valued by the adults around them.

A FINAL STORY

At BPHS, we discovered just how powerful a strong sense of community could be and how the internal culture and the surroundings of a school interact, when a tragic and disturbing event occurred. In our second year, one of our students was shot and killed one weekend, back in his own neighborhood.

The kids heard the news Monday morning and reacted with great emotion. The Board of Education sent out its contingent of grief counselors, but the students responded scornfully—"You don't know us! You can't know how we feel!"—and walked out of the library where they'd been gathered. As kids wandered the halls, we feared things would spin out of control. We had to struggle to keep some of the angriest boys from running out of the building to seek some kind of revenge. Down the hall, we spotted a cluster of students and rushed to investigate, only to find that they'd pulled out the school's video cameras, and were recording testimonies about their fallen friend, for his family. Back in the computer lab, kids headed to the terminals to compose poems and letters about him. Others went to their advisory rooms, where they knew teachers would let them sit and cry, or talk quietly. Gradually, kids and teachers began to organize a memorial service, held several days later. A group of the boys, black, Hispanic, and white, joined together to write a tribute and stand manfully before the school and the family, unashamed of the tears streaming down their faces, to read it to us.

We never want such an event to happen again. But when this tragedy struck, the students' reaction showed us that we had indeed created a community where people cared about one another and knew how to use the resources at hand to respond to life's most difficult situations in a constructive and educated way.

FINDING YOUR NEXT STEPS

Remember: How would you describe the climate of the high school you attended? What were some of the groups and cliques, and which did you belong to? What advantages or disadvantages, hurts or encouragements, did this create for you? Were there kids who were labeled or bullied? Did any adults intervene in any way? In retrospect, what might they have done? Jot down the names of some adults who took a special or personal interest in you in high school. What were the circumstances? What difference has it made in your life? How do these memories compare with conditions in the high school you are now associated with? For example, how many adults, in your estimation, get to know many students well? How often might those adults have opportunities to talk with one another about those students?

Survey: Circulate a questionnaire among students at your school, asking them about some of the issues introduced in this chapter—how well known they are by how many adults in the school, the cliques and groups that exist, conflicts they are aware of, how students are labeled by their peers, and how often students encounter racial slurs, name-calling, taunts about homosexuality, or sexual harassment. Ask, too, about students' perception of how the adults in the school respond to these problems. Share the results with individuals and groups that might help initiate programs to improve school climate.

Organize: Bring together people who hold various roles in your school to discuss the kinds of conflicts and divisions that occur in the building. You might start by inviting the group to read together *Lost Boys: Why Our Sons Turn Violent and How We Can Save Them* by James Garbarino, on factors leading children to violence and effective interventions, or *There's Room for Me Here* by Janet Allen and Kyle Gonzalez, on students who struggle in regular classrooms. The group can choose one new structure or strategy for improving climate that people consider most likely to gain acceptance and begin planning for its adoption. This may begin with forming a teacher or parent group, or with one-on-one meetings with administrators and others who are influential. Help people to see the effort as positive, not a threat to their position. If you anticipate lots of resistance, consider trying out the new strategy with a small subgroup in the school. This is easier with classroom instruction approaches or a program like peer mediation that does not alter major school structures. But also consider such steps as inclusion of special education teachers and students in just one department or several pilot classes. You'll need to gather information—research on the effectiveness of the strategy you are advocating, examples of schools where it's successful, guidance on the concrete steps for making it work. But there's plenty of help out there. Many smart and thoughtful people want to see high schools become better, more supportive places to be. You can find them.

Chapter 4
Voice and Leadership

Both students and teachers exercise choice and make decisions in all elements of school life.

t's January, after the end of the semester, and the BPHS teachers, on a two-day retreat (thanks to some grant money), have just returned from lunch to review the school's performance on the main features in its vision. People begin by talking about size.

Mark: *I know we're a small school, but it feels much bigger, now that we have all four grade levels.*

Vanessa: *There's just no way to know all the kids. In the halls, if they know that I don't know them, they don't listen to me the same way.*

Aiko: *The hallways are much more congested, which means there isn't enough time for kids to get where they need to go.*

Tom: *At least the grade-level teams help to keep a smaller feel. But it's harder to communicate among us teachers, too. When another team schedules a special event and doesn't let the rest of us know about it, I run into problems.*

Michelle: *Maybe we can fix that by choosing a "point person" for each team and have them report at Monday faculty meetings.*

BPHS teachers determine a great deal of what happens at their school on their own, in deliberations like this one. What led us to such a governance style? Let's flash back to spring 1996. A small band of about half a dozen Chicago high school teachers and their three university partners have come to New York to observe a variety of new, small high schools there. It's the end of a long day visiting sites in every corner of the city—a school on a university campus, a school linked with a museum, a school that hasn't begun yet, another famous for its innovative success and longevity. To keep within budget, we're housed at a funky apartment hotel with fading flocked wallpaper everywhere. We've gathered in Harvey's room to drink rosé, munch barbequed potato chips (this after a huge dinner in Little Italy), and talk over what we've seen, what we'd like to emulate, and what we'd rather do our own way.

One pattern we've noticed is that so many of these special schools started with one strong principal who designed the program and whose vision is being implemented by the teachers. We're aware that in a big-city school system, a courageous and well-organized principal is a vital asset. And yet we realize we've already begun a different way. We've been primarily doing this work as a team, a group. We've been operating on consensus decision making, involving everyone in our choices, listening to everyone's voice. It has been slow and cumbersome at times, but it also feels democratic and exhilarating. Perhaps because several of our founding faculty are strong union advocates, one a longtime union representative at her school, we are acutely sensitive to the need for a broad and clear teacher voice in the governance of our school-to-be. We are very wary of any one person becoming the "boss."

And so the flocked wallpaper in our New York hotel room witnesses our resolve: ours will be a teacher-led school. As much as we admire these amazing, idiosyncratic, visionary schools with their one key leader, we're going to do it Chicago-style, where everyone leads (and at worst no one follows). And we are committed to this belief in full: if having a voice leads teachers to take more risks, to be more effective, and to make more of a commitment to the school, won't it be true for students as well?

This participatory aim may seem idealistic, or even contradictory—a strong principal, and yet extensive decision making by the teachers; strong teachers, and yet plenty of voice for kids. Nevertheless, good corporate managers recognize this principle just as clearly as good teachers and educational administrators do: an effective leader enables those around him or her to take more initiative, maybe even fail a few times, and grow in the process.

We realize that as we advocate this principle for American high schools, we're urging it upon a complicated institution, highly authoritarian, with a principal who can make decisions single-handedly at the top and teachers who tell students what to do, meting out rewards and punishments. Even *Breaking Ranks*, the National Association of Secondary School Principals document that boldly supports many of the ideas in this book, offers only a hesitant statement on teacher leadership and then moves on to clearly endorse the present reality: "the principal occupies the pivotal position" in a school (NASSP 1996).

At the same time, teachers organized in departments are often fiercely territorial. They can block changes they believe will threaten jobs or cut registration in their best-populated courses. And whatever the school or departmental mandates, individual teachers go into the classroom, close the door, and do what they believe best. Ironically, those in a school who promote more teacher decision making and student voice may face colleagues whose very vote might be to oppose their efforts. So the recommendations in this chapter may arguably be the most challenging in this book, and the politics and logistics of implementing them can be daunting.

There are ways to respond to this challenge, however. One is to begin with small teams and groups of teachers who want to have and to give more voice, even if change can't be instituted in the whole school at once. We've already described this in Chapter 2, as a way to help big schools feel and act smaller. But effective teaming goes beyond mere reduction in size of a working educational group. When teachers work in small interdisciplinary teams, they can focus together on a single group of students and make their own decisions about how to provide the teaching and support and coordinated adult attention the kids need—which is what happens in a small school. And if the team has a block of several class periods to work with, it can make many of its own decisions about using time, connecting subject areas, and designing instruction.

This doesn't alter governance of the entire school, but it increases teacher initiative at the crucial level of curriculum and instruction. And it builds everyone's confidence in the effectiveness of shared decision making. But why is teacher voice so important? Is it indeed effective for improving and helping guide a high school?

A LOOK AT RESEARCH ON TEACHER COLLABORATION AND LEADERSHIP

Studies of teacher job satisfaction make clear that autonomy is extremely important and strongly related to teacher retention. A 1997 study by Marianne Perie and David Baker, issued by the National Center for Education Statistics, concluded that:

- Although certain background variables, such as teacher's age and years of experience, are related to teacher satisfaction, they are not nearly as significant in explaining the different levels of satisfaction as are work-place conditions such as administrative support, parental involvement, and teacher control over classroom procedures.

■ Teachers with greater autonomy show higher levels of satisfaction than teachers who feel they have less autonomy. Administrative support, student behavior, and feelings of control were consistently shown to be associated with teacher job satisfaction.

■ Teacher satisfaction showed a weak relationship with salary and benefits.

The effect of increased teacher decision making on student achievement has been harder to document, particularly because the main attempts at implementing it have been diluted and piecemeal. The initial concepts were promising, however. Through the 1990s, many school districts adopted a variety of versions of "site-based management," in response to the thinking that "teachers perform intellectually complex tasks, are most effective when working collegially or in teams, and face uncertainty in their day-to-day work. Therefore, a high-involvement and decentralized management strategy is appropriate for schools" (NCREL 1995, 1).

The results were something else. In some districts, like Chicago, site-based management meant community control, which, though it has its own virtues, particularly in highly bureaucratized large-city school districts, doesn't necessarily bring teachers into the process. In other districts, the main approach was merely to delegate more of the previously centralized administrative work to principals. And even in those districts that set up building-level teacher committees, so many key decisions were still made elsewhere in the system that the teachers were often left frustrated or confused. They found themselves with more meetings to attend but little real result (Noble, Deemer, and Davis 1996). And while teachers rarely received training in how to work effectively, principals hesitated to share power (Holloway 2000).

Teacher teaming, which is another mode of teacher decision making, presents its own implementation challenges. It's unlikely to work if teachers are just thrown together willy-nilly in teams and ordered to "cooperate." Some individualists find cooperation little more than an intrusion, while more socially oriented teachers often treasure it. Some teams see more eye to eye on pedagogical issues than others, and some develop better collaboration styles than others. Clearly, careful planning and staff development are needed for team approaches to work.

An outstanding example that shows the possibilities of shared decision making and teacher voice is Fairdale High School, near Louisville, Kentucky, a school that serves twelve hundred students with 25 percent of minority and 60 percent of low economic status. Responding to its high dropout rate and low attendance, the school began to reform itself in 1986, with a participatory committee comprised of faculty, parents, and community representatives. Extensive collaboration, teacher teaming, and teacher leadership have characterized the school ever since. At the instructional level, teachers have developed integrated learning through teams of five to seven teachers each. Math and science teachers work in pairs. Experienced and novice teachers are also paired to insure continuity of innovations as new staff comes aboard. And the faculty devised a flexible, hybrid schedule of traditional and block-period days very similar to that at Best Practice High School.

Fairdale operates with a "School-Based Decision-Making Council," a policy-making body that receives reform proposals, consults all faculty, and oversees investigation and trial of new approaches. The school is widely recognized for its success at reform and serves as a demonstration site for the Southern Regional Education Board's "High Schools That Work" program. By 1993, the school's dropout rate had shrunk to 5 percent, and attendance had increased to 92 percent ("'So Now What'" 1993; and National Center for Research in Vocational Education website document).

The Coalition of Essential Schools has tracked the sensitive work of bringing teachers into the change and decision-making process at Fairdale and a number of other schools, in its journal, *Horace* (Jan. 1993). The coalition authors urge an orderly process that includes training for participants in how to work in a more collaborative structure, lots of consultation and communication among all parties, and thoughtful attention to—rather than just hostility toward—the resistors among the staff.

WHAT IS GOOD TEACHER LEADERSHIP?

After learning from schools' struggles with site-based management, we can say what teacher leadership isn't. It isn't just teachers voting on whether to change a schoolwide policy or practice. It isn't teachers gaining power only to maintain the status quo. It isn't teachers simply divided into teams and told to do something about their curriculum. And it isn't just a teacher steering committee meeting with the principal to make decisions about everyone else.

 What then, are some characteristics of strong, effective teacher leadership in a school?

- It begins with a staff or department or interested group of teachers who want to improve their school or program.

- A shared vision is developed for the work of the teacher group.

- Teachers obtain training in how to work effectively as a team and learn how to deal constructively with conflicts or differences that may emerge.

- The focus of leadership is primarily on improving instruction, curriculum, and school climate.

- Teachers develop a process, whether formal or informal, for considering an issue carefully and working on it with others, including administrators, community, and students. All concerned parties are consulted and respected.

- Teachers gather information about a problem and about ways for solving it.

- Leadership may develop gradually, as various constituencies are brought on board.

- Efficiency is valued, and debate or investigation is not prolonged endlessly. Interminable, unproductive meetings can kill any program.

- Time is provided, either during the school day or in limited after-school periods, for meetings and planning.

- Teachers have the authority and control of resources to address important academic issues.

- Administrators in the school and district support the teacher-leadership effort. When other district rules, mandates, or lines of responsibility become involved in a teacher-led initiative, teachers receive support in resolving problems thoughtfully.

From our own experience, from schools we've visited and others we've studied, it's clear that there is no one formula for developing or carrying on good teacher leadership. The strength of a good decision-making structure comes from the input and initiative of the participants, as they create a structure of their own that serves them well.

TEACHER LEADERSHIP AT BEST PRACTICE

We offer our story of how teachers exercise voice at Best Practice High School, understanding the need for other schools to find their own path. And, of course, we have our share of imperfections and unmet goals. At least, however, we can show how one effort has developed, with all the struggles and limitations that are bound to present themselves in any organized group of human beings.

One advantage we've been blessed with at Best Practice is a principal who believes in teacher autonomy and balances it gracefully with her own leadership. Best Practice shares a building with two other schools, Foundations School, which is a K–8 program, and Nia School, which includes grades 3–8. The principal is in charge of all three. The Chicago Board of Education holds her responsible, just as it does all principals, so she evaluates teachers, signs off on budgets, hiring, and the school improvement plan, and responds to a constant flow of demands for reports and data. But two of the schools already existed, and Best Practice had a specific plan when Sylvia Gibson was interviewed for the job, so plenty of momentum for teacher initiative existed before she joined the effort. Nevertheless, she was the only candidate willing to state with confidence that she believed in teacher-led programs. Others, after agreeing, would add, "But of course, when there are disagreements or conflicts, the buck stops with me." Sylvia, instead, added a more participatory "I want to be a part of the process of developing and creating new approaches."

A second advantage, which just about any newly starting school would have, was that we had so much to do, no one person could begin to handle all of it, and the Board had provided no release time for either of the two lead teachers—so there was plenty of room for individual initiative. Finally, because we started with only 137 freshmen, the staff was at first so small that consultation was constant and informal.

Not that starting a new school was easy. Every teacher had a full load of classes, except for the computer lab teacher, the internship coordinator, and the librarian. Every aspect of curriculum, every school policy, every fresh problem—like what to do with students who disrupted the classroom—had to be addressed outside of the class periods. The school day was a roller coaster, with the teachers hanging on for dear life.

Discipline, for example, devolved to the office staff. No one else was available to address the issue, and so problem students simply ended up in front of them. With no special training, our loyal and hardworking clerks, Gwen Downing and Olga Lamourt, followed their own leanings in handling the kids. Because so many other pressing issues filled the meeting agendas, teachers for a long time had no chance to work out a policy to guide them. It took time for us to learn that in a new school, with a teacher-led program, solving problems and working out new structures would in fact take time.

As a result of repeated faculty discussions and committee recommendations, a series of steps has ultimately addressed the discipline issue. Experienced teachers help newer staff with strategies for maintaining order in more positive ways in the classroom, so fewer students land in the office. And a referral form is used for more serious events, so they can be handled later in the day by one teacher, Peter Thomas, who agreed to take on the duty. Thus, problems get addressed, students remain in the classroom where they can learn, and the office staff is unburdened.

As for our larger governance, what has evolved naturally and gradually over four years is a free-flowing yet orderly process of teacher leadership. Lead teacher Kathy Daniels is now released from the classroom full time, and handles the endless flow of paperwork required to run a Chicago Public School (we won't bore you with the details, but it's enough to keep at least one administrator busy nearly full time). Whatever the paper load, however, as a leader and founder of the school, Kathy also feels a deep responsibility to maintain its core vision and focus. Our second lead teacher, Mark Fertel, is now in charge of the computer lab and shares leadership and administrative tasks with Kathy.

Regular Monday after-school faculty meetings are led by teachers on a rotating basis, using an agenda sheet that people fill in during the course of the day, listing items they want to introduce and the time they'll need. A typical agenda might include:

- whether to change the following week's schedule because of a Monday holiday
- what to do about students who are late to class
- topics to put on the agenda for an upcoming faculty retreat
- how to determine scholarship awards for seniors
- faculty needed to staff a table at a student recruitment fair
- how to help students learn stronger research skills.

While discussions at the faculty meetings can grow deep and thoughtful, the facilitator keeps things moving and does not allow perseveration. If a problem needs more discussion or the design of some new policy or plan, volunteers form an ad hoc committee that goes to work and reports back within a week or two. Committees have addressed such issues as discipline, portfolio assessment, and what to do about teaching research processes in a meaningful way.

Often, individual teachers simply go to work on issues or projects that interest them. In the first year, special education teacher Sonja Kosanovic decided the students would appreciate an annual talent show, and so she simply organized one. For over a year, math teacher Tom McDougal has been gradually developing a grading system that more accurately reflects the learning and activity he most values in his students' work. The science teachers are comparing their curricula to articulate more effectively from physics to chemistry to biology. Though the stereotype of participatory democracy sometimes suggests endless debate and inaction, or disconnected individualistic activity, that certainly doesn't characterize Best Practice self-governance.

Grade-Level Teams

Jenny: I was really amazed when I read all those letters our students wrote to the Board about not cutting teachers from our staff. It was the best writing I've ever seen them do. I'd like to know how we can have more authentic occasions for writing like that.

Marilyn: Wouldn't it be good if we used public events more? Like the Elian Gonzalez case right now!

Laura: Yes, but it has to be something that matters to our kids. I've been running "choice-time" sessions on Cuba, and this Elian thing seems very distant to them.

Steve: So "authentic" means it's also significant for *them*.

Mike: It seems as if what Laura did, taking the kids down to Pilsen [a Mexican American neighborhood in Chicago] really worked.

Harvey: Yes, because it was a fresh experience that really grabbed them.

And so the sophomore team hashes over a curricular issue with the university partners. Grade-level teaming provides the other main focus of teacher leadership at Best Practice. These teams originally developed through their work on integrated learning units. As will be described in Chapters 5 and 6, on curriculum, about four times per year all the students and teachers at each grade level pause in their learning of separate subjects to spend several weeks studying a single theme or topic. The themes, teaching tasks, uses of time, and logistics are worked out by the grade-level team. The teachers coordinate their instructional contributions, each taking an aspect of the theme or each providing an option for students' deeper study or mode of expression.

Thus, these teams have become close working groups. They meet on Wednesdays, while their students are off at their internship sites. The meetings were initially just for planning integrated learning units, but it didn't take long for teachers to begin discussing the students they all share, trading detailed knowledge of individuals' needs and strengths, and coordinating strategies to address kids' problems. At some point they also discovered that it was more effective to meet with parents as a team rather than one at a time.

We observed the teachers' level of commitment on the retreat that was pictured at the start of this chapter. At dinner in the spacious dining room of the rural retreat center, one teacher team began running through their mental list of students, reviewing who was doing well, who was in trouble lately, and each one's attitude toward school. As the dinner courses kept arriving and the catalogue seemed never to end, Steve kept trying to lighten things up by shifting the conversation to movies people had seen or vacations they'd taken. Surely they'd thought enough about teaching for one day. "Don't you guys have a life?" Steve asked. This, however, is the kind of professional focus that insures no students fall between the cracks.

Our naturally developed leadership structure not only has served the school well, but has created a high level of teacher enthusiasm, involvement, and mutual support. In a survey conducted by the Consortium on Chicago School Research, with the most recent data obtained in spring 1999, Best Practice teachers rated their professional working conditions, involvement, and academic effectiveness within the top sixth of Chicago schools on almost every measure. They saw the principal as a strong yet inclusive instructional leader, toward whom they felt a high level of trust and respect. One hundred percent viewed themselves as having influence in the school's decision making and considered the school's program coherent and consistent with its mission. They believed they communicated well with parents, and they felt trusted and supported by them. They asserted that they worked hard to understand their students' cultures. They saw themselves as highly collaborative, engaged in reflective dialogue about teaching. They indicated that they shared collective responsibility for the school and felt high mutual regard for one another. They supported innovation and believed others, including the principal, supported it as well. And they felt involved in a high level of professional development. Clearly, giving teachers a well-organized, efficient voice in how their school works leads them to feel highly committed to the hard work that they do.

We further discovered the teachers' level of commitment at a hiring interview one day. The candidate was a burnt-out veteran from another high school, looking for a berth to finish out a couple of years until her retirement. It had been a mistake, we thought. Who invited her in the first place? But since interviews are open to all staff, a tableful of teachers sat around, trying to get acquainted with our hapless candidate. With each question about some aspect of Best Practice instruction, the poor woman had to admit she didn't know much about the topic, nor did she seem particularly eager to learn. As a result, each questioner responded with an explanation—about integrated curriculum, or literature circles, or classroom workshop. As the explanations grew longer and more fervent, English teacher Beth Meeker whispered to Steve, "Why are we wasting all this time?" But these were the teachers' passionate declarations of what they'd come to believe. Some of us decided that about once a year we should invite an unsuspecting drone to an interview, just so we could restate our beliefs about why we're here.

STUDENT VOICE

Sophomore Seth Frazier walks into the Best Practice High School office and hands a sheet with twenty names on it to Kathy Daniels. "These are the guys who want to play football," he mumbles shyly. She points out some unreadable scribbles that need names printed next to them—and Seth has learned one of the niceties of submitting petitions. Fortunately, he knows everyone who signed, so he fills in the information. One advantage of having a new school without sports teams and other extracurricular activities is that students realize if they want these things, they have to take action. Gradually, they learn to organize and discover that their voices can have an effect.

But if teacher voice is faint in the governance of high schools around the country, student voice reaches barely a whimper. Yet, psychologists tell us that a sense of control over one's own actions is a prime need that humans have (Glasser 1986, 1998). Students, just like all the rest of us, are more likely to stay involved in an activity if they have some control over what takes place. The need for ownership sounds like a platitude, even as it's neglected, but remains essential nonetheless.

A LOOK AT RESEARCH ON STUDENT VOICE

What role does having a voice play in students' success in school? A classic psychological analysis of student behavior and performance is provided by William Glasser in *Control Theory in the Classroom* (1986). Now more sensibly renamed "choice theory," Glasser's thinking challenges traditional behaviorist psychology and asserts that people's actions are guided by five basic needs: love/belonging, power, freedom, fun, and physical survival. Further, people develop mental pictures, based on experience, of what will fulfill these needs. Children who have difficulty in school erase their picture of the classroom as a place where their needs can be met, and as a result, neither threats, nor punishments, nor rewards succeed in changing their behavior (Glasser 1986, 1998).

To construct—or reconstruct—students' mental pictures so that they choose to work hard and learn in school, Glasser says we must address students' basic needs by organizing classrooms around:

- cooperative learning
- student choices about what and how to learn
- plenty of support for achieving success
- caring attention from adults.

The first two of these, of course, are essential forms of student voice. Glasser describes the success of this approach in several schools where he has worked (Glasser 1998).

Another passionate advocate of student choice in schools is Alfie Kohn. In "Choices for Children: Why and How to Let Students Decide" (Kohn 1993), Kohn lists a range of reasons for involving students in decision making in school. First, people who experience self-determination are healthier physically and emotionally. Second, students learn responsibility and self-control by being taught to make thoughtful decisions. Third, academic achievement increases when children make choices of what and how to study. And finally, teachers find their work more exhilarating when students are deeply involved in work they're committed to.

But if psychological theories urge us to give students more voice, do studies confirm that it actually results in greater student achievement? The research is actually quite extensive, though much of it isn't specifically labeled as data on "student voice." Cooperative learning, for example, means students are talking with each other, rather than listening to a lecture—and summaries ("meta-analysis") of hundreds of studies confirm the superior learning students demonstrate when they work cooperatively (Johnson, Johnson, and Holubec 1991; Slavin 1991). Studies of individual teaching strategies that involve active student interchange also confirm the psychologists' assertions. For example, students learn vocabulary more effectively when working cooperatively (Fisher, Blachowicz, and Smith 1991). And small-group literacy projects lead to better comprehension scores, language expression, and metacognitive awareness (Stevens and Slavin 1995).

Going further in the classroom, educational thinkers have for many years urged teachers to help students ask questions, rather than just answer them, and researchers confirm the value of this effort (Commeyras, Sherrill, and

Wuenker 1996). Teaching students to guide their own discussions about books, in literature circles and book clubs, has grown extensively (Daniels 1994; Raphael and McMahon 1997). Many schools and teachers have discovered the value of having students give exhibitions on their learning, rather than take tests, carrying out their own self-assessments (Porter and Cleland 1995), and of running student-led parent conferences (see Daniels, Zemelman, and Bizar 1999 for more extensive lists of studies).

Not surprisingly, considering the traditional structure of American education, research on the role of students in the larger governance of classrooms and schools is much scarcer. Fortunately, there are many accounts of success at individual schools. Many members of the Coalition of Essential Schools, for example, feature student governing bodies that go beyond traditional student councils to address significant issues and policies—schools such as Bronxville High School, Scarsdale Alternative High School, and University Heights High School in the New York area, Souhegan High School in Amherst, New Hampshire, and Fenway High School in Boston. One popular strategy is to address issues in regular student "town meetings" (*Horace*, Sept. 1994).

These structures require explicit nurturing, since students unaccustomed to responsibility don't automatically welcome it or understand how to exercise it. As the Coalition journal, *Horace*, states, "Unless the structures exist in their schools to support student involvement in change, however, young people often experience the same problems teachers face when . . . inspired by new ideas" (*Horace,* Sept. 1994, 4).

Two other promising projects that are helping schools develop student voice are Partners in School Innovation in California and the Manitoba School Improvement Program, in Manitoba, Canada. In each of these programs, consultants work in schools to help teachers and students create new ways for students to make decisions and take active roles in their own education and in the operation of the school. At one MSIP school, for example, students were helped to redesign the role of the student council, to create new cross-grade groupings of students, and to provide training in facilitation and leadership skills for forty to fifty of their peers (Lee and Zimmerman 1999). Teachers at schools involved in Partners in School Innovation observe that their students show increases in their sense of accomplishment and involvement in the school as a result of participating in student empowerment projects (Philips 1998).

The outcomes are frequently more far-reaching than teachers and planners anticipated. At Bronxville High School, for example, a student protest over the town's decision to install parking meters near the school resulted in students' regular attendance at town council meetings and one student's run for mayor (*Horace*, Sept. 1994).

BRINGING STUDENT VOICE INTO THE LIFE OF A SCHOOL

How can student voice be exercised in a high school? Clearly, it must be heard both in the classroom and throughout the school. Since learning is the main purpose of school, we cannot simply establish a schedule for student town meetings while kids listen to lectures all day and expect that the kids will feel they are heard. On the other hand, if classrooms are more active and participatory, but students have no say in larger school concerns, that also tells them they are not truly citizens in their community.

So we outline here a number of levels of student participation and decision making, and while they range from the narrowest to the widest arena of influence, each contributes to students' sense of efficacy in the life of the school. And obviously, some are more frequently found in schools today than others.

Ways to exercise voice in the classroom:

- Students choose activities or strategies for getting assignments done.
- Students assess their own work.
- Students choose topics or materials to study (negotiate curriculum).
- Students guide their own work, in cooperative groups and/or individually.
- Students teach other students, one on one, in small groups, or through individual or group presentations to the class.
- Students choose among seminars or activities to attend among several classrooms.
- Students help plan study units or courses for groups of classrooms.
- Students teach units or courses of their own design across multiple classrooms.

Ways students can have input on wider school issues:

- Students discuss issues in advisories.
- Ad hoc committees focus on special needs or problems—for example, to address the need for conflict resolution, to promote interracial understanding, or to redesign the freshman program.
- Student representatives sit on committees and councils previously comprised solely of adults.

- Standing student committees participate in governance functions—for example, student committee that interviews new teacher candidates.
- Student town meetings deliberate on school policies, problems.
- Students sit on the school board or community council.

Whatever the venues for student voice, it is essential to employ effective processes for establishing them, and for preparing students to use them meaningfully. Support needs to be built among faculty and administrators. Procedures are needed for sensibly balancing student input with that of the other constituencies in the school. No one is proposing that kids simply run the school. On the other hand, if students perceive that decisions are predetermined and their votes are just for show, they'll quickly grow cynical. A good way to build trust in the process is to establish an orderly and accepted pathway for considering proposals. Teachers need staff development to help them expand their repertoire of alternatives to the traditional classroom lecture. And teenagers who aren't in the habit of taking initiative don't all become active citizens without help and training. They must be taught leadership skills—how to communicate ideas effectively, gather support, facilitate meetings, and negotiate conflicts. Of course, these are all excellent skills schools should teach anyway, for success in the adult world.

AVENUES FOR STUDENT VOICE AT BEST PRACTICE

Student Input on School Governance: At the end of the school year at Best Practice, the internship coordinator holds a lunch meeting for a representative group of students and the supervisors from the many businesses, nonprofits, museums, and schools where our kids attend weekly half-day internships (a program we'll describe in detail in Chapter 7). Over pizza and cokes, the participants discuss what worked well during the year, what students think they learned, and what might need to be changed or improved in the program for next year.

"So who can tell about a problem at your internship this year?" Marilyn asks. Morgan responds, *"Well, at the Children's Museum, they just had us licking stamps and sealing envelopes week after week. So after about three weeks of that, we decided we wouldn't do it anymore. We just got up and walked out in the middle of the morning and waited outside for the bus to take us back to school."*

"It was a mutiny!" internship coordinator Shelley Freeman adds. *"I*

got a call from Peggy Beidelman, their supervisor, asking why they did it, what was wrong. So I met them at the bus, and we had a talk about how people at work can try to talk with their boss when they've got a problem, before they just go out on strike. The kids hadn't learned that, and it was hard for them to overcome their shyness."

"The next week we had a good discussion, and they listened. We learned how to talk with adults, so maybe it was all worth it," Morgan concluded.

This was not a deliberative body, but the information was vital for strengthening and refining an essential part of our curriculum. Students were not just being "heard"; their ideas were sought to help guide the program. And initiating this kind of respectful consultation in a high school does not require buildingwide restructuring or lengthy consensus-seeking campaigns with countless faculty committees.

Student input in governance at Best Practice occurs in a number of other ways as well. A student committee interviews new teacher candidates in tandem with the faculty-led interviews. Seniors meet and plan their many pre-graduation functions and are consulted as a class on policies for awards from our school's own scholarship fund. The Local School Council (the local body at each Chicago public school that governs many major aspects of its program) includes one student at the high school level. And daily advisories provide occasion for students to discuss and share with teachers both personal and community concerns.

However, faculty and students both recognize that student participation is not yet all that we'd like. In a survey of students conducted to help us write this book, only the more active students felt that they were heard and heeded. A certain portion of this response represents normal teenage attitude—"Why can't we go off campus for lunch?"—but it's widespread enough that the sentiment must be listened to. And some obvious steps can be taken: regular class meetings, student representatives at faculty meetings, leadership training—perhaps within advisories—to help students participate more effectively. We must value students' input, even if we don't always like what they say.

Voice and Choice in the Classroom: For a research unit she calls "Take Control of Your Education," sophomore English teacher Jenny Cornbleet begins by asking students to plan their own ideal school curriculum, complete with a daily schedule of classes and a list of the ideal teachers of the subjects (e.g., cooking taught by a favorite aunt). From the student schedules, the class identifies four or five topics that are widely shared, and then organizes in groups, each focused on one of the topics. Topics this year were spirituality, love and relationships, fashion and appearance, and music (no surprises here, for teenagers). To gather research materials, Jenny takes the kids to a nearby bookstore, where students choose books on their topics that are added to the classroom library (she reports that the kids guard "their" books passionately, with a class-designed check-out system for security). She then provides a guide sheet for preparing study activities on the topics, with steps and procedures to insure the lessons are well organized. The sheet includes sample activities, but Jenny also requires each group to brainstorm at least forty additional activity options. They then prepare "learning stations" for their topics, each station featuring a list of ten possible activities for studying the particular topic. For example, students interested in fashion (other than those who planned the lesson) may choose to create a "fashion book" using a Polaroid camera and conducting interviews of students they photograph around the school. Students thus actively create curriculum and make choices at numerous stages in the classroom process.

In a simpler, but more regularly used pattern, physics teacher Arthur Griffin places students in groups to work on assigned problems. Each group is given a two-by-three-foot white board to write out an explanation of how they solved their particular problem. In a symbolic gesture of ownership, each student signs his or her name at the bottom of the board. The student groups then take turns explaining their solutions to the class. While this is a much more teacher-guided approach than Jenny's, it still asks students to take responsibility and teach one another about the subject.

But there's no one formula for incorporating student voice in the classroom. Rather, when teachers are committed to the principle, they create their own approaches as the need arises. In chemistry, for example, when teacher Michael Cannon observed that students were not applying themselves seriously, he stopped his science lessons for several days to refocus students by asking them to write about and share their goals for learning and their ideas on how Best Practice education could support those goals.

Our latest effort has been to institute portfolios, schoolwide. After several staff development sessions on the topic, a teacher committee created a plan to help everyone try it for the first time. The first steps in adopting the process have been very simple. In each subject, students choose one piece of their work that they're proud of and write a reflection about it during advisory period. Advisory teachers also help students understand the process of reflection—which is, after all, students using their voice. The portfolios are kept in advisory, added to each year, and used by students and teachers to observe student growth over the course of their high school career. Interestingly, teachers decided they wouldn't grade the portfolios. The students, they concluded, would be more honest and thoughtful in their reflections if the pressure of a grade were removed.

In our chapters on Teaching and Curriculum (Chapters 5 and 6) we'll explain more about the many strategies Best Practice teachers use to give students voice in the classroom. Small-group self-guided literature circle discussions, individualized "workshop" time when students focus on their own chosen topics for writing, student debates, and student discussions about how teaching and learning work in our classrooms—all are strategies that any teacher, in any subject area, can adopt, though of course it's always easier to try something new when others around you are doing it too.

Beyond the Individual Classroom: At the multiclassroom level, Best Practice students make choices and offer input in a variety of ways. To help guide creation of some of our integrated study units—when all teachers at a given grade level focus together for several weeks on a single topic—students are asked on a prior occasion to list important questions and concerns they have, and then to compile these into master lists of shared interests. In many of the integrated units, students choose among subtopics and modes to express what they've learned. During the several weeks of work on the units, the students are assigned to the teacher in charge of the particular topic or mode they've chosen (see description of negotiated curriculum and the "Isms" unit in Chapter 5).

Best Practice has also incorporated student choice in the part of the weekly schedule we call "choice time." Every Wednesday, the school shifts to an entirely different mode from either block or traditional periods. While half the students—freshmen and sophomores—head off to internships at local businesses, schools, and organizations for the morning, the other half attend half-day "choice-time" activities. In the afternoon, the classes reverse, with juniors and seniors on internships while the younger students attend choice time (see Chapter 7 for a more complete description of internships, and Chapter 8 on scheduling).

Teachers offer choice-time activities based on their own interests and the needs and requests of the kids, who sign up in advance for their preferred topic. On a typical day, there are chess club, yearbook, yoga, women's issues group, physics lab makeup, math help, peer mediators' planning session, poetry writing, and more. Some sessions are one-time offerings, and others are ongoing for several weeks or months.

A.M. Choice-Time Options
April 12, 2000

Debate Team—Members need to attend.	
SERIOUS NEWCOMERS ARE WELCOME!	Brechling - 305
Nutrition Project work and Biology/English Fable work	
(2 per advisory only)	Bryant - 314
Choir Rehearsal—MANDATORY FOR MEMBERS	
(preselected) REMEMBER TO WEAR BLACK AND	
WHITE FOR THURSDAY!!	Curtwright - 300
French movie (2 per advisory)	Hernandez - 206
Pep Club	Kosanovic - 313A
Study Hall (1 per advisory) esp. seniors who need help	
on Fable	Meeker - 207
Work on Fables (2 per advisory)	Peano - 308
Project work in computer lab (3 per senior advisory only)	Thomas - 208
Entrepreneurs—ALL STUDENTS FROM THE MILWAUKEE TRIP	
SHOULD ATTEND	Tolbert - basement

P.M. Choice-Time Options
April 12, 2000

Rembrandt Art Society (preselected)	Boyce - 307
Young Women's Group (preselected)	Cornbleet - 304
Pep Club	Dulak - 313A
Board Games (2 per advisory only)	Epps - 310
Chess (2 per advisory)	Fertel - 312
Physics/Physical Science After-School Program (3 per advisory)	Griffin - 313B
Arts and Crafts (2 per advisory)	Harris - 301
Movie and Discussion—"Havana"	Linhart - 209
More Probability—A continuation of the fun stuff from	
our Integrated Unit *and math help*	McDougal - 302
Guys' Discussion Group	Myers - 201
Book Club—All members should bring the books they	
purchased on our field trip!!! (preselected; but serious	
newcomers should see Ms. Sanford)	Sanford - 208

Choice time offers a number of important benefits. First and foremost it—very simply—adds choice to the curriculum, no matter what else is going on in the regular courses. It provides a weekly scheduled period when kids can focus deeply on one topic or interest for an extended chunk of time. It offers ways for students to think, explore, and develop that may not be available in any of their regular classes—an especially important opportunity for students who do not see themselves as academically oriented. And finally, it introduces a major change of pace into the week, replacing the monotonous march of the schedule with some variety and surprise.

As with everything else we've described, some of these strategies, like literature circles and student-led lessons, can be readily translated to traditional fifty-minute, subject-specific classes in traditional high schools. Others, like choice time, would seem to require major overhaul of the school schedule. Teachers and schools can, however, make creative adaptations, even if larger restructuring doesn't appear to be at hand. For example, if a small interdisciplinary team begins working together, nothing really stands in the way of the team declaring one period per week a "choice period," with students electing alternative activities that are offered in each of the participating classrooms. For example, a history, English, and art team might on Fridays provide activities on music, dance, and sports in the historical period or country being studied. Or as a break from the curriculum, each teacher might share a lesson on a topic of his own special interest—film, fitness, a political issue, poetry writing. It's good for students to discover that their teachers are well-rounded, inquiring human beings with active lives.

How do students perceive the strength of their voice and breadth of their choices at Best Practice High School? In fact, the perceptions vary widely and show us that even in a small school, there's a still smaller one inhabited by the most involved and assertive students. While we've achieved some real innovations, we still have plenty of work to do.

The students get a fair say in what goes on in BPHS. It's one of the finer points of being here.

The only ways we have a say in what goes on in our school are through the different committees, such as peer mediation, National Honor Society, and Prom Committee. I wish I could have more say through a newspaper, or yearbook, or even through the student government.

When students at BPHS have a problem, we let it be known. We will get together in groups, make petitions, and have our parents complain. Stu-

dent representatives have been invited to staff meetings and the Walloon Institute in Michigan. I wish we had more of a say in curriculum structure.

People have a lot to say but everybody is afraid. I stepped up to the plate. I grabbed people's attention by stepping up. People are scared of what others are going to think or say afterwards. I faced my fears and suddenly became the spokesman for a whole student body.

I feel like the students don't really have a say, unfortunately. Teachers make all decisions, and students are treated as if they were elementary-school students.

Good teaching is one-on-one or very-close-relation teaching, voicing my opinion in English class.

Good teaching is when a teacher is involved with her students. . . . You voice your opinion. However you feel, you can say it and be open.

FINDING YOUR NEXT STEPS

Reflect: What are some first steps for teachers to begin exercising more of a say in the governance of your school? What might be some strategies to encourage administrators to support and value teachers' voice?

On the subject of students' decision making: obtain copies of Alfie Kohn's article "Choices for Children: Why and How to Let Students Decide" (Kohn 1993) and share them with teachers in your department or teachers with whom you regularly exchange ideas. Talk together about ways students can take more active roles and exercise choice within particular topics each of you teaches. What is one classroom strategy for increasing student voice in classrooms that the teachers are interested to learn more about? Or imagine a plan for a school consultative decision-making body and process. How would it include the voices of both students and teachers? How could it be made efficient and nimble, rather than bureaucratic and sluggish?

Search the Web: How do more participatory governance structures work in schools where they have been successful? Find out by checking websites of groups such as the Coalition of Essential Schools (www.essentialschools.org) or New Visions for Public Schools (www.newvisions.org) or using searches on "teacher empowerment," "teacher decision making," and "student voice." Then contact particular schools, like Fairdale H.S., or Bronxville H.S., or Fenway H.S., for more detailed information.

Consult: Talk to administrators in your school or district to learn which among them are most open to more shared governance. Once you find a sympathetic ear, discuss with that person (or persons) what training, internal communication, and support building would be necessary to increase teacher and student involvement in school governance. Talk over ways that departmental barriers and separations can be reduced. Or if the school is large and overall governance likely to be cumbersome, brainstorm ways that increased teacher decision making and student involvement could occur in smaller units.

Chapter 5
Teaching

Teachers collaborate with students to
explore and employ a growing repertoire
of instructional strategies.

Best Practice High School, Chicago, Illinois. *Kids are counting beans. In a hands-on experience, math teacher Mark Fertel is demonstrating what wildlife biologists call the capture-recapture method of population sampling. He asks the class to imagine the problems that would arise if they wanted to count the number of carp in a lake, llamas in a forest, or ferrets tunneling under a field. In his droll style, Mark observes that draining the lake and counting dead fish would not be the desired method.*

For each group of four or five students, Mark provides a plastic cup, two-thirds filled with dried beans, and some nontoxic markers. "Now it's time to go ferret hunting," Mark explains. "Take twenty beans out of your cup, and mark them each with an X." The students put the marked beans back into the cup and shake well in order to distribute them randomly. Next they take out a small handful of beans and count both the number of marked beans and the total number of beans in the "recaptured" sample.

What follows is simple mathematics; the students use the proportion they have identified to estimate the total number of beans in the cup. The investigation is repeated to get a total of five estimates, and the mean of the estimates is calculated. Lastly, they count the actual number of beans in the cup, to confirm that this strategy really does work, and of course the estimates are rarely off by more than one or two beans.

After completing the sampling process, the groups brainstorm real-world applications of this method. They generally come up with political polls and television ratings, and Mr. Fertel invites them to organize their own rating service. Each class is used as a sample for several questions, including the numbers that watch a particular television program, read a specific magazine, or follow the Chicago Bulls. Using these surveys, the students estimate the total number in the school who watch the programs, read the magazines, or cheer for the Bulls.

Jefferson High School, Portland, Oregon. In his American History class, Bill Bigelow's students role-play the 1934 West Coast longshoremen's strike as a part of their study of the U.S. labor movement. Students divide into five groups: longshoremen, waterfront employers, farmers, unemployed workers, and representatives of the central labor council. Each group is asked to propose solutions to the strike, from their own perspective. They face tough questions: Do we want the governor to call in the National Guard to protect the strikebreakers? How will we respond if the guard comes in? This is not just play-acting; students need to gather, understand, and juggle much information in order to represent effectively their group's attitudes and point of view.

Students are eager to devise persuasive arguments and hone negotiating skills. When a group doesn't have a clear, well-defined perspective, they must develop their own creative solutions. The payoff comes as the textbook is set aside and the students live out the strike in the classroom—the longshoremen negotiate with farmers to support the strike, waterfront workers attempt to garner support from the unemployed, and violence is threatened if the governor calls in the National Guard. In this realistic simulation, students can viscerally and intellectually engage some of the big issues in labor history: the complexity of social alliances, the threat of violence, the role of government, and process of compromise. (Bigelow 1994)

Teaching matters. It matters a lot. According to the National Commission on Teaching and America's Future:

- A student who has had a poorly qualified teacher for three years in a row is likely to have standardized test scores 50 percent lower than one who has had well-qualified teachers for the same period of time.

- Between 40 and 60 percent of the variance in student scores on the National Assessment of Educational Progress is attributable to the quality of the teaching students receive (Darling-Hammond 1999).

- One New York study showed quality of teaching to be the single most powerful variable in explaining difference in student achievement—90 percent, in fact—more important even than family income or parental education levels (Armour-Thomas et al. 1989).

- Most of the achievement gap between poor minority children and students in more affluent communities can be explained by differences in the caliber of the teaching.

Of course, no one who has ever been a student needs a research study to tell them how important the quality of teaching can be. Every one of us can remember magical, inspiring teachers, like the two we just read about, who launched us on a lifelong love of the subject they taught—and we can also remember poor teachers who may well have extinguished our interest in what they had to teach.

Therefore, while many new, innovative high schools have concentrated on a special subject or theme—schools for the arts, science academies, health science institutes—we planned Best Practice High School, and even named it, to focus on the quality and style of the teaching. Ours would be a general education program, and more than anything else, we wanted this school to show that good teaching, "best practice," could enable a cross section of normal kids to succeed and to become productive, thoughtful, confident citizens of our city. We wanted a school that would embody the thirteen principles of effective teaching and learning listed in Chapter 1 of this book and expressed in the standards documents written for the many subjects of the school curriculum.

If high schools in America are to be reformed, renewed, restructured, revitalized, the payoff must come in the classroom—in the daily interactions between kids and teachers, in the place where learning is meant to happen. Everything else—small size, positive climate, student voice, and teacher leadership—ultimately leads to this. And so, guided by our national curriculum standards, by the growing body of instructional research, by accounts of successful schools, and by the wisdom of our own hearts, we knew that our students would need classrooms like the ones we just read about.

What makes these classrooms good? They are challenging, authentic, and collaborative, exactly as our national curriculum standards and our best research recommend. All these students are engaged in complex, serious, meaty issues; they are required to think deeply and share their thinking in a variety of modes of expression; they are experiencing *rigor* without *mortis*. Their lessons address real issues in life and in the community, issues that experts in the field still grapple with, understandings gained from careful study that make a difference, work that kids recognize is worth their time. And finally, these classes are truly sociable and collaborative; young people are working in pairs, partnerships, teams, task forces, and study groups; they are learning to lead, to contribute, to carry their weight, to be part of a larger effort; they are learning to operate as most adults do in their professional and social lives—as a member of a community where cooperation and communication are the essence of effectiveness.

Of course these fine teachers did not create these lessons—or their classrooms—easily. There is a deep structure to this kind of teaching that we'll explore later in this chapter. But first, we pause to address one odd and ironic aspect of current high school reform efforts: few people talk very much about teaching.

TEACHING: THE NEGLECTED VARIABLE

When we surveyed the students at Best Practice High School about how they defined good teaching, much like adults, they had lots of ideas. While they didn't use our lingo, their own words conveyed the same ideas.

Good teaching is when the teacher is not predictable. The integrated units have been the best experiences because they are so interactive.

Good teaching is when we learn something and have fun at the same time.

Good teaching isn't rigid. Good teaching is exploring different fields together. Good teaching is getting involved.

Good teaching is when the teacher pushes you to the limit. Physics stands out in that way.

Good teaching is if you're teaching and everyone is "getting it," and you're working with your friends.

Good teaching is when someone gets the stuff to make sense and lets you figure stuff out for yourself like in the chemistry lab. I love getting into the lab myself. I love to see how chemicals react.

And many students wrote about another variable, caring. Kids want to know that their teachers like and respect them as people and care enough to help them learn.

Good teaching is when a teacher listens to you and tries to understand you.

A good teacher listens and cares.

Good teaching is when you have a teacher that you understand and the teacher understands you. Also when the teacher is always willing to help you when you may not understand or when you're having problems. Physics is somewhat hard, and you always have to pay attention, and my teacher is willing to help before and after school.

A good teacher cares about the students in school and outside of school.

Contrary to some people's beliefs, these high school students aren't lazy kids looking to get through high school without doing anything. They want a high school that makes sense to them, a caring community that ensures learning takes place for each student.

Along with the kids, virtually every school reform model afoot in the nation presumes big changes in classroom teaching. Across the continuum of reform models, from the democratic, student-centered approach of the Coalition of Essential Schools to the career-oriented training of the National Commission on Education and the Economy, everyone is calling for new and better pedagogy. There are plenty of adjectives used to describe this hoped-for kind of instruction: "quality," "world-class," "higher-order," "professional," and "outstanding." As the Department of Education's National Education Goals Panel puts it: *What teachers know and can do is crucial to what students learn.* It all sounds good, except that unlike the assertions of the Best Practice students, neither that report nor most of the others in its genre explains exactly *what* teachers should know and be able to do. While many reformers have been admirably specific about structural, organizational, or fiscal reforms of education, they are often silent on the step-by-step process of teacher change and classroom transformation. There is a kind of general faith that if teachers are mandated to teach differently, they will simply rise to the occasion.

So we need to get very specific about what we're offering as a better pedagogy. Fortunately, a good description can be found by studying the best of the national curriculum standards documents and focusing not so much on their lists of content to be covered as on what they say teachers and students need to do together. And so the common set of principles that we've already talked about, in these documents, can also be stated as a list of things teachers can work to do more of, or less of:

COMMON TEACHING RECOMMENDATIONS OF NATIONAL CURRICULUM REPORTS

—**More** experiential, inductive, hands-on learning

—**More** active learning in the classroom, with all the attendant noise and movement of students doing, talking, and collaborating

—**More** diverse roles for teachers, including coaching, demonstrating, modeling

—**More** emphasis on higher-order thinking; learning a field's key concepts and principles

—**More** deep study of a smaller number of topics, so that students internalize the field's way of inquiry

—**More** reading of real texts: whole books, primary sources, and nonfiction materials

—**More** responsibility transferred to students for their work: goal setting, record keeping, monitoring, sharing, exhibiting, and evaluation

—**More** choice for students: picking their own books, writing topics, team partners, research projects

—**More** enacting and modeling of the principles of democracy in school

—**More** attention to affective needs and the varying cognitive styles of individual students

—**More** cooperative, collaborative activity; developing the classroom as an interdependent community

—**More** heterogeneously grouped classrooms where individual needs are met through inherently individualized activities, not segregation of bodies

—**More** delivery of special help to students in regular classrooms

—**More** varied and cooperative roles for teachers, parents, and administrators

—**More** reliance upon teachers' descriptive evaluation of student growth, including observational/anecdotal records, conference notes, performance assessment rubrics

—**Less** whole-class, teacher-directed instruction, lecturing

—**Less** student passivity: sitting, listening, receiving and absorbing information

—**Less** presentational, one-way transmission of information from teacher to student

—**Less** prizing and rewarding of silence in the classroom

—**Less** classroom time devoted to fill-in-the-blank worksheets, dittos, workbooks, and other "seatwork"

—**Less** student time spent reading textbooks and basal readers

—**Less** attempt by teachers to thinly "cover" large amounts of material in every subject

—**Less** rote memorization of facts and details

—**Less** stress on the competition and grades in school

—**Less** tracking or leveling students into "ability groups"

—**Less** use of pull-out special programs

—**Less** use of and reliance on standardized tests.

While these general, polarized advisories identify some key qualities of good teaching, however, they are still not enough to show a teacher just how to make them happen every day in the classroom. They do not directly specify the elaborate political simulations in Bill Bigelow's class, or the math lesson on sampling that Mark Fertel used to connect his students to the real world. So what sorts of instructional strategies, what specific methods, procedures, or approaches enact these principles and bring them vividly to life in school? Somewhere between broad generalities like "lecture less" and the literally thousands of individual recommendations in the standards documents across the curriculum, there must be a clear and useful picture of this new pedagogy.

To better define "best practice" teaching, Harvey and Marilyn began in 1995 to study master teachers in a variety of schools. Looking into the "deep structure" of these engaging, standards-driven classrooms, searching for their fundamental, recurrent patterns, we identified six basic methods or structures of "best practice" instruction. We realized that these highly effective educators were not planning lessons with thousands of national standards in mind. Instead, they were growing and using a finite number of basic instructional patterns that implicitly enacted the spirit—and many times the letter—of the national standards. In *Methods That Matter: Six Structures for Best Practice Classrooms*, we outlined these big building blocks, along with their key principles and practices:

- integrative units
- small-group activities
- representing-to-learn
- classroom workshop
- authentic experiences
- reflective assessment.

We saw that using these basic, recurrent structures, skillful teachers were building lessons, units, and years of engaging activities for young people.

In fact, teachers don't require a deluxe, restructured school in order to put these strategies to work. Even in large, traditional high schools with regular separate-subject instruction, good teachers can and do use these methods to create active learning within their own classes every day. Committed teachers know that standing and telling will no longer get the job done, and they build their instruction upon this repertoire of active learning strategies instead. Of course, in a small, teacher-led school, a faculty can more easily enact and refine such powerful approaches, share them with colleagues, and see them work well with more of their students. But teachers in any high school don't have to wait for large structural reforms. And we suspect that in a school where lots of teachers are using these effective, student-centered approaches, structural reforms are more likely to be initiated, welcomed, and institutionalized.

INTEGRATIVE UNITS

 We begin with the overarching strategy of integrating the subjects of the curriculum. Of course, this teaching strategy is not at all new. In many outstanding elementary and middle schools, including some of the most celebrated and elite private institutions, thematic, *integrative units* are routine. Young children are taught skills of reading, writing, science, math, art, music, history, geography, and more, within the context of long, rich units of study centered on a single theme, including childhood favorites like rainforests or fairy tales and big ideas such as ecology or survival. Of course, this kind of integration is relatively easy in grade school, where teachers have their students for a whole day and teach every subject. In high school, where teachers are specialized and departmentalized, curriculum integration becomes much harder.

The most effective way for high school teachers to tap the power of curriculum integration is to join in interdisciplinary teams, working with the same group of students. In an integrated unit at the Best Practice High School facilitated by the freshman geography, art, and English teachers, for example, students are invited to create their own island nations. In small groups, the students create and map islands that contain geophysical land forms they are studying in geography, represent their island in the form of a sculpture or piece of fabric art, and write an extended piece about the country in a nonfiction genre. In English, Kathy Daniels helps them brainstorm possible genres: a constitution, newspaper, travel brochure, etc. One of our more creative students, for instance, drafted a stockholders' report for the ski resort she pictured on her mountainous island. Students learn about geography, art, and writing, about doing research using technology, and about how disciplines intersect when one investigates real issues.

But even when individual high school teachers cannot by themselves break down subject matter walls and create a fully integrated curriculum for their students, they can build their own teaching around themes, problems, or big questions that help students find meaning in the subject and develop energy for the work. If a history teacher is mandated to "cover" World War II, she can simply assign the textbook chapter with its names, dates, and places—or she can engage students in an extended inquiry, searching for answers to questions like the causes of war and man's inhumanity to man. It's the real-life process of starting with such questions, more than mixing and matching material from various disciplines, that characterizes the most powerful curriculum integration.

At Best Practice High School, Kate Lang took just such an approach with her sophomore U.S. history class, with students not just studying the well-known Holocaust literature but also reading *The Rape of Nanking* (Chang 1997), about the Japanese invasion of China, and other materials that broadened the inquiry and deepened the conversation. Traditional textbooks were not used; instead, Kate integrated the use of book clubs to read biographies and novels about life in China in the 1930s, the study of statistical data to comprehend events, and other strategies usually reserved for English and math classes. Ultimately, Kate's students covered all the state-mandated subject matter about World War II, including the textbook facts and figures, but they also emerged from this thematic unit with a visceral sense of the horror of war and the complexity of its causes.

SMALL-GROUP ACTIVITIES

Because best practice teachers know that intellectual power is garnered when people think and learn together, well-structured small-group work becomes the norm in their classrooms. Science teachers have long used lab partners to conduct experiments, talk about their findings, and leverage each other's thinking. Now the power of such collaboration is being applied in subjects across the curriculum, in a wide range of purposeful pair, team, and group activities. In one especially powerful innovation, teachers of English and other subjects place students in small reading discussion groups that operate much like adult book clubs. They require students to run their own discussions, digging for meaning, making connections, scrutinizing the writer's message and craft, and then reporting back to the whole class, contributing their findings to the wider inquiry. For improving their writing, students have opportunities for peer conferencing about content and mechanics. And as students become a resource to each other, the teacher can also hold conferences where they are really needed.

In Jenny Cornbleet's English class, literature circles are used for much of the reading. Even when the whole class is reading the same book, as they did in *To Kill a Mockingbird*, the students meet regularly in small groups to explore and discuss the ideas and issues raised in the book. In Jenny's class the students sometimes use literature-circle roles such as Discussion Director, Connector, and Vocabulary Enricher (see Daniels 1994).

Jenny has developed her own adaptation of one role, the Passage Master, who looks for interesting and compelling parts of the story to share with the group. In Jenny's class, this role becomes Book Marker. This student finds passages that are important, writes each passage on the front of a bookmark, along with the page number, and writes a personal response to the passage on the back. In each section of the book read, the Book Marker may create five to ten bookmarks. When the groups meet to discuss the reading, these designated inquirers have passages and responses ready to help get discussion started.

Once the students have finished reading, Jenny invites those who held the same roles to meet together. Together, the Book Markers choose the best responses, categorize them into themes, and make copies for the whole class. Thus, when students write essays about a book, they have passages, page numbers, and ideas to work with, so their writing is part of a conversation, instead of just a disconnected exercise.

History teacher Mike Myers, in a unit on family history, uses collaborative work to help his students develop interviewing skills in preparation for going into the community to interview others. Students interview each other first, to learn how to ask probing questions that can deepen the conversation. When the students return to class with their interview data, they again work in teams to compile information on several questions: What were the occupations of those family members interviewed? What were the cities of origin of those interviewed? What percent of those interviewed fought in wars, and what wars did they fight in?

Each small group is in charge of the data on one question, and together the groups build a classroom profile. They also decide on a way to share the data. The city-of-origin group may place pins and colored thread on a large map to indicate migration patterns. The occupations group might create a chart listing a variety of jobs and graph the number of interviewees engaged in each one. Students discover together the similarities and differences in the experiences of their ancestors.

WORKSHOP

A few high school subjects—art, home economics, drama, driver education—have long been taught differently from most "academic" courses. Instead of the usual lecture/textbook model, they use a "studio" method, where students practice the target activity while teachers demonstrate, mentor, and give feedback. Learners in a studio class typically start at different levels and may pursue different projects, and the inherently individualized classroom structure and frequent teacher conferences provide growth for a wide range of learners.

Over the past twenty years, English and reading teachers have borrowed the studio model, revised it, and offered it back as what we now call *classroom workshop* (Atwell 1998). Now, workshop has been translated across the curriculum, both as a metaphor for the decentralized, hands-on classroom and also as a practical pattern for structuring time and activities. Workshops where students actually "do" learning have been adopted in history, mathematics, science, and other subjects.

The workshop model has been especially helpful in meeting the needs of the increasingly diverse, heterogeneous, or untracked high school classroom, where teaching to the middle of the class will no longer suffice. Operating classrooms like the traditional craft shop, where learners of varied backgrounds are apprenticed to a master artisan who models, guides, and coaches, allows for diverse learners to have their needs met amid the inherently engaging process of making real products. Because the essence of a workshop is individual growth, students of varying abilities are able to all learn and operate in the "zone" where each learns best.

Tina Peano integrates writing workshop with literature study for her Best Practice High School juniors by leading them through a process to create magazines together. After kids have read and discussed books of their choice in literature circles, Tina asks them to identify themes in their books, using "mind maps." Then she poses the questions: In what sort of magazine might your book be discussed—for example, a sports magazine? A magazine about family life? Or one about politics and racial issues? Going around the circle, students state the themes they've identified and the type of magazine their book might be linked to. Next, the kids organize around common themes and magazine types, five to eight or nine in a group. In a workshop setting, each student now writes an article related to her book and focused on her chosen group's theme. Tina provides models and guidelines for various writing modes the kids can choose from—editorials, interviews, celebrity portraits, advertisements, poetry connections. Each student must also generate one idea for an extra credit article he or she may optionally choose to write as well.

During in-class workshop time, Tina conferences with individual writers and monitors progress as the students write. After several days' work, students bring their rough drafts to their magazine groups for editorial sessions. At least two other students in a group must read each person's draft. Since Tina gives a group grade for the magazines, the students take their editorial roles very seriously. After revising, students must obtain a final editorial OK from their group to have their piece included in their magazine. Tina regards this project as one of the most successful she has devised.

Regardless of the subject, however, the underlying structure of a workshop class session is simple and similar:

- *five minutes:* Minilesson. The teacher demonstrates one concept or idea that is relevant to the work in which the students are engaged.

- *thirty to forty minutes:* Work Time/Conferences. Students engage in individual work, reading, writing, researching, on topics of their own choice. The teacher facilitates the learning by answering questions, helping to solve problems, and conferencing with individuals and/or groups.

- *ten minutes:* Sharing. The whole class gathers briefly for students to share their work, get feedback from their peers, and review workshop procedures.

Students in workshop are responsible for their own work, and due dates are set for tasks to be completed. Students enjoy autonomy, work in their own "zones" with the help of others in the class, and are accountable for their production and for meeting deadlines.

The work done by educational psychologist Lev Vygotsky (1962) underscores the value of the workshop approach. Vygotsky explained that each of us has a "zone of proximal development," the area between what we can do alone and what we cannot do, which is where we can learn best. Our zone isn't static; in fact, in different subjects, we may have different zones. Because the most powerful learning occurs in that special zone, the most effective teaching helps students operate right on the edge of what they are able to do. Vygotsky's belief was emphatic: what the child can do with assistance today, he can do alone tomorrow. This is why workshop is such a productive structure. Workshop makes it possible for a teacher to work with a class of twenty-eight or thirty students who have different zones. She can provide materials appropriate to meet the needs of each learner in the class. She can offer tasks that meet all students where they are. Workshop is inherently decentralized, personal, and individualized—placing the teacher directly into the mentoring role that Vygotsky prescribes.

REPRESENTING-TO-LEARN

One of the key insights of recent learning research is that in order for students to understand ideas, they must engage them deeply and act upon them. Listening is not enough. So best practice teachers have a repertoire of ways that students can represent, explore, and express their thinking. The kids regularly keep journals or learning logs to reflect on information, play with thoughts, make connections, and act upon what they have studied. Smart teachers also use other representational strategies for the same purposes. Drawing, sketching, mapping, dancing, videotaping, and singing are vehicles that have become staples in many high school classrooms. When students *represent to learn*, they become active inquirers, using a variety of different modes to deepen their thinking. Howard Gardner (1993) has helped us to see that human beings have a combination of learning styles, and that schools can employ the style that works best for each student while also helping to develop his or her weaker ones.

Video artist Dierdre Searcy has taught us a representational strategy she calls Two-Minute Videos that teachers have applied to subjects as diverse as history, physics, and health. Students work individually, in pairs, or in small groups to discuss the ideas they wish to represent and find pictures in magazines to help them convey their ideas. The pictures are cut out and arranged on a table in a sequence that tells their story. They write short captions for

Key Teaching Methods—Principles and Practices

Integrative Units

Principles

Break down subject and discipline barriers

Create extended inquiries or investigations

Focus on broad problems, issues, or themes

Use disciplines of knowledge as sources and tools of inquiry

Incorporate student interests and questions at all stages.

Practices

Thematic Units

Interdisciplinary Programs (American Studies, Humanities)

Problem/Project-Based Learning

Negotiating the Curriculum/ Coplanning with Students

Small-Group Activities

Principles

Decentralize the classroom

Make learning active, prepare students for real-life cooperative efforts

Stress collaboration and teamwork versus competition and conquest

Enhance student choice and responsibility

Jigsaw the curriculum.

Practices

Pair Activities (Lab Partners, Peer Tutoring)

Centers and Learning Stations

Group Investigations and Inquiries

Peer-Response/Editing Groups

Reading Discussion Groups/ Literature Circles

each image, which becomes their script. One by one, the students read the captions into the microphone as each picture is videotaped. The camera is paused, and the next picture is placed on the wall for the next segment. The finished product is a two-minute video that can be astonishingly powerful and meaningful.

At Best Practice High School, Center for City Schools arts consultant Julie Ann Flynn works with the English teachers helping the students to add move-

Representing-to-Learn

Principles	Practices
Trade passive reception for active construction of knowledge	Written and Graphic Thinking in Journals, Logs, and Sketchbooks
Learning theory says: learners must act upon information	Written Conversation, Clustering, Mapping, Webbing, Cartooning
Translating ideas between mediums means deep understanding.	Expression Through Music, Visual Art, Dance, Drama, Websites

Classroom Workshop

Principles	Practices
Create a classroom as a studio or laboratory	Large Chunks of Well-Structured Practice/Application Time
Learn by doing	Minilessons and Teacher Modeling
Metaphor of craft shop equals apprenticeship and mentoring	Teacher and Peer Conferences
Students choose topics	Folders and Portfolios
Be responsible for process and outcome quotas	Goal setting, Self-monitoring and Assessment
Engage process orientation: stages of the craft (e.g., the scientific process, the writing process).	Sharing, Presentation, Exhibition, and Publication

(*continues*)

ment to their poetry. Students in groups respond to each other's poems to deepen the meaning of the words through movement and dance. This use of another learning medium helps students to discover added richness in the stories their poems tell.

In math classes, teachers invite students to keep double-entry journals where they divide the pages of their notebooks in half, working problems on one half of the page and explaining their work in words on the other half.

Key Teaching Methods—Principles and Practices (Continued)

Authentic Experiences

Principles	Practices
Bring school to life, bring life to school	Use real books, primary sources, authentic materials, simulations
Open the schoolhouse door both ways	Bring in experts, parents, elders, artists
Invite the world in, take the kids out	Go on field trips and visits to wild and natural places; earth and nature education
Make community connections for inquiry, involvement, service.	Do community research: observation, surveys, interviews, records
	Do service projects, internships, political action
	Do school-to-work placements.

Reflective Assessment

Principles	Practices
Ultimate goal is student goal setting, reflection, self-assessment	Anecdotal Records and Observational Notes
Grade and score less	Curriculum-Based Checklists
Save and describe samples more	Portfolios, Work Samples, and Artifacts with Student Reflections
Measure not single grades but triangulation of multiple measures	Performances and Exhibitions with Scoring Rubrics
Use formative versus summative	Teacher-Student Conferences; Student-Led Parent Conferences
Use self-referenced versus norm-referenced.	Joint Report Cards Created by Teachers, Students, and Parents

Students learn to communicate mathematically, figuring out what they understand and what confuses them.

Many of the teachers at Best Practice, eager to receive immediate student feedback, often ask students to write exit slips before they leave class. These responses provide information to the teacher: were the activities of the day interesting, boring, too easy, too hard, confusing? This data helps teachers to know how they are doing and where their next day's instruction needs to focus.

AUTHENTIC EXPERIENCES

When we use the word "authentic" for teaching and learning, we mean making it real—connecting with issues important to individuals and the community, and working with whole, large ideas rather than only with isolated subskills. Obviously, offering students authentic experiences is not exactly a teaching method in the same sense as small-group activities or workshop. Although it is an asymmetrical element, we include it on this list because whenever we see truly great teachers at work, there always seems to be an element of realness—of applicability to or engagement with life outside of school.

In most high schools, students rarely leave the confines of their classrooms, let alone the building. Indeed many high schools have "closed campus" policies that (possibly for very good reasons) criminalize the very idea of teenagers leaving the building during school hours. But the school door must open both ways; students should be out in the community, and the community should also be brought in to them. To cut teenagers off from involvement with the real people and happenings outside of school squelches the single greatest source of engagement and energy educators can tap: teenagers' curiosity and concern about their world.

 One simple and powerful way to make social studies or English authentic is to conduct a personal historical investigation, focusing on each student's own family history. Students study their roots, interview their relatives, and learn family stories that they connect and compare to the history of the country. They find out how important incidents in history affected their family's personal history. How and when did their ancestors arrive in America? Where have they lived and moved throughout the U.S.? How did periods like the Great Depression and the Vietnam War intersect with their lives? What artifacts have been saved and passed down? These investigations always start with the self, but end up opening political, social, and economic issues faced by all American families. The story of one of us is, in a very real sense, the story of all of us.

With her seniors, social studies teacher Arlette Harris decided to ensure that the students were thinking seriously about the family stories they were about to gather by using what she calls a "share-fair." She informed them the previous Friday that they'd need to be ready with two stories their families tell about them or stories connected with holidays or family occasions. One story had to be true and one false. The kids then sat in a circle and proceeded to tell their tales. Thus Arlette worked to ensure that an assignment we might easily regard as authentic becomes much more deeply so. Students concentrated intently, listening for clues that a story was true or false. But more interestingly, many of the false accounts—such as one by a boy about the father he's never met—reflect students' deepest feelings and concerns. These stories were authentic even when they weren't *authentic*. And they helped build connections among black and Hispanic kids who hadn't realized they shared so much in common. For more details on planning such investigations with students, see *History Comes Home: Family Stories Across the Curriculum* (1999), written by Steve and three of our Center for City Schools colleagues, Pat Bearden, Yolanda Simmons, and Pete Leki. Examples of authentic teaching and learning in other subjects, including math, science, and foreign languages, abound throughout this book, since strategies covered under other categories almost always include authenticity as a key characteristic.

REFLECTIVE ASSESSMENT

Powerful teaching must be supported and enhanced—not undermined or contradicted—by meaningful assessment. This means making evaluation strategies an integral part of the learning process and focusing on whole outcomes valued in the curriculum, rather than just giving a multiple-choice test at the end of a unit. Too often, assessment occurs only after learning is over, and sometimes it measures something very different from what the teacher was trying to teach or what the kids needed to learn. While we explore this idea more fully in Chapter 10 we also bring it up here to emphasize this crucial point.

There are many ways that assessment can serve as an important teaching tool. Formative assessment helps students to self-monitor, self-evaluate, and set goals for further learning. When student projects or performances are the basis for evaluation, we communicate to students that we value "doing." Student-made rubrics help kids to know what good work looks like and involve them in the process of determining just what the most meaningful criteria really are.

Portfolios provide a body of evidence that enables the students and others to see their strengths and weaknesses and monitor their growth over time. But the most important component of the portfolio process, the part that makes them powerful, is reflection. It is through reflection, rather than just the collected products themselves, that both teachers and students can understand what was gained, what value was added, in the work the student did.

Students at Best Practice keep samples of their work in collection folders, and at the end of each marking period, choose one piece from each of their subjects to go into their portfolios. Students find that when writing their reflections, it is helpful to think of an audience: other students, teachers, parents, and eventually college admission officers. Therefore, each portfolio begins with a letter to the reader telling something about themselves, their families, and what the portfolio represents about them as people, as learners, and as participants in a learning community. Then, in the reflections, students attempt to explain what each item means to them, what they were trying to accomplish, and what they think they achieved that they hadn't done before.

One of the important aspects of the portfolio process at Best Practice is peer evaluation. For one week each quarter, students in advisory read each other's portfolios and give comments and suggestions. Students who work collaboratively in most of their studies welcome the feedback of their peers as they develop a showcase for their growth over time. Tina Peano, the junior English teacher, and the portfolio committee developed and piloted this peer evaluation process. Students are guided by these questions as they give feedback:

1. On a scale of 1–5 (5 being the highest), how would you rate the organization of the portfolio? Why?

2. On a scale of 1–5, how would you rate the overall effort this student put into creating their portfolio? Why?

3. Does the portfolio have a creative introduction? How does the portfolio try to engage the reader?

4. Based on the portfolio, what would you say is the student's strength as a learner? What is he/she weaker in?

5. Which assignment do you feel this student learned a lot from? What evidence do you have of this?

6. Did the student give a reflection for each item submitted? Did all of the reflections fully explain why each piece was chosen to be included in the portfolio?

THE METHODS OVERLAP

The six "methods that matter" often overlap as the Best Practice teachers employ a combination of strategies to make learning more active and engaged. It's a constant struggle to discover how to make all of the strategies work together but when a visitor enters a classroom, it is often hard to locate the teacher because she's meeting with a small group of students or conferencing with someone who needs help. The visitor will notice that much of the learning occurs in workshop sessions where students are actually *doing* physics, art, math, reading, history. Collaboration is the norm: kids are regularly thinking and working with their peers. And teachers try to balance between subject instruction and integrated units across disciplines.

In Arthur Griffin's freshman physics class, students work in groups on each unit of study. He sets up experiments around the room, and groups of students move through the stations to explore the concept being studied. In a unit on wave patterns, a visitor might encounter one cohort in the hall measuring the velocity of a wave by shaking a "slinky" toy to send a blip undulating down its long coil. Another group is measuring how the sound pitch of vibrating glass changes when water is at different levels in a beaker, while another is blowing through straws, noticing that the sound gets higher as the straw gets shorter. Students come to understand how *velocity equals distance divided by time* and *frequency is inversely proportional to length*, as they explore each of the hands-on activities. After students have cycled through a half-dozen experiments, Arthur brings them together to reinforce the concepts and connect them to real life.

One day in Melissa Bryant's biology class, students walk into the room to find the outline of a dead body on the floor with gruesome blood spatters all around. Yellow plastic tape surrounds the area. Students have entered a "crime scene." Their task is to solve the murder, using clues provided by the blood evidence as well as "rap sheets" on a number of suspects that Melissa provides. In this hands-on lesson on blood-typing, they must collect the right size sample and carefully conduct and cross-check their blood-type test. Happily, the killer is identified by most groups.

Downstairs in U.S. history, Mike Myers has divided his junior students into a simulated federal government, with a president and a proportionately sized Senate, House of Representatives, and Supreme Court. Instead of making a chart about How a Bill Becomes a Law, these kids are invited to develop, write, and attempt to pass their own legislation, working through all the constitutional mechanisms. Not surprisingly for this smart-alecky group of high school kids, the first bill to emerge from the House calls for the legalization of marijuana. It sails through the Senate and House and appears on its way to passage when the president, a thoughtful and quiet girl, vetoes the bill. While the members of Congress hoot and razz her, the president asks Mr. Myers if she can get television air time to explain her decision to the public and enlist their support in preventing a two-thirds override vote. Suddenly, the simulation has exceeded its own design, and things are getting real. As the president sits down to begin writing her television address, the kids aren't laughing any more. Back in committees, serious conversation has begun about drugs and the law: do we really want to do this? Within an hour, another bill, this one banning abortion, has polarized the boys and girls, and galvanized a heated debate about responsibility, welfare, and gender issues. What began as a simple simulation, almost like a classroom "game," has opened up not just authentic topics, but thinking that is sophisticated, complex, and deep. In all three of these examples, collaborative work focuses on authentic content.

BEST PRACTICE HIGH SCHOOL INTEGRATED UNITS

Four times a year, teachers and students join in extended integrated, thematic units that involve all disciplines and utilize the whole range of teaching methods. Most times, the units come from specific student questions and concerns about themselves and their world, elicited in brainstorming sessions. At other times, teachers set a broad theme and design a variety of ways for students to engage the topic. Among the units we have developed so far:

- *Who Am I?* a study of self and identity
- *The Community and the City* studying and sharing information on the diverse neighborhoods that are home to our students
- *The Island Nations* combining geography, English, and art
- *Careers* a chance to explore aspirations and choices
- *Isms* the nature, origins, and solutions for discrimination
- *American Democracy* a unit on government
- *Better Pastures* a large-scale simulation of political, social, and economic conflict that highlights environmental concerns
- *Becoming a Researcher* developing the skills of action research.

Some of these units have been used only once, while others have entered the school repertoire and have been repeated and refined.

Whatever the origin of the theme, teachers must backmap its activities to the curriculum mandated by the district. After all, if we are going to spend two or three weeks of instructional time on a project, it had better cover some of the topics required in each subject. And, in fact, we always find this match surprisingly easy to make: among the prescribed requirements in Illinois are skills like "critically evaluate information from multiple sources," "evaluate the usefulness of information," "synthesize information to support a thesis," "present information in a logical manner in oral and written forms," and "apply physical models, graphs, coordinate systems, networks and vectors to develop solutions in applied contexts" (Illinois Learning Standards, adopted July 1997)—all of which come up naturally in the course of our multidisciplinary inquiries.

Newer teachers and freshman students sometimes struggle with the integrated units, which may be their first experience with a curriculum that emerges from real questions and is not clearly located within a single discipline of knowledge. Textbooks and professional materials provide little help for the teachers, especially at the high school level. Kids must learn how to exercise their own initiative. But as the structure of these inquiries becomes familiar, their power for learning and engagement is unleashed.

During these units, teachers learn along with their students, often outside their specific area of expertise. One of the most successful topics that our sophomores have addressed is the "Isms" unit. When students are asked what concerns them about the world and their place in it, invariably issues of discrimination surface. Our teachers designed the Isms unit in response to those concerns. In this unit, students typically study racism, classism, sexism, ageism, ableism, and heterosexism. Each of the sophomore teachers, regardless of his or her regular subject assignment, works with the students to explore one of the isms. Teachers choose the ism they would most like to investigate and help students begin, as all good researchers do, by reading all that they can find on the subject.

After they read, students develop scenarios for discussion that come out of their own experiences and help them to create definitions for each particular ism. Here are a few of the scenarios (the others will be found on the website).

Racism: Shawanda and her aunt go shopping at a popular department store. Shawanda is fifteen and black. Her aunt is in her early forties. While shopping, her aunt decides to look at gold chains. Shawanda's aunt asks the saleswoman if the gold chain is on sale and if she can try it on. The saleswoman proceeds to excuse herself to ask a manager if the chain is on sale.

However, Shawanda overhears her asking the manager if she should allow her aunt to try on the chain. Shawanda hears her say, "Do you really think she wants to try it on, or do you think she is going to steal it?"

Heterosexism: Vanessa has always been used to playing sports. She enjoys athletics, but as she enters high school she is tentative in joining the teams, because her peers begin to label her as a "butch" or "dyke," derogatory names for lesbians. Vanessa does not want to deal with this, and she knows it will stop many of the girls from wanting to be her friend.

Ableism: Taria has a glass eye, and when she enters high school, her peers ignore her in an attempt not to deal with it. In class, students won't look her in the face when they do group work, and they don't voluntarily choose her to be in their group. A teacher finally asks students why they have ignored her. They explain that because of her glass eye they thought she couldn't do the work as well.

These and other scenarios are used in small-group discussions, and each class is asked to create a class definition for each ism. The reading and discussion prepare the students for the next step of the project, in which they choose one ism to investigate more thoroughly. Students work for one full week with the teacher in charge of that particular ism. Once they have some background, the kids reorganize to work with a teacher on creating a communicative piece about their chosen ism. Kids study, think, and create a project to share with the school community and sometimes beyond the school. This year, for example, math teacher Mark Fertel worked with the students who chose ableism. As they toured the city to look for challenges that disabled people face, they grew steadily angrier at the many obstacles and lack of accommodations they noticed. The students wrote letters to inform a variety of businesses and public institutions of their need to provide better service. They also made posters about accessibility problems, entered them in a contest on the web, and won second and third prizes for their efforts.

Social studies teacher Kate Lang worked with her students to create a wall of respect, honoring individuals who had made a difference in fighting various isms. After researching the backgrounds and achievements of these special heroes, students wrote short reports and created graphic representations for the "wall of respect." On the last day of the unit students dressed as their "revolutionaries," gave brief presentations in character, and answered questions from visitors and other students about the challenges they faced and the differences they made. A visitor to Kate's class that day would have seen a panel made up of Che Guevara, Rosa Parks, Malcolm X, Dr. Martin Luther King, Abraham Lincoln, Gloria Steinem, and many others willing to share their stories.

Kathy Daniels, the English teacher, helped students to create books of poetry and children's books that were powerful and creative expressions of students' deep feelings about discrimination. The children's books were a particularly appropriate medium for this unit because they used both pictures and text to tell their stories. Shelley Freeman, the internship coordinator, used photography to help students investigate ageism. Shelley and her students left school to document instances of discrimination. These students learned to look at the world with the eye of a photographer as they walked through the streets of the city observing how older people were treated.

The Isms unit was a success for many reasons: it started with students' own questions and concerns, reflecting problems that these young people of various ethnic backgrounds face every day; it included challenging research to prepare students before they made their own selections; it was full of choices—kids could decide what to study, whom to work with, what to represent, and what to share; the projects and performances were authentic, using tools that real people employ to understand and report on social issues; and, very important, the teachers were learning along with the students, modeling the ways that a skillful adult learner poses questions, gathers information, sifts data, makes judgments, creates a product.

WHEN METHODS DON'T MATTER

Using student-centered methods is no slam dunk. Good teaching doesn't always guarantee that teenagers will be captivated, attentive, and engaged. Surprise! At Best Practice, where students have many opportunities for engagement, on most days most of our kids accept that invitation, but there are always some students who just don't connect. What do we do when kids don't tune in to our wonderful lessons?

Many high schools use an unfortunate strategy for coping with this: busywork and round-robin textbook reading. Teachers who lack other strategies for motivating students, or who think student-centered learning is somehow touchy-feely and loosely structured, resort to boring instruction to keep kids quiet. There's an odd and unspoken bargain between kids and teachers about low-level activities like worksheets. Students seem to say, "We'll be quiet and fill in these stupid blanks if you don't make us do any real work."

Indeed, teaching the "best practice" way is not always easy, even for the most experienced and highly dedicated teachers. Active, student-centered classrooms need to be highly structured so that students know what is required of them and develop the sense of responsibility to themselves and their peers to actually become engaged. But student-centered teaching provides no inoculation against some kids' history of failure or dysfunctional family settings. By the time students reach high school, some are so turned off to learning that it is very difficult to convince them that school can be different and that their time in school can be well spent. So issues of discipline, work habits, and classroom decorum still arise, as they do everywhere. Teachers who create meaningful experiences for kids have to use their whole bag of tricks to help the struggling ones become partners in learning. The teachers at Best Practice are committed to the effort.

At BPHS, when two of our colleagues were having management problems with particular classes, they consulted Professional Development Coordinator Yolanda Simmons. Yolanda described the problem and its solution in her journal:

> *The students in a fourth-period geometry class and a seventh-period English class demonstrated little or no appreciation for their ample opportunities to be placed at the center of their own learning process. They didn't seem to value the fact that their teachers regularly invited them to share their thoughts independently and with response partners, work in small groups to solve problems, participate in collaborative presentations, and make decisions about what they wanted to study. I visited both teachers' classrooms and found many of the students to be downright disrespectful. After conferring with each teacher about possible motivations for the students' behavior, I suggested a tough demonstration—give the students worksheet packets to complete by themselves, with no opportunities for the usual style of collaboration and discussion.*
>
> *After a few days of worksheets, all of the students in the English class told their teacher that they wanted to be taught the "best practice" way again. Within a week and a half, twenty-three out of twenty-eight of the math students also said they wanted to return to "best practice." Things were looking up! The kids were begging to work in small groups.*

Sometimes, the combination of all these teaching strategies pays off more visibly than others. In Chicago's politicized school system, where schools live and die by their standardized test scores, we were delighted when our class of

2000, who worked for four years with cross-curricular investigations and best practice methods, scored eighth in the city in science and twelfth in social studies, out of seventy-five high schools. Even though we have many concerns about the limits of these standardized tests, the scores were especially significant because most schools that scored higher have selective admission requirements, unlike BPHS. We were also pleased because both of these state exams place heavy emphasis on nonfiction reading, a skill which we stress and value throughout our program. No, we don't believe that these tests are a true measure of our hopes for our students or even an accurate gauge of science or social studies content. But something good must be happening when a hundred regular Chicago kids, 80 percent of whom qualify for free lunch and few of whom ever saw a family member go to college, score among the most privileged and talented students in the city.

THE PROGRESSIVE DEBATE

The exemplary teaching approaches described in this chapter, the ones we have labeled "best practice" or "methods that matter," are in no way new. Such progressive teaching has been around for centuries. Often these approaches find a home in elite private schools and seem to be the property of the privileged, who supposedly can handle the freedom and responsibility that student-centered teaching offers. But as the teachers at Best Practice High School demonstrate every day, progressive methods work with all kinds of kids; indeed, this paradigm of education is our best hope of teaching so that students of all achievement levels actually learn.

Yet, the progressive versus traditionalist debate continues to rage, and some policymakers insist that for inner-city kids teaching must stress factual content, skill drills, a classroom atmosphere of tight control. Wrong, says scholar Gloria Ladson-Billings, who cuts through this controversy with her vision of "culturally relevant pedagogy." Teachers should use approaches that affirm the cultural identity of the students they teach, Ladson-Billings explains, and "culturally relevant teaching encourages students to learn collaboratively and expects them to teach each other and take responsibility for each other" (1994, 70). Best practice methodology—progressive teaching—embodies exactly these ideas of collaboration, community, and student responsibility.

Teachers who use these student-centered, best practice teaching methods have a special vision of schools and the students they teach. As progressive educators, they want school to nurture active citizens and creative individuals.

They view schools as the seedbed for democracy. They want students not just to prosper in, but to sharply question and improve, the world they will inherit.

High school classrooms where students are given the opportunity to work in small groups on meaningful projects, workshop style, feel very different from ones in which students are sitting in rows being lectured to or doing worksheets. Students working on integrated study projects about topics important to themselves and to the world are given the chance to become engaged, to help others, to experience choice, and to have a voice in what they learn. This is what we mean by best practice teaching. What better way to make school a valuable, attractive, and relevant place for American teenagers?

FINDING YOUR NEXT STEPS

Remember: Think about your own high school experience. Was there a teacher who stands out? What were the qualities that made this teacher memorable or special? What kinds of learning activities were most engaging in his or her classroom, and why? Invite feedback from parents and teachers about their own powerful learning experiences both in and out of school. Help them identify the features that made the experience productive.

Gather and Read: Bring together a group of teachers and administrators interested in investigating new and innovative teaching activities, and meet regularly in each other's classrooms for "Teacher Talk." The host teacher can begin the meeting with a tour of her classroom, pointing out projects and activities in which her students are engaged. Form book clubs that meet regularly to read professional literature that deals with strategies of interest to the group. Good books to generate discussion are:

Strategies Across the Curriculum

Daniels, H., and M. Bizar. 1998. *Methods That Matter.* York, Maine: Stenhouse.

Integrative Units

Beane, J. A. 1997. *Curriculum Integration: Designing the Core of Democratic Education.* New York: Teachers College Press.

Tchudi, S., and S. Lafer. 1996. *The Interdisciplinary Teacher's Handbook: Integrated Teaching Across the Curriculum*. Portsmouth, N.H.: Heinemann.

Zemelman, S., P. Bearden, Y. Simmons, and P. Leki. 1999. *History Comes Home: Family Stories Across the Curriculum*. York, Maine: Stenhouse.

Small-Group Activities

Daniels, H. 1994. *Literature Circles: Voice and Choice in the Student-Centered Classroom*. York, Maine: Stenhouse.

Sharan, Y., and S. Sharan. 1992. *Expanding Cooperative Learning Through Group Investigation*. New York: Teachers College Press.

Representing to Learn

Fulwiler, T. 1987. *The Journal Book*. Portsmouth, N.H.: Boynton/Cook.

Wilhelm, J. 1995. *You Gotta BE the Book*. New York: Teachers College Press.

Witten, P. 1996. *Sketching Stories, Stretching Minds*. Portsmouth, N.H.: Heinemann.

Workshop

Atwell, N. 1998. *In the Middle: New Understandings About Writing, Reading, and Learning*. Portsmouth, N.H.: Boynton/Cook Heinemann.

Authentic Experiences

Nabhan, G., and S. Trimble. 1994. *The Geography of Childhood*. Boston: Beacon Press.

Reflective Assessment

Hill, B. C., and C. Ruptic. 1994. *Practical Aspects of Authentic Assessment*. Norwood, Mass.: Christopher Gordon.

Porter, C., and J. Cleland. 1995. *The Portfolio as a Learning Strategy*. Portsmouth, N.H.: Heinemann.

Experiment and Observe: In your own classroom, focus on a chunk of curriculum, and try one of the methods that your group has been reading and talking about. Share your experiences, both positive and negative, with your group. Visit each other's classrooms as friendly observers, and exchange feedback. Plan to visit a school that is farther along in the process of implementing student-centered teaching. If possible, visit with a team, so that you can discuss implications for your particular school.

Experiment and Reflect: Identify a cross-disciplinary team of teachers with whom to plan and implement an integrated unit, and share your experience with your colleagues. Be a teacher-researcher; keep a double-entry journal keeping track of your new teaching strategies and how they are working. On one side of the paper record what you did, and on the other side, record your reflections, concerns, and achievements.

Chapter 6
Curriculum

With their teachers, young people engage in
challenging inquiry into topics that matter.

*t is twelve noon on a sunny spring day in Chicago's Pilsen neighbor-
hood, a vibrant Mexican enclave lined with shops, churches, bakeries,
and taquerias. An orange school bus pulls up to the curb and twenty-
five mostly African American teenagers step slowly off the bus, blinking
in the sun and gazing around at the alien surroundings. After some long
moments of hesitation, they gradually fan out in small groups, tentatively
entering different stores, beginning to converse with the people they
meet, and jotting notes as they go.*

*As part of a sophomore interdisciplinary unit on research methods,
Spanish teacher Laura Linhart wanted her students to experience genuine ethnographic fieldwork, while using the Spanish language and
adding to their knowledge of Mexican American culture. So she designed
this day in Pilsen, equipping each group of four or five students with
journals, a disposable camera, and ten dollars in cash. The students were
to document their observations in pictures, in writing, and with whatever
meaningful artifacts they could purchase with their limited budget. The
ultimate goal was to distill and present their ethnographic data to their
classmates a few days later.*

*The students were given two hours to gather information and were
sent off with a set of very specific instructions, not least of which was to
be polite and friendly, remembering that they were representatives of
Best Practice High School. The kids were to speak only in Spanish, never
take a picture without asking, and watch their language. Student groups
were required to visit a grocery store, a bakery, a record or clothing store,*

and a restaurant. Laura was very careful to ask students to be considerate observers, watching, listening, and not intruding:

> *You should take a picture of the outside of each place you visit (you have a limited number of pictures, so make each one count). Take pictures of people and things that you observe. Ask if your group could take a picture, and if they say no, don't take pictures. Don't ask why not, just say* thank you *and move on. This is not a trip to make people uncomfortable. You are there to observe. If you are told not to take pictures, or asked to leave for any reason, do it. However, please make a note of it in your final report.*

Laura challenged the students to look closely at all they saw and, just like ethnographers, to try to make the familiar strange and the strange familiar. Inside each establishment, students were to note what they saw, what they heard, what they smelled, who was around, what they were doing, what products they saw, and why they selected particular artifacts to purchase.

After their trip, Laura's students prepared to share their findings in a variety of formats, supporting their impressions with notes, photographs, and artifacts. Some students featured the leftovers of delicious Mexican pastries they had purchased (and largely consumed), telling how easy it had been to start conversations in the bakery. Another group reported on how the local laundromat seemed to be a central neighborhood gathering place. One group that had seen someone selling false immigration papers on the corner shared their thoughts about being an illegal alien. Many groups, drawing on their experiences with science and history fairs, used three-panel poster boards to mount their pictures and create a story line for their photos. Each group developed a class presentation (in Spanish, of course) to go with their ethnographies, and these were received with applause and laughs. Long after the field trip and the reports were completed, the displays remained in the room, colorful and valued memories of a special segment of the curriculum.

DEFINING CURRICULUM

The everyday, commonsense definition of *curriculum* is something like "the stuff kids are supposed to learn in school." In many American high schools, this "stuff" is simply whatever material fills the textbook adopted for a given course. Within this mundane definition of curriculum, state legislatures can attempt to "raise standards" by mandating additional years of science or math courses for high school graduation. In a similar vein, educational pundits like E. D. Hirsch and William Bennett can issue lists of facts that every third grader should know or poems that every high school student should study. It is both customary and comforting to think of curriculum simply as the body of valuable information and useful skills that schools transmit to students, for their benefit.

At a more sophisticated level, curriculum is better defined as all the educational experiences students have in a course, grade level, or school. This view better reflects the reality that schools teach much more than the content officially listed in a curriculum guide or textbook table of contents. Both implicitly and explicitly, schools teach values, attitudes, and habits of mind just as much as they teach facts and skills. The way kids are taught subject matter, the processes and the context, the tone and flavor, the power relationships, the rewards and punishments—all these constitute "the hidden curriculum." In school, kids learn what they live; they are educated as much by what adults around them do as by what they say.

When we were starting BPHS, we realized that both our official and our hidden curriculum would be, to some degree, compromises. We knew that some of the time we would need to teach subject matter and even enact values that weren't harmonious with our pure, dream-school vision. Well, we had wanted to be a regular Chicago high school, not a charter or private school, right? So, as part of the system, we might be smaller and newer, but we would still be just High School #74 when it came to nonnegotiable systemwide mandates.

Like virtually all public school districts, the CPS has a list of high school graduation requirements, expressed as credits earned over a distribution of required academic courses: four years of English, three years of science, three years of mathematics, two years of social studies including American history, a year each of art and music, two years of foreign language, and four years of physical education (reduced to two during our second year), and other minor items like passing a state and federal constitution test. The CPS also regulates the content of every course with citywide Chicago Academic Standards Exams (CASE) tests given at the end of each semester. These tests are designed to make sure that all teachers of, say, sophomore English, assign at least some of the same readings and teach some common content. Also, over the past several years, the CPS has been gradually issuing "structured curriculum" guides, day-by-day lesson plans with word-for-word teacher scripts, for every single day of every course.

If we wanted our kids to score well on CASE exams—indeed, if we wanted our school to continue to exist—we had to be certain our kids knew this mandated material. Oh, sure, we could moan about how the national standards from most curriculum groups recommended that students delve more deeply into a smaller number of topics—but if the central office mandated broad and thin coverage of a wide array of subjects, we couldn't risk our kids' graduations by pigheadedly adhering to our private, pet curriculum.

Still, we still had plenty of room to maneuver. Chicago high schools are allowed to choose from several different course titles in fulfilling certain requirements. For example, all CPS students must take three years of laboratory science, but each school can select from among seven approved lab sciences and determine the sequence for these courses. We could also decide *how* to teach the mandated material; we could use a textbook or primary sources, organize into separate subjects or conduct cross-disciplinary units. And we could control *how fast* we covered the required stuff. If our instruction was really effective and there was time left over, we could add other, unmandated curriculum to our schedule—things like computer skills, job readiness, and pleasure reading.

So, in this spirit, we created a curriculum over the first four years at BPHS. We accepted the external constraints and requirements, matched these to our own beliefs and priorities, and asked the kids what they wanted to learn. And then we compromised, shared time, and logrolled between all the competing curricular influences. This balancing act is reflected all across our school life—in our schedule, in the materials we use, in the assessments we have adopted, and in all the rest. It's a balancing act that good teachers everywhere learn to do.

All BPHS students are enrolled in a rich and rigorous college-preparatory-level curriculum. There are no "basic" tracks or low-level sections. The program for our students includes:

Freshman	Sophomore	Junior	Senior
Algebra	Geometry	Advanced Algebra	English
Physics	Chemistry	Biology	French/Spanish
English	English	English	Electives in:
Geography	U.S. History	Music	*Science, Social*
Art	French/Spanish	French/Spanish	*Studies,*
Physical Ed	Physical Ed	Elective	*Art, Drama,*
Internship	Internship	Internship	*Music*
Advisory	Advisory	Advisory	Internship
			Advisory

Some of the coursework at BPHS happens in traditional, single-subject classes, taught according to the national standards of "best practice" within each subject field—or as close as the teacher can come on any given day. But at other times, teacher teams or the whole faculty collaborate to develop complex, integrated units that blend learning in several subjects, offering students choice and responsibility in the process. As teachers and students move into these inquiry projects, the school schedule is adjusted to match—and since we use a flexible-block schedule without fixed bells, we can rearrange time to match instruction. To be sure that these multidisciplinary inquiries contain mandated learnings, the projects are carefully "backmapped" to match official curriculum guides. Since our multidisciplinary units always contain lots of reading, writing, computing, investigating, experimenting, and representing, they are invariably full of the required "basic" skills, even as they genuinely put students in the driver's seat and help them answer their own real questions.

CHALLENGING, AUTHENTIC, AND COLLABORATIVE CURRICULUM

The students in Laura Linhart's class didn't have to be convinced that their trip to Pilsen was worth taking, that the work was worth doing, or that it was important to speak the local language. When students are given real work to do, the curriculum comes alive, and kids participate without coercion. Laura's students knew that they were engaged in something that real people do in the real world. They were using their language skills in a place where they were needed in order to communicate.

As the teachers design curriculum at Best Practice High School, we keep coming back to three big ideas that bring together the principles we outlined in Chapter 1: we want students to become engaged in inquiry that is *challenging*, *authentic*, and *collaborative*. Laura's group of student enthnographers were challenged to do something they had never done before: to enter an unfamiliar, perhaps slightly disorienting setting, to document what they saw, and to use their emerging language skills at the same time. The work was authentic because it was a lively experience in a stimulating new environment, and also because it included tangible outcomes, real products and performances for an interested audience later on. And throughout the collection, analysis, and reporting of data, students worked in collaborative teams, adding social energy and problem-solving capacity to the work, and leveraging each other's thinking along the way.

Perhaps the most poignant and most universal question posed by teenage students is "Why do we have to learn this stuff?" (This query's even more pointed, and quintessentially American variant is "When will we ever use this stuff?") To these entirely reasonable concerns, high schools typically respond: "Well, you'll need it later on." Thus, young people are asked to conceive of learning as a bank where one makes timely and regular deposits, saving up knowledge toward some distant, future expenditure.

This is a pretty ridiculous theory of education—not to mention of delayed intellectual gratification—to try selling to young people whose veins are coursing with energy and curiosity, not to mention hormones. Instead, high schools need to find ways to engage kids in work that is important and meaningful to them *now*, at the time of learning. In order to achieve these ends, we believe schools need to provide challenging intellectual work, authentic, real-life experiences, and plenty of opportunities for collaboration. And this, by the way, is exactly what the national standards of teaching and learning call for, across the curriculum.

CHALLENGING WORK

In a study from the Consortium on Chicago School Research, *The Quality of Intellectual Work in Chicago Schools: A Baseline Report*, Fred Newmann, Gudelia Lopez, and Anthony Bryk examined the work that teachers asked students to undertake in urban classrooms, to better understand "students' opportunities to learn and the competencies they demonstrate" (1998, 1). Their analysis produced two main findings:

> The bad news is that in writing and mathematics, both teachers' assignments and student work generally scored toward the lower end of the scale for authentic intellectual quality. The better news is that . . . teachers who assigned more demanding tasks were more likely to get authentic intellectual work from students than teachers who assigned less challenging tasks. At least some Chicago students have some opportunity to engage in more intellectually demanding work, even if such opportunities are not commonplace. While teaching basic skills and preparing for standardized tests has its place, if it drives out opportunities for more challenging work, it deprives students of the education they need for success in vocation and citizenship. (37)

So what do we mean by "challenging"? Every education reform document prides itself on its tough declaration that school must hold kids to higher standards, and some define this to mean more courses, no Ds acceptable, or a higher bar on what constitutes a passing grade. But we don't accept that more memorization of more facts is truly challenging. Instead, we and the Chicago

Consortium authors have something deeper in mind. They define more challenging assignments as those that call for:

- construction of knowledge—creating, rather than just restating ideas
- disciplined inquiry, which involves in-depth understanding and elaborated communication
- value beyond school, including connection to students' lives.
  (Newmann et al. 1998, 6–12)

So what does such challenging work look like, in innovative high schools? One step is to ask students to take challenging courses that do indeed involve "disciplined inquiry." At Best Practice High School, all freshman take physics, and even though they get excellent teaching, and support when they need it, it's still really hard. Why physics for freshmen? Well, Best Practice, like a number of other high schools around the country, has chosen to turn the science sequence upside down—or perhaps we should say right side up—and teach physics first. The traditional, never-questioned science sequence was always biology, chemistry, and then physics. While the story may be apocryphal, it has been said that the original reason for this time-honored sequence, held to so tightly by high schools across the country, was the principle of alphabetical order.

Leon Lederman, Nobel Prize–winner in physics and former director of the Fermi National Accelerator Laboratory in Batavia, Illinois, promotes instead the approach of teaching physics before the other sciences through a project called ARISE (American Renaissance in Science Education). According to Lederman (in Epstein 1999), "Science has a story line when the opening chapter is physics" (7). In order to understand modern biology, students have to understand the chemical reactions that take place in living cells, and so they need to know some chemistry. Chemistry, which explains how atoms and molecules interact, is based in physics, where students first learn about what atoms and molecules are. By studying the sciences in this order, students can learn to see science as a coherent whole, from the fundamentals up. Another advantage of the Physics-First program is that students study the subject while they are taking the algebra needed for solving physics equations, and so the teachers can connect the two disciplines.

Another way of creating a challenging science curriculum is to integrate the science subjects, rather than teach them separately—thereby making it easier to connect science to larger community issues. At Fenway High School, a small school in Boston, ninth, tenth, and eleventh graders study *critical themes in science*. The ninth-grade theme, "What do we need to survive?" explores knowledge about food and digestion (thus including biology) and water and air (covering aspects of earth science). The tenth- and eleventh-grade curricula focus on "Communication" as a larger umbrella theme. This includes the human body as a communication system (thus including biology, especially the nervous system and genetics), plus electricity and magnetism (physics). Teachers use various activities with the school's external partners, the Boston Children's Hospital, CVS pharmacies, and the Museum of Science, to complement topics in the classes. As house coordinator Suzanne Panico observes, "This is not an easy curriculum to design." There are few models or materials ready at hand, and it takes extensive time and repeated trials to get it right. After four years of refinements, the faculty is pleased with the ninth-grade plan, but still working on the upper grades.

Americans like to think of math and science as *the* challenging subjects in school. But we need students to have opportunities to reach high in all subjects. At Best Practice, music teacher Phyllis Curtwright helps her classes learn about various styles of music—modern, romantic, renaissance, baroque, and classical—by immersing them in both the music and the representational art forms for each style. Understanding the importance of models or examples, and wanting to convey the elements of the style in different forms, Phyllis marinates her students in music and art.

When she comes to the baroque style, after a minilesson looking at examples of ornate baroque art and calligraphy, she asks students to create a baroque border with some message in the center. Students use resources in books and on the computers to learn the artistic style (clip art not allowed) and then draw their borders. The ornate style of the music is then addressed by learning a fugue, which Phyllis describes as "a round, like 'Row, Row, Row Your Boat' with extra kicks." She helps the kids see how passages with the same pattern start at different times, like a round, and in different keys. Again, after a minilesson on the elements of a fugue, the choir (which has performed a Bach fugue in citywide competition) comes into each class to sing and to work with students on this complex kind of music. The music for the fugue is put up on an overhead, and the choir members help the students to see where the different lines are sung. The payoff comes when the class, with the help of the choir, takes a stab at singing the fugue. Phyllis presses her students, for most of whom a Bach fugue is a very foreign entity, to acquire a working understanding of this important musical form through hands-on experiences.

AUTHENTIC

The concept of authentic curriculum is so central to good teaching and learning that it must be recognized both in *how* teachers teach and *what* they teach. Carl Rogers and Jerome Freiberg (1994) contrast the learning of isolated facts, which they call "learning from the neck up," with learning at the other end of the spectrum, learning that is "significant, meaningful, experiential." For example, a child who has moved to a foreign country and spends a lot of time with other kids learns the new language quickly, with no language instruction at all. "But let someone try to instruct her in her new language, basing the instruction on the elements that have meaning for the teacher, and learning is tremendously slowed or even stopped" (Rogers and Freiberg 1994, 36).

One meaning of the word "authentic" when applied to curriculum, then, is that the content helps students to immediately see and experience the relevance of what they are studying. High schools, however, are places where learning is too infrequently "real." The fragmentation of the typical high school student's day makes it difficult for teachers to help students connect their learning to the real world and real-life problems. According to George Wood, "lists of facts to be memorized predominate instruction, and tests ask students to choose the right answer, not to demonstrate the right reasoning. But much of this material makes little sense to students. When they do not see how it is used, what they might do with it, or why it matters, they're unlikely to commit to learning it" (1998, 101).

So we must create a curriculum full of opportunities for "doing" that can help students see why they are doing things and how the subject connects with life. At Best Practice, our U.S. history teacher, Mike Myers, often uses simulations to bring historical ideas and incidents to life in the classroom. One day last spring, as Steve proudly conducted a Chicago school board member on a tour, he at first felt chagrined when he led her into Mike's room to find the students at the far table all fiddling with paper airplanes. It took a couple of minutes to realize that the class, in the midst of a unit on the Great Depression, was involved in a simulation of a working economy and the seemingly unruly table was actually the airplane manufacturing company, about to experience the stock market crash. After some background reading about the depression, groups of students had been given role cards explaining who they would be and what they could and could not do. Students would experience what it felt like to be consumers/workers, bankers, manufacturers, and small-business operators.

Mike was the "big bank," and he took charge of the money at the start of the simulation. One group of students, the "small bank," was loaned $100 and was empowered to make loans of $15 to $30. One group ran a candy store and another a stationery store. One group, the paper mill, had a supply of paper for sale, another manufactured "engines" using tin foil, and the last group manufactured paper airplanes after purchasing parts from the paper mill and the engine supplier. In each manufacturing and business group, one student took the owner role, and the others were workers.

The economy began to hum when the manufacturers and businesses took out loans to begin production. The paper airplane manufacturer needed to buy paper and engines and pay the workers. The paper cost $1.00, the engine cost $5.00, and the workers' cards read that they were each to receive $3.00 for a completed paper airplane. In total, then, each plane cost about $12.00 to make, and was for sale for $15.00. With the profits, the manufacturers could make more planes, and the workers were getting paid so they could buy candy and stationery; life was good.

After about twenty minutes of simulation, math teacher Tom McDougal came charging into the room holding up a newspaper announcing a stock market crash. The class took a few moments to deal with the shock, and then Mike, as the "big bank," began calling in his loans to cover his stock losses. A predictable domino effect ensued, and after the dust settled, the groups of students were asked to write from the perspective of their particular role about the effects of the crash on their jobs, their businesses, and their lives. This simulation, which took place during a hundred-minute block schedule, set the tone for deeper inquiry, making the concept of an economic depression personal, so that the students could begin to contemplate, just for a moment, what it is like to be in someone else's shoes. This kind of experiential, even playful connection to content is authentic.

Another side of authenticity in curriculum is enacted when students engage with real events and situations in the larger world beyond the school walls. At Addison Trail High School, Katy Smith, Ralph Feese, and Robert Hartwig, who teach in an interdisciplinary team linking English, social studies, and science, introduce students to the Illinois Rivers Project. In this program, kids from all over Illinois participate in interdisciplinary study of the state's waterways. Students go out to the rivers to perform scientific water-quality tests, study the history and geography of the rivers, and write in response to these real-world experiences. Some of the Addison Trail students culminate this study by writing children's books about rivers and visiting an elementary school to share their stories with the students.

In addition to bringing real-world issues into the classroom and students out of the classroom into the world, authenticity also means that students have a voice and spend at least part of the school day pursuing answers to questions that they themselves have asked. So at the Illinois Math and Science Academy (IMSA) in Aurora, Illinois, we find teenagers from all over the state engaged in real-world hands-on science. Blaine Eubanks, a senior from Eldorado, Illinois, is pursuing something he has dreamed of for years, an experiment in sonoluminescence, using sound waves to create light in the form of a glowing bubble in water. Blaine hopes that the bubble could theoretically serve as a reactor for cold fusion. Blaine understands that the experiment may not be successful, but "sometimes you learn more when you're unsuccessful." Nancy Sethakorn, a junior from Gibson City, became interested in exploring viruses by reading *The Hot Zone* by Richard Preston, a book about a viral outbreak. She and her partner, Eric, decided to look into natural inhibitors of the growth of the illness-causing *E. coli* bacterium. There hasn't been much research on natural inhibition, and because salt and pickling have traditionally been used to keep food bacteria-free, they focused on the antimicrobial effects of spices, to try to explain scientifically their preservation of food.

Frequently IMSA students get feedback from classmates, providing more questions that send them back to look more deeply. Students become researchers, detectives, and thinkers who understand the importance of the work they are doing. They are encouraged to pursue the inquiries of their choice and to become expert in their chosen topics. According to one student, "learning is very interactive here. It's not like they just tell you to turn to a certain page in a book." States another, "Learning is for us to do." Most are delighted to be part of this exciting experiment in teaching and learning: "It's nice to be where learning is held in such high esteem" (Leroux 2000).

In this, the most prestigious school in Illinois, teachers are not so concerned with coverage, but instead with deep investigation into real-life problems. IMSA was established by an act of the Illinois legislature in 1965, "to offer a uniquely challenging education for students grades 10–12 talented in the areas of mathematics and science and to serve the school system of the State of Illinois as a catalyst and laboratory for the advancement of teaching" (B1). But why should this kind of teaching and learning be restricted to an elite institution? If we know that academically able students learn in this way, why hold our other high school students to a bland, textbook-driven curriculum?

COLLABORATION

John Dewey ([1938] 1963) points out that perhaps the greatest of all pedagogical fallacies is that a person learns only the particular thing he is studying at the time. Children spend a major part of their childhood in school. By the time a student has graduated from high school, she has spent approximately five hundred weeks or fifteen thousand hours in school. Schools have many explicit goals for students' learning in all of those hours, but the hidden or implicit curriculum is equally powerful. Studies and essays by Dreeben (1968), Jackson (1968), Sarason (1982), and Apple (1993) have shown the many ways in which the culture of the classroom and the school socializes children to values implicit in the structure of those places.

When we ask students to sit in rows, or when we discourage the sharing of work, we send a very different message than when we have students sit at tables and solve problems together. Students who are given opportunities to collaborate every day receive the loud and clear signal that working and thinking with others is an important skill, valued both in school and in the real world. Since the thinking curriculum requires active participation in the learning process, teachers who value student thinking structure their classrooms to give students time to think, problems that are worthy of thinking about, and other students with whom to think.

Of course, these ideas are not new. John Dewey called for schools where student-citizens would experience and learn about democracy by making choices and working collaboratively. Nowadays, businesses have begun to recognize these ideals and organize their workers in teams and task forces where voice and decision making are valued. Thus, when we ask students to work together to solve problems, we provide them with skills that are highly valued in society.

So collaboration needs to be a mainstay of the curriculum, a skill that is both used as a teaching tool and seen as a central piece of content. At Best Practice, a visitor will see students working together in teams and groups every day, in just about every classroom. Of course collaboration is balanced with times when a teacher provides information and explanation to the whole class and workshop sessions when kids work individually on their own projects. But there are no rows of desks at Best Practice; only tables where students work together much of the day.

A standard collaborative group activity in all BPHS English classes is literature circles, small book clubs formed around novels that each group picks for itself. Modeled upon the real-life structure of adult reading groups, these literature circles blend the principles of good cooperative learning with the power of independent reading. Each BPHS English teacher has his or her own way of structuring the groups so that student-led discussions work well. Tina Peano asks her juniors to maintain informal reading logs in which they jot reactions, connections, questions, or feelings while they read, or just after they have read a section of their book. Then, when students come to the once-a-week meeting of their book club, they can use the inventory of responses in the journals as a springboard to open-ended discussion of the ideas they are finding in their books.

For physical education teacher Beth Jackowski, collaboration is a regular element of teaching and learning, not just on sports teams, but in the health classes that are part of PE. She makes sure that two to three days per week, students are actively studying and sharing in groups. One activity popular with the kids is the role-playing of health and family scenarios. Students pair up, with one playing a parent, the other the teenage child. Sample scenarios: a student wants to take a job with hours running until midnight; another has agreed to a curfew but arrives home three hours late after a party; a girl has become pregnant and announces to her parent that she is engaged. The students take ten minutes to prepare their role-plays. As they perform them, each is followed by ten minutes or more of class discussion about the issue.

Collaboration does not apply only to work in small groups. At times, Beth invites the whole class to work together on a simulation. A recent one demonstrated for students how quickly sexually transmitted disease spreads when people have multiple partners. Each of the fifty students in this double-class activity was given a small cup of clear liquid, a simulated "bodily fluid." All were water except for six that contained a clear chemical. No one knew who had the "infected" fluid. The students were randomly paired and each used an eyedropper to drip a bit of his or her fluid into the partner's cup. Next, the kids all found new partners and repeated the fluid exchange. After one more change of partners came the question: how many students out of the fifty were now "infected" with the chemical? Most students guessed around 20. Beth then went around the room dripping a few drops of a test chemical into each cup, which turned the infected fluids pink. The students were surprised to find that almost the entire class now had the "disease."

Of course, many innovative schools employ group work extensively. At the Robert F. Wagner Institute for the Arts and Technology, in New York City, student collaboration goes well beyond the stage of sitting at tables and solving math problems together. Students are organized in three-year "studios," with each focused on a particular art, such as videography, website design, dance, or theater. Fifteen to twenty-five students of various grade levels, freshmen through juniors, work together in each studio on both individual and group projects. Bimonthly, the school puts on a dinner-theater night, to which the community is invited. Parent volunteers cook, kids wait tables, and one or more of the studio groups mounts a performance. Paintings by the art students are auctioned. The school jazz band plays.

Several times per year larger projects are presented. For one January production, kids took over a Manhattan club for a Superbowl party. Journalism students got media coverage. Graphics students designed the announcements and invitations. Performances included dance, theater, and a fashion show. Along with extensive collaboration, such projects also give new meaning to the phrase "performance assessment," and to the concept of authentic learning.

THE NEXT STEP: NEGOTIATING THE CURRICULUM

As much as we may achieve by making our science, history, English, math, and other content classrooms challenging, authentic, and collaborative, teaching them as disconnected subjects still limits student learning. In the wider adult world inquiring, problem solving, and gaining new skills is rarely as compartmentalized as this. And so pathfinding high schools must find ways to bring subjects together. And this means not just plugging a little statistics or geography into a literature lesson where appropriate. Rather, it involves guiding students to conduct in-depth inquiry that starts with an important question and then to pursue that question by using all the subject-area skills and knowledge needed for that particular investigation. This is the kind of higher-order thinking and problem solving that colleges, the business world, and our communities are asking that public school graduates be able to do.

Yet, while breaking down subject-matter boundaries is a vital step, it's still not enough to make integration fully challenging and meaningful. Kids need to help plan, not just experience, interdisciplinary work. Some teachers initiate integrated units by designing intricate, highly structured projects with all the steps and materials and activities laid out for the kids to march through—only to find that the students experience them pretty much as they have everything else—just another series of assignments the teacher has given. To avoid this trap, curriculum experts Jim Beane and Barbara Brodhagen (1995) have developed a more student-centered version that they call "integrative," in which the curriculum is designed around real concerns students identify about themselves and their world. This approach begins with brainstorming activities that help students to identify the questions and issues they share in common. Inquiry projects are then developed by teachers and students together, to pursue the topics most important to the class. When a project is completed, the teacher can "backmap," comparing the work the students do to the mandated ingredients in district or state standards, to confirm that necessary content was covered. Teachers who use this student-centered investigative structure are invariably surprised and pleased at how much of the required curriculum gets taught without having to plod mechanically through it.

Negotiating Curriculum—BPHS Model

The goal of this process is to develop several student-chosen themes that can become topics to be investigated. Because this conversation is so important and so complex, we expect it to take several class periods.

Step 1. The teacher explains that the faculty need to know students' questions because we want to build curriculum around subjects of concern to them.

Step 2. Students are asked to take about five minutes to individually jot questions and concerns they have about themselves. The facilitator models a few questions: "Will I go to college?" "What will my job be as an adult?"

Step 3. In groups of four or five, students share their "self" questions for fifteen to twenty minutes and determine which ones they have in common. The teacher circulates to help students see how related questions can be grouped together.

Step 4. Group recorders list the common concerns on chart paper and hang their sheets around the room.

Step 5. Students circulate for about five minutes to study the lists.

Step 6. A spokesperson from each group shares the chart with the whole class.

Step 7. The teacher helps the class to combine common concerns into one comprehensive list, again connecting all closely related questions.

These steps are followed a second time, focused on students' concerns about the larger world. The class then chooses a few themes or issues to be investigated over the year.

(Adapted from Daniels and Bizar 1998)

While we do lots of smaller negotiating activities at BPHS, we generally use the full Beane and Brodhagen model once a year, for long-range curriculum planning. Usually, we'll take kids through the process during the spring, and let the big themes and questions they discover guide the teachers' planning for the following year's integrated units. This negotiation process has led directly to some of our very best teaching, including the "Isms" unit (described on pages 120–122) in which students investigated the causes of and possible solutions for the anger, hatred, and discrimination they've experienced in their own lives.

FINDING OUR CURRICULAR BALANCE

When we university idealists were helping to plan BPHS, we started with the naïve vision of an entire curriculum that was thematic, integrated, and negotiated. It wasn't too long before the newly hired teachers told us that we needed to listen to some realities. The algebra teacher, Mark Fertel, said that he needed time with his students to just teach math. How were they going to apply their algebraic skills if they didn't spend some time learning them? How were they going to pass the citywide semester exams if they didn't practice skills that would appear on the test? English teacher and school cofounder Kathy Daniels reminded us that the freshmen needed to read *Romeo and Juliet*, because it was part of the Chicago curriculum on which students would also be tested. Arthur Griffin diplomatically questioned how physics would fare in these vague interdisciplinary experiments.

Still, we all agreed that some integrated, student-negotiated curriculum was vital; it was a core ingredient of our common vision, no matter how hard to actualize. So we sought a balance. Gradually a compromise, a kind of time-sharing developed, and an understanding that integrated curriculum units contributed just as powerfully, if not more, to the abilities students would need to demonstrate on the tests. Today, after much experimentation and with structured student input, the teachers at each grade level organize four integrated learning units per year. When one of these two- or three-week units begins, regular subject classes stop, and teachers reorganize so everyone on a grade-level team helps students with some part of the project. The rest of the time, the other twenty-eight or thirty weeks a year, our faculty works mainly inside traditional subject boundaries—but with many smaller interdisiciplinary collaborations threaded through the schedule.

BETTER PASTURES

After four years, we've gotten pretty good at this balancing act, having conducted many different integrative units, most of which are described in other chapters in this book. One of the challenges that the teachers continue to work on, however, is how to integrate science into the units. We've moved a step in that direction with the following unit, named "Better Pastures," developed by BPHS chemistry teacher Doug Spalding and Victoria Augustine, from Balboa High School, in San Francisco.

When we solicit students' concerns about their world, worries inevitably surface about the environment: what has been done to it already, and how we can be more considerate in the ways we treat the earth in the future. "Better Pastures" is a simulation about a town that must deal with the problems caused by the dismantling of an obsolete nuclear power plant in their community. This unit not only requires some serious and focused science study, it also helps students to see how science plays an important part in their daily lives and to explore the politics that surround technological issues in a typical American community.

While Doug and Victoria's "Better Pastures" simulation is too deliciously complex to reproduce here, these excerpts from the preparatory materials give a flavor for the activity—and the way in which all effective simulations need to be constructed.

Better Pastures: Setting the Scene

 Better Pastures (IL)—A walk down Main Street reveals why people like to live in the town of Better Pastures: it still has that "small-town feeling." Not bad for a municipality of nearly 40,000 that enjoys all the modern conveniences of the city. Thanks to a substantial tax base, the Better Pastures School District is well funded, the fire and police departments are well equipped, and a new county hospital provides state-of-the-art health care. The beautiful location can't be beat: along the picturesque north shore of Lake Michigan, less than an hour from downtown Chicago. Better Pastures represents a slice of the country, far from the hustle and bustle of Chicago. Residents are the envy of many urban dwellers who hum that advertising jingle, "The grass is always greener in Better Pastures." Except for a few long-distance commuters, hardly any of its citizens ever venture into the Loop. Most citizens work for one of the large employers in the immediate area: at one of the pharmaceutical plants, at the Naval Training Center to the south, or at Three Flags Amusement Park immediately to the west. Yep.

Life was grand in Better Pastures—until the largest employer of 'em all (right smack in town) announced it was shutting down.

When Con Ed decided earlier this year to cease operations at the Better Pastures Nuclear Power Plant and powered down its reactors, it meant not only the elimination of several hundred well-paying jobs, but the loss of some $20 million in annual taxes for the city and county. The Green County Planning, Building, and Zoning Committee must seek another source of tax revenues to maintain the level of services county residents have come to expect. The Con Ed Board of Directors is eager to sell the plant facilities and grounds before decommissioning costs for this nuclear power plant over-whelm the beleaguered company. The Board of Directors has set a deadline to make a preliminary decision on June 4. The next shareholders' meeting follows public hearings scheduled for Tuesday and Wednesday, June 1 and 2. Veteran analysts expect several proposals to emerge at these hearings. . . .

These are a few of the twenty-two roles students choose from in the Better Pastures scenario:

Better Pastures City Council

Each of the council's seven seats will be up for grabs in the next Better Pastures municipal election on Wednesday, May 5. Council members are elected to represent "divisions," or voting districts. A special City Council meeting has been scheduled for June 1 and 2 to hear debate over a new power plant proposal.

Green County Planning, Building, and Zoning Commission

The county's Planning Commission will soon unveil a new zoning map. Residents and businesses alike have been vying for important parcels of land in Better Pastures. Among the many proposals are open space for additional parks, land for a new recreation center (to host a proposed midnight basket-ball league), site for a new K–12 school, and a mall. Once the zoning map is complete, the Planning Commission will take on the important issue of how to maintain the county's tax base, assuming Con Ed leaves town.

Potawatami Nation

The Potawatami Indians represent Native Americans who were the original inhabitants of this region, before getting forcibly pushed out by settlers. This community has the lowest per capita income in the region. Tribal elders have struggled over the issue of development, such as a proposal to construct a low-level nuclear waste repository on their land. The plan became controversial when ancestral burial grounds were discovered in the vicinity. Since the Potawatami have complete jurisdiction over the land, the state and federal regulations are not in effect.

Students begin the unit with two weeks of building background knowledge by studying the chemistry and physics of various kinds of energy, the sociology of local city politics, and the roles of the various stakeholders in a community. The students then pick roles for themselves and draft statements to persuade others of their goals. The unit culminates in a town meeting. After last year's debate, held in a large arena-style room in a local junior college, students became so passionate about their points of view that several almost came to blows on the way out. While we obviously discourage violence at BPHS, we couldn't help but be impressed with a learning experience that engendered such fierce passion about ideas.

THE POWER OF INTEGRATING THE CURRICULUM

We interviewed teachers to determine if all the effort needed to develop these units was worthwhile. Teachers listed the following advantages and achievements:

- *Social:* Integrated units build community and create better working relationships between students and teachers and among teachers.
- *Climate:* Teachers get to know students in new ways.
- *Authentic:* Real student questions, rather than separate subjects, drive the instruction and bring out issues that are not often dealt with in school, for example, oppression, power.
- *Curriculum:* Integrated instruction provides opportunities for depth of teaching versus breadth of coverage.
- *Integrating:* Integrated instruction demonstrates the connections between the disciplines and how the disciplines provide the tools to solve problems.
- *Research:* Students learn research and technology skills in the context of what they are studying.
- *Assessment:* These units provide opportunities for students to develop projects that demonstrate competence in many different ways.

While the Best Practice teachers were pleased by these many benefits of integrated instruction, they also spoke of some of the problems or challenges inherent in them:

- The units still take time away from higher-level math and science because it is hard to integrate those subjects.

- In a school system where students and schools are evaluated by standardized tests, the units take time away from test preparation.

Nevertheless, our concern is lightened a bit when we find our school scoring eighth in the city on the state science exam, and when we see our math scores on the standardized tests go up 30 percent in one year. The balance between integrated, student-chosen curriculum and mandated topics can indeed be achieved.

FINDING YOUR NEXT STEPS

Read and Discuss: In order to examine the curriculum recommendations and standards put forth by organizations representing the various disciplines, read *Best Practice: New Standards for Teaching and Learning in America's Schools* by Zemelman, Daniels, and Hyde. In departments or teams, discuss ways that your curriculum reflects the standards and ways that they can be enacted more fully. Many of the recommendations reflect the need for authenticity in the work that students do. Invite people to think of a chunk of curriculum that they regularly teach (e.g., wave patterns, the Great Depression, sampling, *Romeo and Juliet*) and consider how they could make the students' study of the material more authentic. How might they get the students out of the building, try a simulation, bring in an expert on the subject?

Experiment: Think of a chunk of curriculum, and pick one task for students to do in collaborative groups. Be sure that the task involves discussion and group interchange, so the students must work together and compare ideas. Simply giving a group a set of math problems to solve may lead them to just divide up the problems and each do one or two. Afterward, have the students evaluate the experience. Talk as a class about how the groups worked and develop a list of positive behaviors that help groups get work done. In other words, guide students to learn how to participate in group work effectively.

Reflect: What are some ways to add challenge to some part of your curriculum that is the most routine or the least exciting? How might you add this challenge so that the work isn't simply "harder," but deeper, more reflective, more connected with large, important ideas or questions? For example, as Kate Lang's students wound up their study of the rape of Nanking, she asked groups to generate questions for discussion that linked the readings they had done to themes the class had covered throughout the year. The groups then led discussions by the rest of the class around these questions.

Visit: With colleagues, visit a high school that has a program that uses integration: for example, American studies, arts integration, interdisciplinary units, or negotiated curriculum projects. Be sure not only to observe classes but to talk with teachers about how they instituted the program and how they plan together. Meet together afterward and discuss what you observed, what worked well, what fit with your own educational beliefs, what parts you'd do differently. Share what you observed with other teachers at your own school. If the experience was positive, encourage more of your colleagues to make the same visit, to build support for the approach in your building.

Chapter 7
Community Experiences

Young people are engaged in the life of the community and the world of work.

Victor *came to the Best Practice High School as a freshman in 1996 when we opened the doors. When asked why he chose to attend the new, small school with the funny name, he answered tentatively that he wanted to get out of his neighborhood. This answer was typical for many of the new pioneering freshmen; they just wanted to be safe.*

One feature of our new school that Victor had not even heard about was that each student would leave the building on Wednesday mornings to "work" in some business, museum, or community organization. Victor indicated an interest in photography and was placed at Parkway Photo, a lab that handles all aspects of commercial photography. The people at Parkway were extremely supportive and rotated the six BPHS interns through all the aspects of their business. Right from the start, they noticed that Victor had a talent for mounting large posters.

Victor began showing up at Parkway after school just to help out, and before long he was offered a part-time afternoon job. When we asked Victor what he liked about working at Parkway, he said, "The kids in my neighborhood are hanging out and not doing anything good, and since I have been here, I don't have time for hanging out." Victor has made his internship site into a "safe house," and in addition to being safe, he is doing an adult's job and doing it well. The wonderful people at Parkway know that Victor wants to go to college, and they hope he does, but they also know that the skill he has developed will provide him with a $20-per-hour job any time.

Carlton came to Best Practice High School instead of attending a school in a housing project because his mother, like Victor's, wanted him out of his neighborhood. Carlton seemed to have a tough exterior when he arrived and didn't know where he wanted to intern. As a freshman, Carlton was placed with a group of videographers, Community Television Network, where a group of eight interns were learning the rudiments of video. It was clear very early on that Carlton was good with a camera. As early as November of that first year, whenever the BPHS faculty needed something videotaped, we called on Carlton. As a sophomore, Carlton requested a similar type of internship and was placed at the Museum of Broadcast Communications, where his talents were quickly noticed. He was later offered a part-time job working as a cameraperson for $10.50 an hour, exuding a sense of confidence in his abilities.

Candace came to Best Practice as a freshman because she also was looking for safety, but in a different way. Candace had just experienced an act of home violence in which her mother was killed and she barely survived. She was looking for a small community where she could heal. As Candace freely tells people, she could have gotten into any high school, but she chose Best Practice because she was looking for a small, protective community. Her internships provided her with a variety of experiences, and she found that she was interested in science and medicine. As a senior, Candace interned at the Rehabilitation Institute of Chicago, where she worked with patients and found her experience extremely rewarding. She received a paid science research internship for the summer at Northwestern University and was later accepted as a freshman at Northwestern.

Students spend five thousand hours in high school, and too many of these hours are squandered. In *A Time to Learn*, George Wood writes about his experience as a high school principal in Ohio, "Over the last eighty years we have engineered, through a series of quick fixes, a high school structure that often simply spends our kids' time rather than using it, and that is the crisis of the high school. It is this wasting of the five thousand hours that every American teenager spends in high school that should concern us" (1998, 7). Time and the way it is used are at the heart of the problem, especially in America's high schools. The challenge is clear: how can high schools use time in ways that respect students and use the five thousand hours to help them make the crucial transition to adult mainstream society? Allotting some of that time for students to learn in real-world settings like businesses and social service agencies is one part of the answer.

LINKING OUT-OF-SCHOOL EXPERIENCES WITH CLASSROOM LEARNING

From the time of Dewey, high schools have been challenged to prepare students to assume their responsibilities as citizens of the world. Operating only inside the walls of the school limits the opportunities for meaningful participation in the real world. But increasingly, schools are "getting real," offering students the chance to participate in the larger world as citizens. One focus for this connection is service to the community. Two models for involving students in such service are:

- *Service learning:* Students go into the community to help in many different ways: creating a garden, helping to clean up a neighborhood, visiting the elderly, and other experiences that provide help.

- *Project-based learning:* Students complete in-school projects such as designing a system for providing transportation or assistance to handicapped citizens and then take them out to the community.

The other natural connection with the larger community focuses on work and careers. At least one part of American high schools' effort has traditionally been to prepare students for the world of work. However, there is a problem with making this effort purely "vocational": many of the jobs of the twenty-first century have not yet even been created. Adults rarely have one career for life, but instead need to master a range of skills to prepare them for a workplace where the demands are both technical and analytical. Data from the Bureau of Labor Statistics indicate that in the coming years, 15 percent of all jobs will be unskilled, 20 percent will require a professional degree, and more than 65 percent of all jobs will require specialized education—that is, more than a high school diploma but less than a four-year college degree.

These changes in the workplace call for a flexible educational mission that prepares all students for further learning and productive employment. And so high schools are being challenged to provide opportunities for students outside the four walls of the school, to help them to experience the world of work but in broader and more truly educational ways.

There's growing support for this effort, nationally. In 1994, Congress passed the School-to-Work Opportunities Act (STWOA), which provided federal funding for all fifty states to stimulate efforts to bridge the world of school and the world of work. The purpose of STWOA is to prepare students for future jobs by giving them timely and accurate career information along with high levels of academic and technical skills, by providing three education/career alternatives:

- attaining a high school diploma or an alternative diploma or certificate
- going on to postsecondary education for advanced training
- entering the world of work with the option of pursuing further education if desired.

Since the passage of this act, most states and many high schools are now engaged in examining work-related experiences and, in some cases, implementing them. These school-to-work activities take many different forms: cooperative education, internships in local agencies and businesses, youth apprenticeships, mentoring, job shadowing, and career awareness fairs.

One of the continuing problems, however, even where these programs exist, is how to connect the vocational and the academic. A recent national evaluation of the School-to-Work Opportunities Act reported that even in high schools where there are strong commitments to out-of-school experiences, it was rare to see these efforts well integrated with the academic programs.

TYPES OF WORK-CONNECTED MODELS

Cooperative education, the oldest workplace learning program, enables students to combine classroom activities with actual work experiences. Students enroll in school for half a day and are employed the other half. Stern (1997) found that co-op participants who remain with their original employer earn more money than students who don't participate in such experiences. In addition to greater earnings, cooperative education leads to high self-esteem and a desire by the students to learn useful skills (Stone 1995).

Internships place students in paid or unpaid work settings to gain exposure to a variety of career opportunities; students spend from a few weeks to a whole year in a particular site. The passage of the School-to-Work Opportunities Act has been influential in encouraging high schools to participate in internship programs. However because these programs require a great deal of planning, with at least one full-time person needed to locate sites, assign students, and monitor their performance, few high schools have well-developed internship experiences. Yet one study that evaluated student performance in a summer internship program sponsored by the Boeing Corporation found that participating students increased their technical competence, and reported that they better understood how academics related to their work experiences (Wang and Owens 1995). The schools with intensive four-year internship programs, such as Central Park East Secondary School and Best Practice High School, have much anecdotal evidence that students learn a great deal they wouldn't have encountered in classrooms. It is important to conduct studies that closely examine the effects of these programs in order to encourage other schools to undertake the substantial work involved.

Another way of familiarizing students with the world of work and the skills needed for it is the *school-based enterprise* in which students, as part of their in-school experience, produce goods or services for sale and participate in the many aspects of the enterprise. School-based enterprises are more easily linked to the academic curriculum because they take place in the school. Research on these in-school programs is scarce. However, there are indicators that the availability of such programs in rural communities, where there are few businesses to support internships, could greatly benefit students there (Stern et al. 1994).

Career academies, which originated in Philadelphia in the late 1960s for poor urban students, have grown in the last five years all over the country (*New York Times*, 7 Nov. 1999). The idea is to integrate work-related classes into traditional curriculum so that students can fulfill college entrance requirements while developing job expertise. These schools-within-schools combine study in an occupational or industrial field, like technology, health care, or criminal justice, with regular courses. There are now about a thousand career academies nationwide. Oakland, California, has incorporated them into all its high schools, and other cities are considering doing the same.

Much more research is needed to learn how these kinds of programs help students to learn. The stories so far tell us the benefit is great. A growing body of evidence points to lower dropout rates, better college attendance, and an increase in the number of college credits earned during high school.

PROMISING PRACTICES

At Tawa School, a suburban school in New Zealand, eleven-, twelve-, and thirteen-year-old students use the Wellington central business district as an internship-type classroom (Rush 1999). Students in the high school may choose a city experience, and out of seventy students each year, about twenty opt to attend the City Site Classroom Program, which, according to Perry Rush, acting principal of Tawa School, enables students "to gain access to the rich resources in a large city" (63). Students work with business and arts organizations on projects that are concrete and mutually beneficial. In one project, for example, students designed and created artwork to display in a corporate boardroom. The principles that undergird the program are freedom, ownership, responsibility, and openness. Students receive cell phones and call the school when they arrive at and depart from a site. Using weekly planners, students plan their own learning time and schedule meetings with their teachers and their project groups. In this project the lines between the worlds of work and school are blurred, and students take responsibility for completing projects and reporting their results.

On the in-school end of the spectrum, career academies are popping up all over the country, focusing on diverse occupational paths. At James Monroe High School in North Hills, California, students in the McComb Firefighting Academy study chemistry, computer science, and firefighting principles. At Farrington High School in Honolulu, juniors and seniors in the Travel Industry and Tourism Academy learn communication skills such as phone etiquette and the Japanese language. In New York City, the Gateway to Sciences program at the Life Sciences Secondary School provides opportunities for students to collaborate with the Mount Sinai School of Medicine, where they learn about careers in science and health. All these programs help students to connect school to the community in very real ways.

COMMUNITY EXPERIENCES AT BEST PRACTICE HIGH SCHOOL

Of all the program elements we've developed or stolen for BPHS, we consider the internship program the "jewel in the crown." This program has two goals: first, to provide students with opportunities to experience the worlds of work and service and, second, to give teachers time to meet together. Teacher teams meet while the students are out of the building, and the internships have enabled students to operate outside the school as responsible young adults, exposing them to a rich range of employment opportunities of which few teenagers are aware. Our program has been named an exemplary site by the Corporation for National Service Learning.

Throughout this book, we've talked about the importance of authentic school experiences as a way to tap into students' natural curiosity and desire to learn, and when we started the Best Practice High School, we knew we wanted to do an especially good job of opening the school doors so that students wouldn't spend their five thousand hours in a school building isolated from the real world. The remainder of this chapter will walk the reader through the design and implementation of our whole-school internship program.

In the year before we started the school, as we interviewed and hired our first cohort of teachers, we not only talked and planned together, but also visited other model high schools. These visitations deepened our conversations about what to do with those five thousand hours, and on our visits we admired some strategies and discarded others. One of the key visits was to Central Park East Secondary School in East Harlem, New York, where we learned about their internship program. One morning per week each CPESS student in grades seven through ten spends three hours engaged in community service. We knew it when we saw it! This was an important way for students to spend time. It had all the elements we were looking for: real-world experience, using the city as an extension of the school, and helping students understand the world into which they would graduate.

But we quickly discovered that the task was huge. We started with one-hundred thirty-seven students, and as we grew, the program expanded along with the student body. Our commitment to our internship program is not only philosophical, but monetary, with funds from our small discretionary budget to support one and one-half teachers who plan and implement this program. One key task of the internship coordinator is to find sites around the city that are willing to have student interns one-half day each week. She must be willing to make cold calls, conduct site visits, and act as a strong advocate for the school, the students and the program. As a result, the city has responded and many organizations, museums, hospitals, and businesses have shown a willingness to help. Through much legwork, our intrepid coordinator, Carolyn Smith, has found placements for all 440 students, a feat that reveals the eagerness of businesses and organizations to participate. In Chicago, the community has demonstrated that it is concerned about education and opportunities for kids. Our current list of sites can be seen on page 156.

JOB FAIR–GETTING STARTED

At the start of each school year, our internship coordinator organizes a Job Fair where representatives from every site come to the school and set up displays that inform students about their choices. A visitor to the Job Fair would see a dynamic bustle of young people gathering materials and interviewing the site representatives. The gym and auditorium are filled with the noise of inquiry and response. It is easy to see that the freshman aren't quite sure about *where* they want to "work" or even *if* they want to "work." But the seniors

Internship Site List 1999–2000

Anti-Cruelty Society
American Red Cross
Business and Professional People in the
  Public Interest
Cardenas/Fernandez and Associates
  (advertising)
Carole Robertson Center (day care)
Carson, Pirie, Scott and Company
Chicago Academy of Sciences
Chicago Annenberg Challenge
Chicago Architecture Foundation
Chicago Children's Museum
Chicago Department on Aging
Chicago Department of Consumer Services
Chicago Fire Hockey Team
Chicago Historical Society
Chicago Lighthouse for the Visually
  Impaired
Chicago Public Libraries: Mabel Manning
  and Harold Washington
Chicago Public Schools: Dett, Herbert,
  Irving, Orozco, Ruiz, Suder, and
  Telpochalli
Chicago Tribune
Chicago Women's AIDS Project
ChildLaw Center, Loyola University
Cole Studio (art studio and gallery)
Community Television Network
Cook County Juvenile Court, Art and Nature
  Room
Cook County Department of Planning,
  Census 2000 Project
Cowpainter's Studio (art studio)
Exito! (Spanish language newspaper)
Field Museum of Natural History,
  Department of Education
Garfield Park Conservatory Alliance
Geodesic Systems
Goodman Theater

Illinois Council Against Handgun Violence
Illinois Masonic Medical Center
Irene's Place (shelter for homeless women)
James Jordan Center (community center)
Jascula/Terman and Associates (advertising)
The Levy Restaurants: Dos Hermanos
Lincoln Park Zoo: Education, ADOPT
  Program, and Guest Services
  Departments
Lower West Side Public Health Clinic
Make a Wish Foundation
March of Dimes
Merit Music Program Administrative Offices
Mexican Consulate
Museum of Contemporary Art
Museum of Broadcast Communications
National-Louis University
New City YMCA
Northwestern Memorial Hospital
Parkway Inc., Advanced Visual Imagery
Victor Powell Photograph, Inc.
The Peace Museum
Reach Out and Read @ Cook County
  Hospital
RDI, USA, Inc. (advertising agency)
Recording for the Blind and Dyslexic
Rehabilitation Institute of Chicago
Ronsley Special Events
Rush-Presbyterian St. Luke's Medical Center
Salvation Army: Midwest Head Start
Shedd Aquarium
Street Level Youth Media
Terra Museum of American Art
United Negro College Fund
United Neighborhood Organization
University of Illinois at Chicago, College of
  Education
U.S. Equities Real Estate
Warren Barr Pavilion (senior citizen care)

zero in on sites connected with their hopes and dreams. Some focus on hospitals, because they are interested in a career in a medical field. Others want to go to juvenile court, a law firm, a restaurant, or an advocacy group for public-housing residents. Many hope they can find a much needed part-time job, while others are just looking for a future. Each job site provides a one-page information sheet introducing the site and describing the jobs that interns are asked to perform. A visitor to the Job Fair would see a powerful example of a city's business and service community supporting students. Some sample job descriptions are shown on page 158.

After the Job Fair, students write five essays on their first five choices, and every attempt is made to ensure that students get one of their choices. As students get older, they become more aware of the kind of placement they want and what they are good at. They are encouraged to explain the skills they offer and to write persuasive arguments for the internship they seek. Choice comes with the responsibility of writing a good essay and of doing a good job in the world outside the walls of the school.

Over the course of their high school career, our students come to understand the equation. Here is an example of one student's request to be placed at Rush-Presbyterian St. Luke's Medical Center:

Ever since I was five years old all that I wanted to do was to be a pediatrician. This has been a life long dream. Now this would be a good chance to actually experience and find out what it would be like to help children and be a pediatrician. Since I have always wanted to work in the medical field when I grow up, I have looked into safety stuff. I have been first aid acknowledged ever since I was 6 years old. I was able to do this through the First Aid for Little People by Red Cross, and now by Girl Scouts which is sponsored by Red Cross. Right now I am first aid and CPR certified. As an assistant leader with Brownie and Junior Girl Scout troops I have had many experiences helping young children calm down and not think about how much pain they are in when they are hurt and I am trying to help them. This happens mostly when we are on camping trips and a lot of times on hikes. I have earned my Emergency Preparedness Interest Project Patch as a Cadette Girl Scout. I would be successful in this site because since I have always wanted to do this. I will put my mind to it. I am really determined to accomplish this and I will accomplish it. I will not give up for anything.

Jeanette

Job Descriptions

Lincoln Park Zoo
Guest Services

Thank you for your interest in the Guest Services operation at the Lincoln Park Zoo! Your help is greatly needed as we attempt to provide our visitors with a good time as well as providing them with information on what the Lincoln Park Zoo is all about.

As a Guest Services intern, your main responsibility is customer-service oriented. You should be able to work with staff and volunteers in order to provide the zoo visitor with everything (in the friendliest manner possible) that he/she might need in order to have an enjoyable and educational experience at the zoo. You will be encouraged to greet the visitors as they walk in the gates, or as they stroll the grounds in hopes of making them feel welcomed at the zoo. We invite our guests to ask their questions and let them know that staff is readily available to help them with their every need.

The Guest Service operation consists of one coordinator, Robin Biehler, an assistant, Deborah Jones-Miller, three other support staff, and about 100 volunteers. We all work together in fulfilling the very important role of providing an exceptional customer service to our visitors. As the last free cultural institution in the city of Chicago and one of only three free zoos in the country, our department is able to indirectly help support the animals and operations at the zoo by assisting our visitors in a friendly, professional manner.

If you would enjoy working in the unique environment of a Chicago public park, interacting with the general public as well as being around animals, then the Guest Services department at the Lincoln Park Zoo can offer you an exciting and rewarding experience. Please call me if you have any more questions about the Guest Services area or any questions about the zoo (312-742-2353).

Thanks again for your interest!

The Art Institute of Chicago

The Art Institute of Chicago is one of the largest and most famous art institutions in the world. It incorporates the museum of the Art Institute, which houses one of the world's most distinguished collections of fine art, and the School of the Art Institute, which ranks as one of the top independent colleges in the United States.

The museum was founded in 1879, and today the permanent collection has grown to include 250,000 objects. Last year, over 145,000 students toured the collection and nearly 1.5 million people visited the museum.

Internships

Data Resource Management: The Data Resource Management department manages central information systems, personal computing, programming, and telecommunications and networking. An intern will process requests for accounts payable checks; process purchase orders for the ordering of equipment and services; learn to troubleshoot telephone equipment; and learn to run forms, reports, and other print jobs.

Museum Education: The Museum Education department develops programs and educational resources for the museum, including tours, art projects, and lectures. An intern will participate in three areas of Museum Education: Community Programs, Student Programs, and ArtExpress. An intern will be involved in office work, meeting the public, and observing tours and lectures.

Museums in the Park: Museums in the Park is an affiliation of nine museums (Adler Planetarium, Art Institute, Chicago Academy of Science, Chicago Historical Society, DuSable Museum, Field Museum, Mexican Fine Arts Museum, Museum of Science and Industry, and Shedd Aquarium) working together on common interests. An intern will assist with day-to-day office duties including mailings, data entry, copying, filing, and organization.

Purchasing Department: The Purchasing Department purchases and delivers all nonart items at The Art Institute of Chicago. An intern will be involved with the day-to-day operations of the department, including exposure to general office work; monitoring and distributing supplies to the Museum and the School of the Art Institute; conducting inventories; processing invoices; maintaining vendor records; and participating in the recycling program.

Loyola University Chicago
ChildLaw Center and Clinic
High School Internship Opportunities

The Loyola ChildLaw Center

The Loyola ChildLaw Center oversees the fellowship program that trains up to 30 law school students a year on how to address the physical and emotional needs of abused and neglected children. In addition to the curriculum and internship requirements, the training of the fellows involves inviting several national and local leaders to discuss topics such as child development, juvenile court, and the treatment of child trauma due to abuse and/or neglect.

The Loyola ChildLaw Center also conducts the Courtroom Testimony Training, which is a program that trains caseworkers from the Department of Children and Family Services and private agencies to testify in court on behalf of abused and neglected children.

The Loyola ChildLaw Clinic

The Loyola ChildLaw Clinic represents abused and neglected children whose cases are in Cook County Juvenile Court. Students in Loyola Law School work under a clinical supervisor and provide direct representation to children, including interviews, investigations, and courtroom advocacy.

The Loyola ChildLaw Clinic conducts Child Mock Interviews in order to train the Loyola Law School students on how to interview child clients before going to court. The Clinic seeks out child volunteers who are willing to play the role of abused and neglected children being interviewed by an attorney.

As a high school intern, you will be given the opportunity to:
Experience the working of the academic aspects of Loyola University Law School
Meet attorneys and law students who are strong child advocates
Sit in and listen to a case being reviewed in Juvenile Court
Play the role of an abused and neglected child for the Child Mock Interview Program

The job responsibilities of a high school intern are:
Assisting in the preparation of programs such as the Courtroom Testimony Training, outside speakers, Child Mock Interviews, etc.
Preparing packets for mailings
Light typing
Some answering of phones

The Illinois Council Against Handgun Violence
Internship Available

Organization

The Illinois Council Against Handgun Violence (ICHV) is dedicated to reducing death and injury caused by the easy accessibility of firearms in society. For almost 25 years ICHV has worked to prevent handgun violence through educational and public awareness programs. Throughout the year, ICHV hosts several events generating large numbers of participants and media exposure such as the Midwest Action Conference, the Lincoln Award event, and our Annual Walk Against Handgun Violence.

Position

Internship responsibilities include:

Providing assistance with ICHV event logistics, media outreach, etc.

Assisting with research relating to gun violence

Assisting with mailings, answering phones, light data entry

Qualifications

Qualified candidates are energetic, resourceful, detail-oriented, and possess good written and oral communication skills. Knowledge of IBM computer programs and basic office skills are essential to this position.

Another student wrote requesting a placement at Juvenile Court:

 I want to be placed here because I know and have family that often visits this place very unfortunately. I don't believe I know a lot about this but I would like to understand the mechanics and how juvenile court works. I will become successful here because when I grow up, I would like to become a police officer and when it happens, if it happens, I'm sure the chances of me having a few run-ins with kids will be somewhat high.

Luciano

The Internship Coordinator reads and evaluates each student's essays and gathers information from teachers to make good placement decisions. Each year some placements are a good fit right from the start: the students enjoy the jobs and have a variety of responsibilities, while the supervisors at the sites like the interns and approve of their performance. Many times, however, problems arise, converting the internship coordinator's role to one of problem solver. Sometimes the internship is just not a good fit, or there is a personality conflict, and the student can be placed elsewhere. Other times, student interns, experiencing the most freedom they have ever had in a school-based situation, choose to test the limits. We have seen it all: students who leave their site early to stop at McDonald's for lunch, students who just don't show up even though they're bused to the sites, students found shopping at a mall next door to their site. If the interns don't arrive, our coordinator receives a call from the site, and parents are contacted. Most students understand that they are being trusted and step up, while a few need to be counseled about the impression they are making, not only about themselves, but about Best Practice High School, in particular, and Chicago high school students, in general.

Sometimes we decide that a few students are not ready to leave the building, and they are placed as aides in the two schools we share space with. One particularly difficult student—we'll call him Ken—presented a placement problem. His teachers unanimously agreed that he was being disruptive in his classes, was "hanging by a thread" academically, and he had not even written an essay to indicate his internship choice. It was decided that Ken would work in the kindergarten class of the Foundations Elementary School, part of our school multiplex. Teachers didn't expect much from this placement, but we knew that the able kindergarten teacher could probably handle him.

Ken surprised us all. Before long, the teacher was asking if Ken could come to her class more often than once a week. The kids loved him, and he really seemed to enjoy working with them and reading to them. Whenever Ken walked by the first floor on the way to lunch or gym, the kindergartners would accost him, hang on his arms, and hug him. Ken had a talent that we never would have predicted for working with small children. The internship program gave Ken a place to excel, perhaps for the first time in his school career.

Some of the internship sites provide rich experience, while others just give students filing and other menial tasks. But as with some of our other efforts at Best Practice, "even when it's not working, it's working." Spending some time in a "bad" or "boring" site can help students to know what they don't want to do for the rest of their lives. Of course, when it works, it really works. At Rush Hospital, the doctors took twelve of our students under their wings and provided them with whole-day real-life hospital experiences. One day the students donned scrubs and sat in the gallery to watch surgical procedures. Another day, they examined preserved human brains, with the guidance of doctors.

At the Anti-Cruelty Society, interns are taught humane ways to deal with animals, a truly hands-on experience. At the Shedd Aquarium, interns have helped design an exhibit on sea horses. At the Chicago Historical Society, interns serve as docents and also as exhibit planners. One year they developed an exhibit on the clothing and styles of "west-side" teenagers. At the Museum of Contemporary Art, student interns "dress for success" in order to attend meetings of the board of directors.

When the students return to school, they use time in advisory to keep journals about their internship experience. These journals become the running record of their reflections, a kind of action research project in which they move beyond the experience to reflect upon it. Their reflections are shared with each other and with their advisors as a way of problem solving and celebrating progress. In this way, we attempt to do the important work of connecting their internship experiences to what they do in school. Here is a student's journal about her day at the Museum of Contemporary Art:

Dear Journal, Today was a rough day, we had so much work to do. We had lots of materials to sort into different groups: 1-media, 2-magazines, 3-mail from competitors. It was sort of confusing, but my supervisor, Susan, checked in to see what we were doing and if we were doing OK. Well, after we sorted the papers in three different groups we checked them off on a list.

The problem was: all of the material wasn't on the checklist and that meant that we had to add them in order to file the material.

Like I said, today was a really rough day, we did a lot of reading, and although our project was tiresome and "overwhelming," as Marasila said, we really accomplished a lot!

That's A Good Thing.

So next week when we go back, we'll scratch out the ones we've done and completed and start on a new pile.

Kia, Freshman

Another student wrote about stocking a food pantry for a volunteer organization called City Year:

Well, my morning was a mess! I woke up at 4:40 A.M., turned the alarm off and laid back down. I did not get up till 5:30 A.M. I was together by 6:20. I left at 6:30 to wait till 6:55 to get on the 7:05 train. I got downtown by 7:45. We got started at 8:00 with our huddle. That was good. The Pep Talk took f-o-r-e-v-e-r. And it was so COLD outside! L wasn't there so Biam said you're coming with us. So I went to Open Hand. This time it was work. The truck driver said it was a "small" load. But NO! It was big. There were over 5 cases of cereal and an assortment of mixed cereals. There were also boxes of juice, gyros, tortillas, and cookies. I stocked the shelves. The only part that I did not like was that my back was hurting, and the guy with the key was late so we were out in the

COLD again. We were finished by 11:00 and we did our third huddle. One good announcement was that the Chicago Bulls signed on as national sponsor for two years, and they can use the logo on the City Year jackets. The whole group was excited because they might get free tickets. Well, that was my morning. I hope yours was as eventful as mine.

Candace, Junior

In the second year of the school's existence, sophomores asked if they could take junior college courses as part of the school-to-work program. Shelley Freeman, our internship coordinator, and Assistant Principal Juanita Tolbert contacted Malcolm X College, located just three blocks from our school. A program was custom-designed for forty-five juniors to take courses in lieu of internships, not for college credit in junior year, but granting credit in senior year. The students rotated through four courses that provided students with information and hands-on career experiences in medical fields, computer technology, and entrepreneurship. These classes not only provided exposure to career fields, but also gave the kids a taste of college. Many of our students will be the first in their families to seek higher education, and this experience has helped them deal with their anxieties about it. Just as with the work internships, when students returned to the high school, they journaled about their courses and how the skills they were learning would fit into their lives.

TRANSPORTATION

At Central Park East Secondary School, all of the children take public transportation to their sites. In fact, the New York City Transit Association helps with the program by donating subway tokens to the school. When we imported the program to Chicago, we were surprised to discover that in Chicago, freshmen and sophomores were not allowed out of the building unaccompanied by a teacher. We had to scramble to find money for buses, and our internship coordinator had the very complex job of developing bus routes. In the first year of the school, there were 137 students to deliver to sites, the following year there were 240, and now there are 440. We were not at all sure that when we grew to four full classes, the bus system would work, but all of the students get delivered to their sites, and the internship program remains a core component of the school's mission.

Now that we have a complete high school, the freshmen and sophomores take buses up and back to their sites in the morning, while the juniors and seniors use the same buses to go to afternoon sites and then take public transportation home. As one would imagine, internship day is a hectic buzz of teachers and students assembling in the auditorium and hustling to board the buses. More than once, students have taken the wrong bus and returned to school. The first few Wednesdays are manic and confusing, and we all wonder if it's worth the effort. But practice helps, and after the kinks get worked out, the program more than justifies all the time and money that it requires.

ASSESSMENT

In addition to keeping journals, our first internship coordinator, Shelley Freeman, developed forms for students to evaluate their own performance and for site supervisors to give feedback on student performance. These evaluation instruments deal with skills and attitudes necessary for performance in the workplace, such as following directions, working in teams, appropriate dress, and positive attitudes. Samples of self-assessments can be seen on page 166–167.

GRADES

Students also receive grades for their internships, and one component of the grade is the summary that students write at the end of each semester. Our current internship coordinator, Carolyn Smith, reads each of the 440 summaries and writes a short note back to each student. Here are some examples of student summaries along with Carolyn's notes:

Dear Miss Smith,

For internship I go to the Chicago Tribune *and I work with computers and my job responsibility is to help Wolfred and the technology department. I work here and learn at the same time. I think that's the best part of internships. You work and learn at the same time.*

What we do at the technology department is to fix problems with the computers around the Freedom Center. People would call you or e-mail the technology department for help and we have to fix it up. Sometimes we set up computers in offices. The goals of the technology department are to work like a team and get the job done quick and easy so the equipment is operational. And I'm there to make it easier.

Self-Assessments

Name: _Alex Chaparro_ Advisor: _MS ROSENSTEIN_ InternshipSite _CTW - AT SCHOOL_

STUDENT INTERNSHIP SELF-ASSESSMENT #1

Directions for Internship Self-Assessment:

Please take the time to think about your internship activities and responsibilities. There are two sides of this form--please complete both the **checklist** on this side and the **question and comments** portion on the other side of the page. For the checklist, read each statement carefully and then check the column that appropriately describes your performance in each category. Your additional comments* or suggestions* on the other side of the page will be helpful to me in making your situation the best that it can be for you!!

5=excellent 4=above average 3=acceptable   2=poor   1=unsatisfactory

	5	4	3	2	1
I make the effort to follow dress code requirements (this category may not be applicable for some internships)					
I listen carefully & try to follow supervisor's directions	5				
I have a pleasant, POSITIVE attitude toward my work	5				
I understand my responsibilities	5				
I treat all co-workers, peers & students with respect	5				
I respond to new situations with enthusiasm*		4			
I am gaining a greater appreciation for the demands of my job and my workplace		4			
I am able to be assertive when necessary	5				
I assume a leadership role when it is appropriate	5				
I show motivation in my effort to succeed	5				
I come to my internship prepared to work hard	5				
I ask appropriate questions to gain understanding		4			
I am given appropriate responsibility & enough to keep me busy each Wednesday*	5				
I am making an effort to overcome any shyness & communicate effectively with my supervisor*	5				

THIS COMPLETES THE **CHECK LIST** PORTION OF THE ASSESSMENT. PLEASE TURN THE PAGE AND COMPLETE THE **QUESTIONS AND COMMENTS** PORTION ON THE OTHER SIDE.

Self-Assessments (continued)

Irene's Place
Daytime women's Shelter

Internship Self-Assessment

1. Internship helped me improve in: alot I've learned to respect my self and others cause usually I'm very disrespectful twards people. But I've learned in order to get respect you have to respect others.

2. My strengths at Internship were: Helping the women and especially washing dishes. I liked communicating with the ladies and having nice conversations with them

3. My weaknesses at Internship were: Speaking up when I wanted something, or scared to yes or no.

4. One new thing that I discovered about myself through Internship was: I can be a very interactive person. I usually don't talk but I've talked more since I've been going to internship

Give yourself a grade on the following things (A, B, C, D, or F):

At Internship, I was:

1. Adaptable and responded to situations with enthusiasm   C

2. Able to listen, follow directions, and understand expectations   A

3. Able to show initiative, starting new tasks before asked   B

4. Courteous and treated others with respect   A

5. Showed good work habits and seldom wasted time   A

Wolfred is my supervisor and he is the chief of the tech. department in the afternoons. And he's like one of the guys because he's cool and a friend. I also work with Edgar. He's my friend from school and we work together. There's Sandell, Peter, Joe and a lot of other people. I feel that this is the best internship I have ever been to because I'm learning about computers and computers are the jobs of the future. So it's like I'm going to school for free and I have a good time. I think that there's only one thing I hate about Internship and that is that we do mostly the same things every week. It would be sweet if we did something new.

Leon Gonzalez

Comments:

Leon,

I'm pleased that things are going well at the Tribune, *after your somewhat rocky start. The exposure to computers sounds great as does your supervisor. I hope that this internship helps prepare you for a successful future working with computers.*

Miss Smith

Another student works with the elderly:

Dear Miss Smith,

Hello my name is Shalena Brim. My internship for this year is at the Warren Barr Pavilion. My job as intern consists of many different jobs. I play games with the clients like bingo, dominoes, putting puzzles together, etc. I work in the Adult Day Care where the elderly people come while their children are at work. Some just come because they are retired or bored. I work with 5 different women. They all have taught me many things, like how to be patient and treat them with the love and respect that I would want when I get older. The elderly people do many different activities. They exercise, they watch tv, they dance, they take naps, etc. This internship is never the same, we always do something different. I love this internship and I would never want to change it because it helps me mature for my time as a future psychologist.

Shalena

Comments:

Dear Shalena,

Nice work on your summary! Even though I knew how much you love your internship, it was great to see why on paper. Warren Barr Pavilion is extremely fortunate to have you.

Miss Smith

Students have two final projects for their internship program. First, they each have to write a résumé. Students are given models for résumés, and our internship coordinator works with advisory teachers to help them guide the students through this process. Then each student designs a brochure about his or her internship to interest other students in the site. These brochures are composed on computers and provide a way for students to apply their growing abilities in computer technology. (See pages 170–171.)

LESSONS THAT ARE NOT LEARNED IN SCHOOL

We interviewed our students and asked them what they thought they had learned at their internships that they wouldn't have learned at school. Some of their answers surprised us. First, almost universally, they said they had learned to use some piece of equipment. For some students, it was a fax or a Xerox machine, but a few of our students even ran the $5-million sky show at the planetarium. Second, the students told us that they learned how to talk to adults. Many of the students served as docents in museums and found themselves in the position of talking with authority to both staff and visitors. Third, many students learned to work in teams and negotiate problems, both with each other and with their supervisors, determining how to divide up and share tasks, and how to ask a supervisor for more challenging activities. Finally, some of the students reported that they had learned to speak to groups.

When high school students leave their buildings, they find that there are many lessons that they are eager to learn, and that are discovered naturally through authentic experiences from which they grow in many different ways. The SCANS report that we've repeatedly referred to notes that basic skills are just one aspect of what high schools need to cover in preparing students to participate in mainstream society. Students need to be able to think and to

Sample Résumé

Leon Batiste
406 South Hamlin
Chicago, IL 60624
(773) 533-5514

<u>Objective:</u>
To obtain a position in a successful company in which I can utilize my skills to enhance the company's growth.

<u>Experience:</u>

June 1996

Jr. Architect: Participate in building a miniature playground on the property of the Board of Education. My duties consisted of mixing cement, brick laying, painting, digging ditches, planting grass and an assortment of flowers.

1997 - Dett Elementary School

Art Teacher Aide - taught the students to paint, draw pictures, make a straight line and build different shapes with construction paper.

1998 - Rush Hospital

Orderly in the Volunteer Services Dept.

I ran errands for the nurses between departments. Transported patients being admitted into the hospital to their rooms and transported patients leaving the hospital going home to their cars.

1999 - Anti Cruelty Society

Cleaning the animal cages, walk the dogs and created a build board sign that is now being displayed at the Anti Cruelty Society with my artwork.

<u>Education:</u>
King Elementary School - 740 South Campbell - up to 5th grade

Washington Irving School - Oakley and Polk - 6th grade to 8th grade (graduated)

Currently attending Best Practice High School. Due to Graduate June 5, 2000.

<u>Reference:</u>
Available upon request.

Sample Brochure

My Internship Experiences

My experience as a volunteer at Henry Suder School has been very exciting this year because I worked with the teachers and helped be a great role model and mentor to children younger than myself. I also learned what being a teacher is all about and you help many children to excel in life as a teacher.

Jamil Johnson " My internship is fun.

Kia Griffin " I enjoyed working at the MCA (museum of contemporary art) because it's a place I never visited or knew about, that made it interesting. "

Tewanda Palmer " I learned how to care for animals. "

"Steering you in the right direction"

Best Practice High School

B.P.H.S Internship Brochure

Introduction

What is an internship?

An internship is a site you choose to volunteer your service at the whole year. But before that you have to write a short essay on 5 specific sites you want to volunteer at. At your site you learn a great deal of things concerning the site. Most intern sites are very interesting to learn about and have tasks that will help you in the future. You visit your site once a week on Wednesday. You are exposed to career options and preparation for future jobs. You learn to be responsible and it assists in finding summer jobs.

What freshmen should know/will learn about internships

* Learn and develop new skills
* Gain work experience
* Challenging, exciting activities
* Fun
* Students choose sites
* Networking opportunities
* Learn responsibility
* Educational
* Volunteering
* Great life experience

List of some sites available in 1996 - 1997

* Architreasures
* Anti-Cruelty Society
* Chicago Historical Society
* Chicago Children's Museum
* City Year
* Computer Consultant
* Dett School
* Foundation School
* Victor Herbert School
* Washington Irving
* DCFS/ Juvenile Court
* Lincoln Park Zoo
* Mabel Manning Library
* Mid-City National Bank
* Marwen Foundation
* Museum of Contemporary Art
* Nia School
* Henry Suder School

New Sites To Be Added For 1997-1998

develop personal qualities such as responsibility, self-esteem, and integrity. They have to arrive on time, work in teams to solve problems, apply technology to specific tasks, and evaluate, organize, and communicate information. Often high schools just concentrate on the teaching (or transmission) of basic skills. Where do students, who pass through high school following a long list of rules, learn the other important components of success in the real world?

In many large high schools, following rules is the hidden curriculum: listen for the bell, be in your seats when the bell rings, take notes for forty to fifty minutes while your teacher lectures, and move on to your next disconnected subject. In the high school of one of the authors, there were one-way corridors, and going the wrong way was punishable by detention, even if the correct route required circling through the entire building to get to the class next door. The hidden curriculum often demonstrates to students that they aren't smart enough, responsible enough, or reasonable enough to deserve the choices and responsibilities that an internship program presents. When we invite students to leave the building and, for at least part of a day, participate in the real world, our hidden curriculum whispers that we think they can.

When each freshman class enters the high school, they have limited ideas about careers. Many of the students' most visible career opportunities involve some form of illegal activity. Some have observed firsthand the spoils of gang involvement in the jackets and jewelry worn by gang members and their families. Others come to school like small children saying they want to be basketball players or rap singers, or sometimes teachers. They have limited knowledge of the world of work and of the kinds of jobs available. This program, and the sharing around it that takes place back at school, lays bare the many options that exist, shows what kind of education is needed to pursue these options, and ignites the desire to find a responsible, challenging role in mainstream society.

FINDING YOUR NEXT STEPS

Remember: Think back to your own high school experience. In what ways did school help you make explicit connections to life and work? Did you take shop or home economics? Were these helpful experiences? Did you have any jobs or participate in service activities outside of school? If so, what kinds of things did you learn from those experiences? How may these have helped you in your adult life?

Visit: It is important to see models of community participation in action. Central Park East Secondary School in New York accepts visitors on Tuesdays by reservation. Best Practice High School in Chicago accepts visitors on Thursdays by reservation with our professional development coordinator, Yolanda Simmons. Visiting the school enables you to talk to the students about the value of these internship experiences in their high school careers. Be sure to ask about how the school connects kids' work experience to their academic studies. Visiting businesses or organizations that have student interns is also highly instructive. Talk to persons who supervise the interns to get their perspective on what the students gain from the activity.

Experiment: It is not necessary to involve your whole student body in the first internship experiment. Plan a small pilot program that places interns in a few community organizations, businesses, or elementary schools in your area. The placements can be of a shorter duration and involve a small segment of your student body. It might be organized as a one-semester elective, supervised by one teacher. Have the participating students keep journals documenting the activities they are involved in and their reactions and reflections about the quality of the placement. Interview them about what they learned in their placement that they might not have learned in school. Brainstorm with interested teachers how to link the internship experiences with the students' academic work.

Find Funds: If you school is interested in organizing an internship program, it may require funding to support the program. The School-to-Work Opportunities Act (STWOA) provides federal funding to all fifty states to support partnerships. Many states and some foundations have funding programs as well. Business groups are also a valuable resource (see Chapter 12). Often, if such groups don't provide funds, they have considerable influence with the foundations that do.

Chapter 8
Scheduling

The school day and calendar provide flexible and variable blocks of learning time.

When we began dreaming up Best Practice High School back in 1995, our vision included a pure block schedule. We planned to deliver 100 percent of our instruction in 103-minute periods on Monday, Tuesday, Thursday, and Friday—with Wednesday set aside for the kids' service learning internships around the city. After the school was approved and we gathered our faculty, the new teachers began expressing some doubts about full-time block scheduling. No one had ever actually taught a double-length period, and many were concerned about filling a big block with valuable activities. After much debate, we decided to develop two different plans: the A schedule, which was the block plan, and a B schedule, a traditional seven-period day of fifty-minute periods, which we could revert to if necessary.

Our first day of block scheduling, with the 137 newly recruited freshmen, back in September 1996, was a mess. Both the teachers and kids—few of whom had ever experienced 100-minute periods before—struggled with the new structure. Even though the teachers did their best to provide plenty of variety and hands-on work, the day still seemed to drag on forever. When the kids finally went home, the nine faculty members sat down around a table in the library, discouraged. Finally someone said, "Well, *that* sure didn't work." The kids' exit slips confirmed the teachers' perceptions. The message seemed clear: block scheduling didn't work—or it didn't work for us—or maybe we just weren't ready for it. Whatever the reason, the teachers decided to try good old fifty-minute periods for a while. The next day, we posted that schedule on the front door so that the kids would see it on their way in. Since there was no computer-driven bell system to reprogram, this was all we had to do to change our schedule. The kids arrived the next day, read the memo, and obligingly marched off into Plan B.

Thus began our three-month quest for a schedule that worked. The teachers tinkered and experimented every week, mixing different combinations of block and regular scheduling, moving advisory periods around, trying to figure out what to do with kids on Wednesday afternoons when they returned from their internships. Everyone felt pressure to make the block work—after all, we were supposed to be an innovative school, right? But then the Board of Education would announce another mandate or standardized test, and everyone would start worrying about covering the material, fearful that any schedule tinkering might undermine kids' performance.

By Thanksgiving, the file folder marked "schedules" contained nearly thirty different variations, some of them still bearing the folded-over scotch tape that had affixed them to the front door. Along about this time, many of us were feeling guilty about our floundering. What business did we have running a school when we couldn't even devise a schedule that worked for our staff and kids? But then we remembered something: this was why we started a new school in the first place, so we could experiment freely, take risks, and try things out. And just about then, we also realized that we had finally stumbled into a pattern—approximately schedule thirty-seven—that was actually starting to work. Here's what we ended up with, a schedule that has now served us well, with minor modifications and variations, over four years.

	MONDAY	TUESDAY	WEDNESDAY	THURSDAY	FRIDAY
	Regular	*Block*	*Internships & Choice Time*	*Block*	*Regular*
1st period	8:30–9:20	8:30–10:13	8:30–12:00		8:30–9:20
2nd period	9:23–10:13			8:30–10:13	9:23–10:13
3rd period	10:16–11:06	10:16–11:59			10:16–11:06
4th period	11:09–11:59			10:16–11:59	11:09–11:59
5th LUNCH/	12:02–12:32	12:02–12:32	12:00–12:35	12:02–12:32	12:02–12:32
ADVISORY	12:35–1:05	12:35–1:05	12:38–1:08	12:35–1:05	12:35–1:05
6th period	1:08–1:58		1:39–2:51	1:08–2:51	1:08–1:58
7th period	2:01–2:51	1:08–2:51			2:01–2:51

Like so many other ingredients of our school life, the class schedule at Best Practice is the product of compromise, time sharing, and the balancing of competing needs. It is also an intentional hybrid of different schedule types. On

Mondays and Fridays, we operate like a "regular" high school, meeting for seven fifty-minute periods. On Tuesdays and Thursdays, we utilize a block schedule with 103-minute periods: the odd-numbered classes (periods one, three, and five from the regular schedule) meet on Tuesday, and the even-numbered classes on Thursdays. That means kids meet each of their classes three times a week—two single periods and one double. On Wednesdays, freshmen and sophomores meet at school and then are bused to their service-learning internship sites for the whole morning, and after lunch and advisory they select from about ten "Choice" classes and activities. For seniors and juniors, the schedule is reversed, with Choice and advisory in the morning and internships in the afternoon.

The above schedule represents what we do for about twenty-four weeks of the year. The other fifteen weeks are somewhat different. For the first six weeks of the year, since our internship program does not commence until mid-October, the weekly schedule alternates between regular and block days. During this time, we are firming up all 440 placements around town, matching the kids to the available spots, and training the students in the skills they need to be successful in their internships.

The other ten weeks are devoted to our integrated curriculum units. Four times a year, working in grade-level teams, we suspend the regular class schedule and dig into broad interdisciplinary problems, themes, or inquiries for a couple of weeks. During these integrated units, teachers often step out of their subject-area role and become the mentor to a group of students pursuing a question they have selected. Kids are assigned to whatever teacher is facilitating the subtopic they have chosen, and a schedule is built to suit the project at hand (sometimes it parallels the block schedule—other times it is created anew). Often this includes teachers spending whole days with one group of students, a configuration that the faculty have increasingly favored as they mastered block scheduling and came to treasure big chunks of time with kids.

Whatever schedule we use on any given day, the kids move between classes when teachers release them—not when a bell rings. Indeed, one of the things we were careful not to fix when we inherited our 1902 building was the broken controller box in the main office. So, how does it work without bells? What about teachers who let kids out of class too early, so they disturb others—or keep them too long, so kids are late to their next class? At our school, this is a recurrent but minor problem. About every two or three months, teachers begin to drift from the printed schedule, and then we do some fine-tuning. Usually someone raises the issue at a faculty meeting, and people basically say, "Ooops, sorry," and everyone agrees to tighten up the transition times. This has never been a point of conflict or taken up more than a minute or two. The last time that class ending times became a problem, a colleague simply posted this note on the office door:

COLLEAGUES!

Can we please synchronize our watches? There are too many kids getting out of afternoon classes four or five minutes early and bothering classes on the third floor. Help!

No meeting time was required—everyone knew what to do.

How did we come to our own particular scheduling compromise after so many experiments? Because we live under the same constraints as other Chicago public high schools, our teachers feel they need a portion of each week for traditional separate-subject instruction to ensure that our kids will test well on required citywide exams. This means that, even though we have a small school, our teachers still see about 140 kids on Mondays and Fridays, just like teachers in big, traditional high schools. On Tuesdays and Thursdays, they see an average of 70, and on Wednesdays, they see from a handful to 25—depending on however many kids sign up for the Choice class the teacher has announced for that day. Looking back, if we had adopted the Coalition of Essential Schools model of putting kids and teachers into small teams—and factoring in local Chicago constraints—we could have reduced the number of students that each teacher saw every day to seventy or eighty, a decision some of us have sometimes regretted.

Another goal of our schedule was to provide ample teacher planning time, and one of the wonderful side effects of our Wednesday internship program (which we stole unabashedly from Central Park East) is a full half-day of planning time for teachers every week. An off-campus service-learning program has to be the greatest win-win discovery in the history of secondary education: the kids get a powerful, often life-changing experience, while teachers get a half-day of precious collegial time together. Our whole faculty also meets every Monday after school, around 3:15 P.M., with the intention (not always fulfilled) of taking care of our administrative and busywork at that session, leaving the "big stuff"—matters of curriculum and instruction—for the longer Wednesday sessions. We also get some more half-days by using an arcane, Chicago-specific practice called "time-banking." If you schedule an extralong school day, you can save up minutes and use them to dismiss kids at noon about eighteen times a year. In addition to meetings, we schedule teachers so that they have lunch every day with their grade-level team and have their planning period with their department colleagues. With all these structures in place, BPHS teachers probably enjoy better planning and professional development time than faculty at most other high schools—though it never, ever seems like enough. And even though our teachers have lots of time with colleagues, they still spend more time in class than regular Chicago teachers. In fact, to make the schedule legal, our faculty must vote to approve a waiver of local union rules each year.

One of the cumulative benefits of our odd, hybrid schedule is *variety*, for both teachers and kids. Since no two consecutive days are scheduled alike, there is texture and diversity to the week. Every day is a little different from the last one. For students, going out into the real world every Wednesday seems to act like a sorbet between courses at a fine dinner—it cleanses their palate for the following two days back at school. We also appreciate variety and texture over weeks and months, as the integrated unit projects cycle in and out of the schedule, as old Choice classes are retired and new ones are introduced, providing for stretches of interesting and varied work. So we enjoy variety from day to day, week to week, and throughout the year—and it feels far more energizing and adventurous than the monotonous death march to June that many of us remember as students and as teachers.

PRISONERS OF THE BELL

One irreducible fact about education is this: in the end, all we have is *time* with our students. If you ask teachers to identify their biggest problems, as we often do in workshops, *TIME* always appears at the very top of the list. Probe this response and teachers will explain that there never seems to be enough time to cover all the content in the curriculum, to respond fully to student work, to call and talk with parents, to develop new courses and units, to hold individual student conferences, to meet and collaborate with colleagues, to study and implement new teaching methods—not to mention coach sports, moderate after-school activities, and have a bit of a personal life as well.

And how is this precious time allocated? One of the most consistent features of American high schools, from coast to coast, from affluent to poor communities, from small schools to big ones, is the use of an automated bell system to structure the day and govern the movements of both students and teachers. Now, practically ever since it was invented around 1911, the bell schedule has been attacked by critics as a problematic and peculiar instrument. Every school reformer worth his or her salt has taken a whack at this mechanical anachronism. But still, the practice has endured for almost a century—so that now generations of students see this as the "normal," indeed the *only* imaginable way to organize a school day.

The "bell schedule" gives rise to myriad dysfunctional behaviors. Just for one example, think what happens seven or eight times during every high school day, at end of each fifty-minute class period. As the big clock above the blackboard ticks down to the class ending time—let's say 10:50—the same series of events plays out throughout our country's high schools, as it has across generations:

10:45 As the teacher talks, the students begin glancing with increasing frequency at the clock.

10:47 Although the teacher continues talking, students begin quietly closing their books, gathering their materials, packing their backpacks. From this point on, no student will volunteer any comment or ask a question.

10:49 Students are now fully packed up and have finished paying attention to the teacher. All eyes are on the second hand of the classroom clock; students know at what exact second the bell is programmed to sound.

10:50 The bell rings and students bolt from their seats. If the teacher continues talking, she will be ignored and possibly run over. If the teacher foresees the upcoming bell and asks students to stay for an extra few seconds, they will grudgingly, squirmingly remain in their seats. They may even appear to listen. But they will remember nothing.

Now imagine the same high school, just without the computer-driven bells. There is still a multiperiod schedule with five-minute passing periods between each. But now, instead of bells ringing at the same split second in every classroom, the end of each class is individually determined by the teacher. The instructor—not an arbitrary computer programmed by an outside consultant seven years ago—decides, within a minute or two, one way or the other, when the work is done, when activities are complete, when the last question has been answered, when a graceful and intellectually satisfying ending has been achieved.

A single minute's leeway doesn't sound like much of a distinction—until you are teaching. Even fifteen seconds changes everything: it can be the difference between driving home a last crucial point, making a last key connection—or being stampeded as kids bolt for the door. It can even mean allowing a few seconds for students to quietly pause and digest the day's lesson. Then, instead of the whole school's students bursting into the halls at the same second, creating an instantaneous, self-feeding roar, the kids filter out gradually. Of course a din will arise soon enough, but this way even the passing period can begin with a little less abrupt urgency.

When we combine jangling, incessant bells with an incoherent and overstuffed curriculum, we create disjointed experiences for students. It isn't the least bit unusual for an American high school junior to experience a day like this:

Period 1—Physics—properties of waves in a liquid
Period 2—English—Act III of *Hamlet*
Period 3—Social Studies—the battle of Gettysburg
Period 4—LUNCH
Period 5—Geometry—quadratic equations
Period 6—Physical Education—rules of badminton
Period 7—Art—drawing in two-point perspective

The many grown-ups who proudly boast, "I don't remember a thing I learned in high school," probably had schedules just like this one.

So what's wrong with having a school day divided into seven or eight fifty-minute segments, signaled with bells and separated by four-minute "passing periods"? A handful of problems immediately come to mind:

- Fifty minutes is simply too little time for significant intellectual engagement in many important school subjects.

- Short periods encourage teachers to lecture, rather than use more experiential, interactive teaching methods.

- Different school subjects need different amounts of instructional time.

- Bell-driven schedules create difficulties with beginning and endings of classes.

- A seven-period day contains too many time-wasting transitions.

- The uniformity and tedium of 180 identical days taxes students' motivation.

- The symbolism of marching students around at the sound of a bell is demeaning.

- The bell schedule reflects (and reinforces) a distorted view of knowledge and learning.

The final concern is the gravest one. Dividing a student's studies and her days into many separate subjects and periods sends a deeply wrong message about the nature of knowledge and learning in the real world. Life doesn't present problems to us in neat subject-matter disciplines, but rather in complex, intertwined, multidisciplinary realities.

Now it actually would be possible to coordinate some elements of the comically chaotic curriculum above: students could draw the Gettysburg battlefield in two-point perspective. The math teacher could teach students the algebraic formulas behind the action of waves. In PE, badminton students could trace the origins of the court games that existed in Hamlet's time. Come to think of it, a really creative math teacher could pose Hamlet's personal paralysis as a kind of equation, with outrage balanced by fear and inertia. But while these slightly forced parallels might lend a degree of coherence to a smorgasbord curriculum, an even better answer is whole days or weeks focused on a single overarching theme or topic, looked at through the lenses of the different disciplines of knowledge.

But in practice, such coordination or curriculum integration happens very rarely—usually only in specially designed programs like American Studies. Instead, what occurs—as most former high school students can clearly recall—is days and months and years of chaotic conceptual blur. From class to class, period to period, hour to hour, nothing fits together, nothing connects to anything else. High school means four years of sitting through seven cognitive U-turns a day.

In addition to its misrepresentation of knowledge and thinking, the bell schedule is freighted with some deeply unpleasant imagery. The behavioristic, even Pavlovian implications of a bell-driven school day are worrisome on their face. Indeed, there's rich irony afoot when secondary English teachers assign *Brave New World*, a novel that describes a mechanistic, assembly-line-run-amok society not much unlike the average high school. The idea of managing students' movements with bells was originally embraced by the "school efficiency" movement of the 1920s, a national trend toward reorganizing schools more like industrial plants. Looking back a century later, we may find it hard to fathom the enthusiasm for the factory model among school superintendents and principals of the era, who were entirely comfortable with the assembly line as a metaphor and delighted to adapt mass-production procedures to the business of schooling (Callahan 1962).

Over 90 years, the seven-period day has grown deeply into the culture of American schools, its roots twisted around other ingredients, such as ability-group "tracking." In a school with thousands of students and hundreds of teachers, scheduling these fragmented days becomes a staggeringly complex and cumbersome undertaking. We begin with the necessity that each student meet certain course requirements and be in some specific spot during seven segments of the day. Then we concoct four or five "ability" levels for each class, and label each individual student by their presumed "ability" in each subject. Already the mathematical combinations are soaring from the arithmetic through the geometric and on into the exponential. Given this boggling complexity, it's not surprising that, for example, most of Chicago's large public high schools have a special employee called a "programmer," whose full-time job is creating and mending student schedules—and often, saying "no" to kids who ask to switch classes for any reason.

Indeed, the house-of-cards quality of high school scheduling comes into sharp focus when a student tries to change her schedule in the middle of the year. Let's say Sally wants to switch her language choice from Spanish to German. She's completed the first semester of Spanish, attending a level-three class that met during fourth period. To accommodate Sally's request, the programmer would have to find a level-three section of first-year German during fourth period—the same time as Sally's former Spanish class. Too bad—there's only an honors section fourth period. We can't put her in there. Well, let's see. There is a section of level-three German I during third period—maybe Sally could switch her English classes. Now we've got to find a level-two English class during fourth period. Great—here's one. Oh, no, that won't work. That class is already too full. Maybe if we moved chemistry. . . . You know what, Sally? This just isn't going to work.

Teachers, too, have suffered under the reign of the bell schedule. Just like the students, their days are chopped into seven disconnected parts. The typical day for a high school English teacher—let's call him Bob—might look like this:

1st period	Freshman English (Remedial)
2d period	Speech (Regular)
3d period	Shakespeare (Honors)
4th period	A Lunch
4th period	B Lunchroom Monitor
5th period	Freshman English (Remedial)
6th period	Planning
7th period	Speech (Regular)

Bob has five classes with three "preps," which means he teaches sections of three different courses—the maximum allowed by the union contract. He also spends a half-period monitoring the lunchroom, enjoys a twenty-five-minute half-period for his own lunch, and has a fifty-minute planning period in the afternoon. Each time the bell rings, Bob has to move just as fast as the kids, because his classes and duties are scheduled in different rooms across the building. That means that each morning Bob has to carry along all the necessary handouts, books, and teaching materials for his first three classes—English, speech, and Shakespeare. During lunch, he repacks his briefcase for the afternoon.

Bob sees 150 kids per day, every day. When he gets to his one planning period, he finds a random assortment of colleagues in the faculty lounge, since the scheduling process at his school pays no attention to which teachers have planning time together. This means that Bob and his English department colleagues cannot gather during the school day because some of them are teaching during every period. So the English department meets occasionally after school, when there's pressure for meetings to be short so people get to their coaching assignments, plan the next day's classes, grade yesterday's homework—or pick up their own children and go home for dinner.

When teachers work a seven-period day in a typical American high school, with a large enrollment and an elaborate tracking system, a variety of collateral difficulties arises. One example is course assignments: every teacher may teach five classes a day, but which five? In high school departments, there's always plenty of politics and bargaining around who teaches what. The honors or advanced placement classes are usually viewed as prizes or goodies, and so there's plenty of maneuvering to get these sections. Higher-"ability" classes are coveted for many reasons. First, of course, they are easy to teach, since they are, by definition, composed of students who work hard and do well in school, without presenting major discipline problems. Further, some of the prestige of honors classes seems to rub off on the instructor; if the students are gifted, the teacher must be, too.

On the other hand, most teachers try to avoid a load of basic or remedial track students, both because the kids are harder to teach and because being assigned there implies that the teacher is also a lower-level performer. Of course in every American high school there are vivid exceptions to this rule—skilled veteran teachers who volunteer for lower-level classes and newcomers who somehow snag a section of advanced placement. But in general, the veterans get the upper-level classes, and those with less departmental seniority or clout get assigned the lower-level classes and the younger students.

ALTERNATIVE SCHEDULES

As part of the federal government's Goals 2000 education efforts, President Clinton impaneled a National Commission on Time in Education, and its *Prisoners of Time* report made a variety of recommendations about scheduling in American schools (1994). Among the key recommendation was an increase in the overall time spent on core academic subjects. Arguing that American pupils receive about half the instructional time of students in Germany and Japan, the commission called for a longer school year and the relocation of nonacademic pursuits (driver education, physical education, etc.) to after-school programs. Most relevant to high school restructuring, the commission also strongly endorsed the idea of flexible block scheduling.

Flexible block scheduling simply means using longer, variable chunks of time (instead of seven short and equal segments) to better match the learning needs of different subjects and students. To date, somewhere between 10 percent and 30 percent of American high schools have begun experimenting with some form of alternative or block scheduling, and literature on the various models and their outcomes has burgeoned in recent years.

Probably most popular variant of block scheduling is the *alternate day* model. In this arrangement, students still take the typical six classes, but these meet in ninety-minute segments every other day. Thus students might have English, mathematics, music, and an elective on an A day, and science, social studies, foreign language, and another elective on a B day. In another variation, called the *4×4* model, traditional yearlong courses are compressed into semester-length versions, so that students take only four classes at once, meeting in ninety-minute periods. The *Copernican* model, derived from the highly intensive summer school programs offered at many high schools, divides the year into three sixty-day segments during which students take a few concentrated courses. An interesting variation is the *trimester* model, in which students take five courses each in two seventy-five-day sessions, followed by a thirty-day spring trimester designed for intensive study of one or two subjects—or making up lost credits.

Of course, each of these different models brings with it a set of management problems, as well as conflicts with the old scheduling system, that must be worked out. What about students who transfer from a traditional school to one on a 4×4 block schedule—or vice versa? What about subjects, like music, where daily practice all year long seems like a better instructional approach than longer sessions for just half the year? How do kids make up for absences when every day missed is a double dose of curriculum? What about kids who fail a class—how can they catch up? How will students do on Advanced Placement Tests administered in the spring when they finished the course in the fall? And so on. For every one of these difficulties, schools around the country have found answers that work for them. Because block scheduling has been piloted, tested, and explored for many years, there are abundant resources available to assist schools and districts with working through these issues.

In 1990, Wasson High School in Colorado Springs became one of the early adopters of the 4×4 version of block scheduling, in which students take four courses per semester. As recounted by foreign language department chair Roger Schoenstein, the switch was designed to address high student-failure rates, teacher and student stress, and a general feeling that the seven-period day created an untenable "time crunch" for everyone at the school. Though the change created some fear among faculty and the community, its results were prompt and encouraging:

> We began to see major changes throughout the school. Teaching styles changed as our teachers moved away from the "sage on the stage" role and encouraged more student involvement and student-directed learning. Instead of just lecturing, teachers started guiding kids in cooperative learning, critical thinking, and problem solving. We developed new interdisciplinary and team-taught classes that stressed the connections between separate subjects. When students saw the relationships between subjects, learning began to make more sense. As a result, more kids "bought into" the idea of learning.

After five years, Schoenstein reports, Wasson had documented significant positive changes using the block schedule:

> We've seen an increase in the average daily attendance rate from 91.7 percent to 93.9 percent and an increase in the percentage of students on the honor roll from 20.8 percent to 26.5 percent. The number of credits students earned jumped from an average of 4.8 Carnegie units to 5.8 Carnegie units. (At one point, we worried that everyone might graduate early, leaving us with no senior class, but that hasn't happened.) Class size dropped an average of three students per class, and the average number of students a teacher taught in a semester was cut in half. Our failure rate is down, and our college enrollment rate is up. In 1990, 31 percent of our students had failed at least one class, and 40.4 percent of our graduating seniors enrolled in four-year colleges and universities. In the first year under the block

schedule, the failure rate dropped to 22 percent; the five-year average has been around 25 percent. And 50.4 percent of our graduating seniors now enroll in a four-year college or university.

Standardized tests scores, on the other hand, have remained largely unchanged during the same period. SAT tests—taken by only a handful of Wasson students—declined slightly, while ACT scores went up a bit. During this time span, the previously tenth- to twelfth-grade school added a ninth grade, bringing six hundred more students into the building. Also, during these five years, the minority student population rose from 22 to 34 percent, and the proportion of low-income families grew to a quarter of the student body. As Schoenstein reports:

> With so many factors at work here, it's hard to tell what caused what. But we have to consider the results that can't be graphed or measured. We have a calmer and quieter school than we had before. The hectic pace has slowed down a notch or two, and stress levels have been reduced for staff and students alike. We've never been able to graph the change in "smiles per hundred students," but if we could, I know we'd see a sizable increase. The block schedule has changed more than the timing of our bells; it has changed the entire culture of our school.

Block scheduling seems to work in many of the other places it has been tried. Since the early 1990s, a substantial body of research has suggested that longer and more flexible chunks of learning time bring many benefits for students. Several studies have shown improved academic performance as measured by course grades, by courses completed, and by credits earned (Visher et al. 1999). Attempts to link block scheduling to elevated standardized test scores, on the other hand, have been inconclusive thus far. Block-scheduled schools have documented improvements in attendance, which researchers attribute to greater student engagement, stemming from more interesting and coherent classrooms, and closer relationships with faculty. Reductions in discipline problems have also been reported in block-scheduled schools—which, given a more focused instructional program and halving the number of daily passing periods, seems predictable. Block scheduling has also earned the support of both teachers and students, even though it causes growing pains for both when first introduced. Block scheduling remains in place in the majority of schools that have adopted it—an enviable record of permanence in the notoriously transient world of educational innovation.

But block scheduling works only if teachers take genuine advantage of the time and flexibility it provides, moving beyond lecturing to enact the wider repertoire of powerful, interactive, hands-on teaching methods that large time blocks afford. This opportunity (indeed, obligation) isn't always recognized or welcomed by teachers who are newly arrived "on the block." We'll never forget the faculty lounge conversation we once overhead at a school where the staff was contentiously debating a move to flexible block scheduling. One history teacher turned to another and said: "Hundred-minute periods? I don't know if I can talk that long!"

This not atypical response reminds us that, as schools move toward longer, more flexible classes, they must offer teachers ample staff development time and training. After all, the point of block scheduling is not to facilitate more uninterrupted stretches of teacher talk—but rather to open up the kind of challenging and powerful learning activities called for in our national curriculum standards. Teachers need time and help as they rethink and expand their instructional repertoires, assistance and practice as they refresh their command of methods that can create active, well-paced classes of substantial length and engaging variety.

For many large, traditional high schools, the enormity of switching to a block schedule—or the power of inertia, or the fear of change, or the clout of the person who does the programming—can freeze change in its tracks. So it is very important to recognize the possibility of incremental change. Scheduling changes can be tried on a partial, experimental, and pilot basis. In the Addison Trail High School Interdisciplinary Studies program that we've repeatedly returned to in this book, each three-member teacher team has about seventy-five students, rooms located close to each other, and the first three periods of the day to do their work. The teachers decide, for the first 150 minutes of the school day, how to schedule their activities, and the students move freely among the three classrooms and other learning sites around the building (the library, etc.). Meanwhile, all around them, other students march along on the regular school schedule.

STARTING TIMES

One special scheduling problem in American high schools is that the day starts too early. This anomaly reaches a peak of absurdity—and even danger—during Midwest winters when high school students stand in the frigid, pitch-black night waiting for buses to pick them up at 6:00 or 6:30 A.M.—hours before dawn. The high school kids must wait in the dark, of course, so that the buses can drop them off and make a second, later circuit for the elementary kids, who get to sleep later.

Once the teenagers are deposited at school, the adults in charge notice that they are, to say the least, not quite ready to go to work. It's a common faculty-lounge joke that the kids are asleep through much of the morning. Teachers (and parents) have typically attributed this lack of morning engagement to the defective character of generations of teenagers—and have not stinted in their criticism of layabout youth.

This adolescent sleepiness phenomenon has been noticed and more thoughtfully addressed by some people outside of education, including the researchers at the Center for Biological Timing at the University of Virginia. They note:

> Parents, teachers, scientists, and young people themselves have noticed that in our society there seem to be an unusually high number of teenagers who are frequently tired and sleepy. In many places, students drag themselves out of bed before the sun rises; pull on some clothes and maybe eat a few mouthfuls of breakfast; ride, drive, or walk to school; try hard to keep their eyes open during first and second period; start to feel alert just before lunch; and then get sleepy again later in the day. Even if they feel tired at night, the teens have trouble falling asleep at bedtime.

The researchers explain that adolescents' biological clocks, as a side effect of puberty, can cause a "phase delay" in sleep time. As a result, most students are not ready or able to fall asleep early enough (say, 10 P.M.) to be fully rested for the early-morning wake-up required by most high school attendance schedules. In other words, the typical American high school schedule is out of biological alignment with the students it serves.

After generations of griping by parents that their teenage offspring were merely lazy, it turns out that their brain chemistry is crying out for more sleep and later sleep. Few American high schools, needless to say, have leapt to adjust their schedule to accommodate these medical realities. Schedules, like other ingredients of high schools, are organized around the convenience of the adults who run them, not the learning needs of the students who attend them.

At our own school, working within the administrative constraints of the Chicago public school system, the best we could do was push our opening time back to 8:30 A.M., not quite biologically optimal, but better than the predawn reveille enforced by some neighboring schools. And, yes, our kids are still sleepy when they drift in, often sociably late. Our first period teachers still face the perennial problem of waking the kids up—but they are quite good at it.

FINDING YOUR NEXT STEPS

Shadow: Follow a student through a whole school day, accompanying him or her through every period, every shift in the schedule, including after-school activities or sports. If you are part of a group or class that's studying the school, each can pick a student with a different sort of schedule, class levels, and program. While your shadowed student is at work in class, make notes in a journal about how time is divided and used in each class, how the transitions work, how the pace and texture of the day feel. Drawing on your notes, make some judgments about the schedule: how it affects learning, what works and what doesn't, how the day is experienced by kids, what might make it better.

Discuss: Review the Best Practice High School weekly schedule on page 175. What appear to be some of the advantages and disadvantages of a schedule like this? If your own school were to adopt this schedule, what might be the outcomes? In this spirit, gather some schedules from other neighboring high schools and study them for possible ideas. Drawing from all these sources, try to develop an ideal "hybrid" schedule that might work for your own school.

Surf the Internet: Search the term "block scheduling," and you will come upon a variety of websites and articles, many of which promote block scheduling and offer research supporting it. There are also websites authored by upset citizens who are trying to prevent or abolish block scheduling in their local high schools. Using these sources, develop a complete list of the pros and cons of block scheduling, and then apply them to your own school. You might want to add a third column to your chart—"possible solutions" that might work to allay fears and solve foreseeable problems.

Study: Teaching hundred-minute classes is a challenge for teachers accustomed to forty-five- or fifty-minute periods. While longer classes do allow time for the deeper experiential learning recommended by national curriculum standards, if they are not engaging and well planned they will just be a bigger dose of the same old stuff—an invitation to student apathy and misbehavior. Block periods require a broad range of teaching strategies, along with some strong organizational skills. Though this is a lifelong effort for every teacher, you should start now to grow your repertoire of these crucial teaching methods and experiment with them in the classroom. Appraise your own tools: what classroom strategies already work well with your students? What's missing? What's your next step? Study some lesson plans from colleagues who are teaching "on the block," to see how they allocate time within a hundred-minute period, what activities they use to create variety and pacing within their class session. Seek ideas from the main professional organizations in your discipline: each will have a standards report that details teaching recommendations suitable to longer class periods.

Try Out: Experiment with a new schedule at your school. A big step, requiring wide participation and planning, would be moving toward block scheduling. On a more modest scale, a small group of teachers (ideally in one corridor or geographic area) could be freed to try out a new schedule for a week or two, documenting results and sharing their findings. This can work especially well within an existing interdisciplinary program, where a team of teachers can reschedule their shared students—perhaps for a whole morning or afternoon. Or you can start even smaller, changing the schedule for just a few students for just one day at a time, to see how different uses of time feel. High School District 230 in suburban Chicago developed a model called "in-school field trips" in which a group of about seventy-five kids and ten teachers could go off together for a half-day's study of a special theme, making their own schedule and allocating time to the tasks at hand. You can read about these in-school field trips in *Methods That Matter: Six Structures for Best Practice Classrooms* by Harvey Daniels and Marilyn Bizar.

Chapter 9
Technology and Materials

Contemporary technology and rich
materials support students as thinkers,
researchers, and authors.

After twelve years in a progressive pre-K through eighth-grade "demonstration" school, Harvey's daughter Marny entered the local public high school. It was quite a shock. Gone were writing workshop and literature circles, interdisciplinary curriculum units, exciting trips and projects, artists and storytellers in the classroom, reflective cumulative portfolios, teachers who have watched you grow for years, and a small cohort of classmates who developed—not without struggle—a powerful and wholesome community amid shared childhoods. Instead, Marny's nationally celebrated public high school handed her a forty-pound stack of textbooks, a map of the building, and a schedule full of multiple-choice tests.

Marny put her head down and coped. She was responsible and dutiful, showing up, participating in class when she was interested, doing her homework, and studying for these strange new events called "tests." Marny's ability to meet the everyday demands of this "regular" high school probably owed largely to the sense of responsibility and pride she'd developed at her K–8 school. As a freshman, she also found time to have a normal teen social life, talking on the phone and getting together with friends, many from her old school.

But Marny's passion was directed elsewhere. Because she had become accustomed to conducting her own investigations, designing her own artworks, and creating a community rather than being conscripted into one, she turned to the Internet. Over the first six months of high school (during hours when she might have been checking over her homework) Marny spent most of her out-of-school time creating a complex and sophisticated website honoring her favorite rock band, Queen.

Let's follow her down to the basement as she fires up the computer. What does Marny do as she works on her website for two to three hours a day? She reads, researches, organizes, designs, categorizes, writes. She creates detailed bibliographies. She conducts extensive written conversations with friends all around the world—many of whom are working adults of varied backgrounds. She composes critical reviews. She writes historical essays on the origins of individual songs and the vagaries of different band members. She maintains a gallery of four hundred photographic images collected from books, magazines, and other websites. She orders out-of-print books from around the world, pays for them from her summer earnings, reads and digests them, and includes their insights in future pages of her site. She conducts on-line opinion surveys, calculates the results, and presents the statistics. She negotiates agreements with other websites for cooperative mutual promotions. She arranges official links with vendors like Amazon and Music Boulevard to connect her visitors with their sites. In the first year of operation, Marny's site enjoys nearly six thousand hits.

Marny is never satisfied with her site, and she is constantly scanning others for features she can adapt. She subscribes to services that critically review websites and provide written feedback on a variety of features. She revises something every day. She adds new columns and retires old ones. She changes the basic look of her home page perhaps a dozen times, seeking the elusive and perfect representation of the spirit of Queen. When technical glitches occur, she can dig behind the surface and fix things in HTML code, which she has taught herself to write. She's taken on a couple of small, paying jobs designing websites for others. And now, more and more often, Marny is patiently advising other would-be website designers, beginners who are seeking her experience and expertise.

In other words, Marny has used the technology of the Internet to create her own high school curriculum, and it is a surprisingly broad and challenging one. It incorporates reading, writing, mathematics, humanities, music, art, business, and even a couple of languages—HTML and Front Page. There is plenty of craftsmanship, reflection, and critical self-assessment, but no textbooks, no "ability groups," and no "Scantron" tests. And the biggest difference between Marny's homemade curriculum and that found in most schools, of course, is *choice*. After nine years in a progressive school, Marny had the tools, the drive, and the need to direct her own inquiries.

In her sophomore year, Marny decided to branch out from her private on-line curriculum. One great advantage of her extravagantly funded suburban high school was that it has several state-of-the-art computer labs and courses that use them. Marny signed up for a class called "computer imaging," which put her in front of a brand-new Macintosh G3 one period a day, doing something she loved and was increasingly skilled at. At midyear, a photo collage she had created was hanging in a local art exhibition. At the same time, Marny auditioned for a show on the high school FM radio station and began appearing every Saturday afternoon with her "RIP radio hour," playing "upbeat music from six feet under"—i.e., featuring music by deceased artists. Looking ahead to her junior year, Marny was delighted to see a new course listed in the catalog: Website Design. Against the advice of a counselor who warned that too many of these computer art courses might detract from her eventual college applications, Marny signed up.

We hope that Marny can continue to strike her own balance between interests and obligations. As long as her parents don't start placing class rank or GPA above her learning, and as long as her school provides state-of-the-art technology and some courses that use it wisely, Marny can chart this course.

The story of Marny's on-line curriculum is not just a tale of technology. It is also about young people advocating for themselves and about high schools making some room for kids to pursue their own interests and make some of their own decisions. But a key ingredient is also the availability of *tools*—of the materials, resources, and technologies that can help kids find their voice and use it, loud.

What can we say about educational tools, technology and other learning materials in high school? That there should be plenty? Needless to say, all schools should have whatever helps kids to learn, from books to computers, from science labs to sports equipment. Equally obviously, teachers, who are the ones closest to the learning process, should have a major voice in deciding what materials are ordered and used. And of course, students should also help choose their own educational materials; at Best Practice High School, we bus our freshmen to a local bookstore to personally pick out novels for their classroom libraries.

When we talk about resources like books and computers and chemistry labs, the issue of money immediately arises. As Jonathan Kozol scorchingly reminded us in *Savage Inequalities*, in American education the distribution of materials and technology, not to mention funding for teachers and programs, is not fair. Marny's suburban high school (which coincidentally appeared in

Kozol's study) spends about $15,000 per year per student. A few miles away in Chicago, schools like Best Practice receive just $7,000 per student annually. The only things that separate these two districts are a strip of asphalt called Howard Street, an intervening suburb, and a hundred years of inequitable school funding, a condition that's sadly paralleled all across America. The solutions to this intractable problem are legislative and long-term; in our state and many others, principled school leaders are now lobbying state governments to create a taxing and school finance system that's more fair. Meanwhile, as we all seek to address this deplorable inequity, the goal should be not merely to redistribute scant dollars, but to grow the overall funding pool. We don't want to take away from Marny's school the gleaming computer labs, the radio station, or the improvisation classes—we want to get those same resources for *all* schools, on both sides of the street.

In this chapter, we focus mainly on the two educational resources today's high schools rely upon most: textbooks and technology. In doing so, we don't mean to underestimate the importance of novels, plays, nonfiction books, film, videotapes, magazines, journals, CD-ROMs, or any of the other information media that high schools can use—and probably should use more than they do.

But textbooks have inarguably dominated American high schools for more than eighty years. In most classrooms and courses, the textbook has been the main, often sole, source of information and authority. Now, with the rise of technology and access to the Internet, information is available from a multitude of sources—and not all the sources agree. Will the dominance of textbooks be challenged or undermined by technology? Would this be good for students? And does today's educational technology promise a genuine step ahead for kids, or is it just the same old stuff in a new guise?

TECHNOLOGY IN THE HIGH SCHOOL

Technology! It's a mantra, a mania, a panacea—and, some say, a placebo. Today, everyone is scrambling to get computers into their community high schools, to guarantee their kids a seat on the technological bandwagon. This technophilia seems to affect people in schools even more than out in the general public. School boards that would hesitate to fund smaller class sizes or teacher workshops will cheerfully spend hundreds of thousands of dollars on computer equipment they don't even understand and couldn't possibly operate, just so the district will be "up-to-date."

There's no question that the world is changing, that technology is important, and that schools hoping to prepare their students for the emerging world outside need to have good technology resources and programs. But what exactly are technological "best practices" in a secondary school? How can technology help students and teachers reach for the national curriculum standards? In what ways can technology help make high schools more collaborative, authentic, and challenging?

A first decision is whether we view technology as a tool or as a topic. A few high-tech advocates, like the International Technology Education Association (ITEA), want to make technology itself a new school subject, right alongside English, math, and history. According to the ITEA's standards documents, American high school kids should be learning how to select and use "manufacturing technologies," "transportation technologies," "medical technologies," and seventeen other subjects. Programs following this lead are likely to schedule students into separate computer classes, teaching different applications apart from the rest of the curriculum, and perhaps teaching computer programming to older students.

However, there is a widening consensus that technology is better thought of as a cross-curricular tool rather than a new school subject. Most effectively voicing this view is the International Society for Technology in Education (ISTE), a partnership of key education organizations, including the American Federation of Teachers (AFT) and National Education Association (NEA), as well as the major curriculum groups in English, mathematics, science, social studies, and foreign language. The ISTE's National Educational Technology Standards (NETS), cosponsored by the National Aeronautics and Space Administration, Apple Computer, and the Milken Exchange on Education Technology, set goals for technology use by students K–12, stressing that these experiences should be embedded not just in content areas, but in multidisciplinary, problem-based units.

According to the NETS high school standards, by the end of twelfth grade, students should be able to:

1. Identify capabilities and limitations of contemporary and emerging technology resources and assess the potential of these systems and services to address personal, lifelong learning, and workplace needs.

2. Make informed choices among technology systems, resources, and services.

3. Analyze advantages and disadvantages of widespread use and reliance on technology in the workplace and in society as a whole.

4. Demonstrate and advocate legal and ethical behaviors regarding the use of technology and information.

5. Use technology tools and resources for managing and communicating personal or professional information (finances, schedules, addresses, purchases, correspondence).

6. Evaluate technology-based options, including distance and distributed education, for lifelong learning.

7. Routinely and efficiently use on-line information resources for collaboration, research, publications, communications, and productivity.

8. Select and apply technology tools for research, information analysis, problem solving, and decision making in content learning.

9. Investigate and apply expert systems, intelligent agents, and simulations in real-world situations.

10. Collaborate with peers, experts, and others to contribute to a content-related knowledge base by using technology to compile, synthesize, produce, and disseminate information, models, and other creative works.

These goals are certainly harmonious with our technology program at Best Practice High School. We don't think of technology as a subject in our curriculum—though we certainly study its impact in our history and science classes—but rather, we are trying to ensure that our students have systematic, continuous, and broad experiences with the contemporary tools for gathering, reviewing, using, creating, and sharing information.

A good example is our art teacher Aiko Boyce, who used a wide range of technology—and embodied the spirit of the NETS standards—in the culminating project for her senior studio art class. Each student was asked to select a single world artist whose work they were eager to investigate deeply. The only constraint was that the artist's work and life had to be fairly well documented and accessible. The kids' first task was to immerse themselves deeply in the artist's oeuvre, studying samples, learning about favored subject matter, work habits, style, and techniques. To gather this information, students used books and museum visits where possible, but a major portion of the research was done on-line. Today, the Internet has become, among other things, a virtual gallery where students can view artworks from around the world, along with biographies, news items, and critical reviews.

Once kids had spent some time "marinating" in Picasso, Jasper Johns, or J. M. W. Turner, Aiko asked them to create an artwork that somehow reflected their understanding of this artist. This could mean a painting or sculpture in the artist's style, an approach to similar subject matter, the artist's style moved into a different medium, or a piece that somehow embodied the spirit or concerns of the artist. When this piece had been created, the students had to write a reflective essay explaining the connection between their own work and that of the chosen artist.

Next, Aiko asked the kids to "go public" in several different media. First, they created a video presentation of their "homage" artworks; the camera rolled as each student stood before an easel that held her artwork and explained the connections between her own work and that of the artist—in essence, another version of the thoughts in the reflective essay. As a final step in publishing their work, a group of students prepared web pages for the school website. While the web designs varied widely, most contained samples of the famous artist's work, a photo of the student's own piece, the reflective essay, a segment of video from the classroom presentation, and a list of links to sites featuring the artist's work—as well as the student's e-mail address, of course, so members of the cyberpublic could respond to their project.

Building a Technology Program from Scratch

Throughout this book, we've told stories about Best Practice High School, often apologizing first for how easy we've had it. We're new and we're small, and everyone at our school is here by choice. We've acknowledged repeatedly that it is easier to start a new school than to turn around an old one, reversing decades of habit, tradition, and momentum. But technology is something else. We wish we'd had a little momentum, some history—or even some computers—to start with. Here's how our technology quest has unfolded so far.

When we wrote the original proposal for Best Practice High School, one of its key features was what we called a technology-rich curriculum. Most of our founding crew of teachers were at least proficient—and some were enthusiasts—in educational computing, and we wanted to use technology in every class. We dreamed that our graduates would be able to use a wide array of computer applications—word processing, publishing, image composing, graphics, spreadsheets—as well as being skilled and discriminating users of the Internet.

We put our money where our mouth was in the staff budget: we assigned a full-time faculty member, cofounder Tom Daniels, as our computer teacher. Tom did not approach the job as a hardware enthusiast (he was definitely not a nerd, a geek, or a wirehead) but as a veteran English teacher who saw computers as powerful tools of authoring and investigation. Our plan was to begin with a computer lab, where teachers of all subjects would regularly bring classes, team-teaching with Tom and helping kids to learn applications appropriate to their discipline. Later, we hoped to add four to six computers to each classroom, networked to the building server, to widen the program and enable more extensive use by students.

The first problem was that we had no computers, and the school district was not about to buy us any. During the months before our school was set to open, we kept looking blankly at each other and asking, "You mean they're going to let us start a new public high school, but not provide a single computer?" When we finally accepted that we would have to fend for ourselves, we turned to Chicago's notably generous foundation community for help. The Prince Charitable Trust (still a major benefactor of our school) wrote us a check for $50,000 to equip our computer lab—and we were off and running.

We decided to create a twenty-four-station lab with half PCs and half Macintosh clones, and we placed our order. Around the third and fourth week of school, the boxes gradually started to arrive, a few per day. Whoever had a free period when the truck came in would carry the cartons upstairs, unpack them, and help Tom load the software. By Halloween, Steve Zemelman was home in bed, nursing a miserable back injury from carrying equipment up too many flights of stairs, and our new computer lab was ready to open.

Ironically, even as we had been begging money for desktop computers, our building already had state-of-the art computer wiring that connected most of our classrooms. This installation involved a classic case of Chicago politics. The summer before we were to open the school, our building was loaned out by Mayor Daley as a support facility for the 1996 Democratic convention, held in the United Center across the street. This loan-out meant our faculty could not enter our own school during the whole summer before our initial opening—a horrendous inconvenience. On the other hand, we perked up when we heard that the main occupant was Ameritech, the local phone company, which was handling all communications services for the convention. To run their own operation from our school, they installed a small temporary computer network.

Through a variety of intermediaries and negotiations, we were able to get Ameritech to wire almost the whole building and to leave the wiring behind as a form of "rent." So when we moved in on August 23, 1996, gleaming aluminum wire traces snaked along all of our ceilings and into our classrooms. Unfortunately, we still had no computers to use them. Nor did we have the routers and hubs needed to actually connect. In fact, though the individual computers would be up and running shortly, it would be fifteen months before we had a functioning buildingwide network.

Despite these difficulties, our roomful of twenty-four stand-alones really worked. From the day we set it up, the lab was buzzing with enthusiastic, non-stop usage. Sure, we had read the articles claiming that computer labs were a thing of the past, that bringing students to centralized labs was inefficient and cumbersome. The new thing was supposed to be computers in the classroom. Well, we didn't have any computers in our classrooms until our second year of operation, so we couldn't really make any comparisons. But we loved our lab. The scheduling calendar on the big brown cabinet always showed the room booked weeks or months ahead, for every period of the day. Teachers across the whole curriculum were using the lab intensively, just as we had envisioned. Some of the typical projects and studies:

Physics teacher Arthur Griffin brought kids to study astronomy using a program called Hands-on-Universe, which enables students to call up photos of any portion of the sky, using a network of cooperating computer-controlled observatories around the world. Some other students in the HOU program have actually discovered new stars—a fact that kept our kids motivated as they scanned the heavens.

In *art* class, Aiko Boyce wanted students to learn drawing in two-point perspective. After kids had tried their hand with paper and pencil in the art room, she moved them to the computer lab where they used the graphics programs to re-create and elaborate their pictures on the computer.

In *algebra* class, one of the key early concepts is tessellations, the idea of recurrent interlocking patterns. In order to make this concept clear to students, teacher Mark Fertel partnered with Aiko Boyce to help students create their own tessellations on the computers.

In *English*, students routinely use the computer lab for word processing, document design, and publishing of various sorts. Three years later, in the senior class, kids worked on creating digital portfolios containing selections of their best work over four years. Some seniors have chosen to simply save their best work in their folder on the network, while others have elected a more ambitious project of creating their own web page on the school's website.

Social studies teacher Peter Thomas has a personal enthusiasm for the complex historical immigration patterns in Chicago. Using the on-line availability of

U.S. census tracts, Peter was able to help the kids investigate patterns and changes in their own neighborhoods. Because our students come from neighborhoods all around the city, they could compare notes how their own communities had developed.

Every week, one of our Wednesday *Choice* classes, organized by teachers and/or students, utilizes the computer lab. Twelve students recently created the "Magix Studio" with the help of music teacher Phyllis Curtwright, a "recording company" where each week they produce compilation tapes, hot mixes, and other musical products.

An unexpected bonus was that our computer lab became the school's central gathering place, living room, and nerve center. The way our building is laid out, the computer lab is the first room you see when you come up the stairs from the entrance. It is a big room with two doors that are often open— an inviting sight. From the very first week, kids who came early to school or stayed late took advantage of Tom Daniels' long hours and made themselves at home in the lab. Before we got on-line, they would play computer games and chat with friends, or Tom, or whatever other teachers happened by. It quickly became official school policy that the computer lab was open an hour before school and an hour (or more) afterward. Given its location, as well as the huge meeting table in the center of the room, we began welcoming all visitors to the school in the computer lab as well. All tours would begin with Tom explaining and demonstrating our technology program.

For the first year and a half, our network didn't work, so we weren't on the Internet, the lab computers weren't hooked up to each other, and neither were the classroom computers that we had been slowly adding to every room. The best Internet access we could achieve was by stringing a regular school phone line over to a single machine, and then hooking that computer up to a projector. For kids to get hands-on time on the Internet, they had to wait their turn for this Rube Goldberg arrangement. Just as bad, kids couldn't access their personal folder on the school server—which had been our plan for building student portfolios.

Looking back four years later, now that our network and its Internet access are so central to everything we do, it seems amazing that we could have allowed this deficit to continue for so long. The reasons for our network failures are complex, arcane, and tedious. Suffice it to say that when technology mixes with bureaucracy, the combination can be toxic—and paralyzing. Board policies prevented us from using certain required equipment or restricted us to buying from approved vendors. The CPS would promise that free equipment or enticing grants were just around the corner, but they were always delayed. It seemed as if we were always waiting for the missing link. Finally, after we hired our own computer consultant and he put countless days into the project, the happy ending arrived late in our second year—connected at last.

Why did our basic computer lab work so well, so promptly? The first key to our success was having a full-time teacher, Tom Daniels, in charge. Tom was personally committed to technology in the service of inquiry and curriculum integration, and provided the philosophical consistency and leadership. Being in the lab full-time meant that Tom was a coteacher to every faculty member who brought in a class—whatever the topic, there were always two adults to help students. The other strength of our program was that the faculty were deeply and steadfastly committed to using technology in their classes and making it work.

In recent years, as we have been adding computers to individual classrooms, our teachers are learning a variety of ways to use them. But in general, classroom computers tend to be used for minor projects—word processing, a quick lookup on the Internet, and so forth. We know that this incidental role will soon change. If we look at the longer-term picture, we realize that we are living in a transitional time in educational computing. Probably within ten years, every student will have their own personal computer, either built into every desktop or as an ultralight portable carried from class to class.

Looking back over the first four years of our attempted "technology-rich" curriculum, we realize the program peaked in its second year. Since we were adding a new class of students each year, growing from 137 to 440 students, our kid-to-computer ratio steadily worsened. In year two, we had one computer for every five students; in year four, now it was one for every nine. And now our machines are getting old; they are dirty and beat-up looking. On any given day a half-dozen machines have an "Out of Order" sign hanging on them. Our outside computer consultant dutifully comes in once a week and fixes them—but under constant use, they promptly break again.

Of course these aging machines are also totally obsolete—in the computer world four years is a generation. We remember the delight and excitement back in 1996 when we unpacked our gleaming new state-of-the-art Compaqs and Macintoshes. Now, these machines are electronic dinosaurs: Pentium I's with 2 MB hard drives, 16 MB of RAM, and floppy drives. They have no CD drives—not to mention DVD drives. They cannot handle the applications that have been developed in the intervening years. They're too slow to do decent website design—they cannot even run a 300 dpi scanner at a reasonable speed.

Needless to say, the Chicago Board of Education does not have a special fund to upgrade obsolete computers. Given our small pool of Chapter I money, we must choose between new computers and expenditures for security, the buses for our Wednesday internships, and other key ingredients of our program. Finally, in the spring of 2000, just as we were graduating our first class and the computer lab was starting to look like an electronic antique shop, we pooled some long-hoarded money and made two big orders: ten new Macintoshes and ten new PCs, almost enough to replace the entire lab (the old machines will go into classrooms for lighter use), and a "lab-on-a-cart"—a set of twenty laptops with a server that can be moved from room to room.

Though we have been struggling with growth and equipment issues, during our fourth year we did create a school website (www.bphs.org). Because we had no significant web-building expertise on our own faculty, we turned to a few outside helpers. First to volunteer was Marny Daniels, Harvey's daughter, a high school sophomore whose website honoring the rock band Queen we described at the beginning of this chapter, and who is friends with a few of the kids from BPHS. Marny went to work creating a template for us, using existing school logos and artwork. Then our friend Daniel Cheifetz, a former teacher who had built a successful high-tech company and left to create his own charitable foundation, offered the help of his talented young staffers.

The key ingredient we wanted to get on the website was student portfolios. To jump-start the process, we got four senior volunteers to bring their favorite writing and artwork to Daniel's new Enterprise Development Foundation in Evanston, Illinois. It was a treat for these kids to work one-to-one for a whole day with a professional website designer—and that afternoon we published their rough-draft pages. Since then, we have been gradually building the site—certainly not one of the first nor one of the most extensive school websites around, but one that has been a joy to work on and provides our students with a publication opportunity for thoughtfully selecting and polishing their work.

One reason we wanted so badly to jump-start a BPHS website in the fall of 1999 was that Tom Daniels had fallen ill and we wanted to make this part of Tom's dream come true. We wanted him to see the technology program he'd designed reaching its goals. Tom was confined to his home, but we knew he could follow our progress on-line, if we could get the site up. Everything took longer than expected; everything that could go wrong did. We kept promising Tom: pretty soon, just a couple more days.

By then, Tom could no longer make it upstairs to his computer, so we brought a laptop to the house and strung a phone line over to his chair by the window. But there was still nothing to see. Finally, toward the end of October, using a borrowed server and donated tech support from the Enterprise Development Foundation, our simple, primitive rough draft of a website went up. It wasn't much, but Tom seemed to approve. He beamed as he clicked through the site for the first time, chuckling at the kids' writing and pictures, making suggestions for future additions and changes. We took notes.

Tom didn't have much energy in those days, but every time friends or family came to visit, he'd slowly reach over, click on the computer and show them proudly what his kids and colleagues were doing back at school. Just two weeks after the website went on-line, Tom passed away. At his funeral, the senior class ringed the room, and several kids took the podium to speak of Tom's mentoring, in class, in the computer lab, in advisory. Over the following weeks, as we all walked past the two darkened doors of Tom's lab, it was a grievous reminder of how much we had lost.

Between our personal paralysis and the fact that it was the middle of the year, we couldn't fill the vacant position, so the teachers cobbled together the technology program as best they could. Finally, in late spring, math teacher Mark Fertel transferred into Tom's position and lit up the lab again with his special energy and enthusiasm.

Year after year, our kids have become more and more confident in their ability to use technology. As one senior put it, "I know how to surf the net well. I can type really fast and I can do reports that are the envy of my friends from other schools." Another noted: "With the technology available at school I have the world at my fingertips. I was able to take a video production class, and last year I was able to talk to a UN delegate about the mock United Nations. I was representing his country, so I e-mailed him to get his position on the Kosovo crisis."

But even as our students enthusiastically use all this technology, and we devote more dollars and staff time to support it, we sometimes ruefully note that there is no citywide test of computer proficiency. Our kids, who have used so many different applications across the curriculum for four years, would probably score at the very top of any such assessment. Yet, because computer fluency isn't tested, because in our system the only data that matter are TAP reading and math scores, any efforts we make outside of readin' and 'rithmetic earn us no official credit from the central office and only "steal time" from test preparation. Of course, we try to look further ahead with our technology efforts, beyond our district's narrow testing system. We know that the minute our students step out of the Chicago public schools, they will immediately be evaluated (by employers or colleges) on a much wider scale of proficiency—one that definitely will include their ability to use contemporary technology. Even though it is costly in many ways now, we are trying to do the right thing for our kids in the long run, offering them a technology-rich curriculum.

Hype or Help

When we put aside all the hope, hype, and hysteria—what can computers really do for a high school and its students? We think that some aspects of computers actually may contribute to better teaching, though they also bring along inevitable problems and frustrations. While computer-based classes are certainly no guarantee of good teaching, they have certain characteristics that at least favor better instruction. To begin with, the spatial dynamics of a typical computer laboratory classroom are different from the traditional classroom in some important ways. The layout of our lab at BPHS is shown on page 205.

While the focal point of the regular classroom is the teacher, in the lab there are twenty-four focal points—the students' individual screens. This floor plan inherently discourages whole-class presentations by the teacher just as it invites one-to-one coaching. It encourages teachers to look over the shoulders of students, observing, advising, or commenting. Interestingly, the student is the person in charge of this interaction—she's the one running the machine, driving the mouse. There's a kind of control here that's very different from, say, taking notes on a lecture. Of course this kind of coaching in a laboratory setting is nothing new to teachers of art, science, or driver education, who have always tapped the special power of one-to-one conferences.

Another healthy dynamic of new technologies is that they can challenge traditional ways of doing things in high school. At BPHS, we'd been debating the value of the traditional research paper, and a lively conversation ensued about the role of computers in the process. Here's a memo Harvey wrote to the teachers:

Dear Colleagues:

Since our lively discussion about research papers at the January retreat, I have been thinking about the impact of technology on our research assignments.

We have all agreed as a faculty that one of our whole-school goals is for kids to become skillful researchers. And we all recognize that technology has changed the way people gather, organize, and share information. But schools—including ours—sometimes cling to ancient research practices

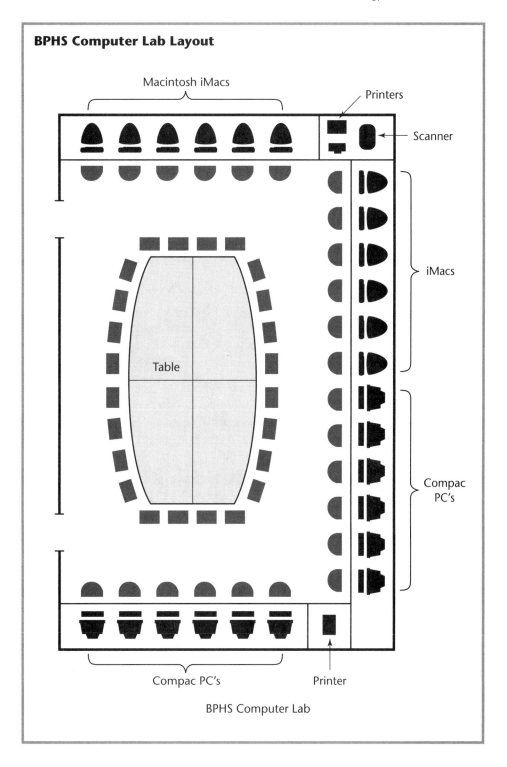

BPHS Computer Lab Layout

Macintosh iMacs

Printers

Scanner

Table

iMacs

Compac PC's

Compac PC's

Printer

BPHS Computer Lab

anyway. For one example: today, real-world researchers do not hand-copy text onto three-by-five note cards. Instead, they photocopy important stuff, or cut and paste it from the Internet. Technology has made the important task of clipping and saving potentially useful material both faster and easier.

So why would we require kids to do an arbitrary number of note cards, just because *we* did it back in high school? Not only do the note cards exhaust and demoralize the kids (just like they did to us, back in the 60s and 70s), but they also distort the research process. Come to think of it, why do we still teach roman numeral outlining when computer programs like Inspiration actually help kids brainstorm and display ideas in a much more realistic and productive format? And even more challenging, why should we think of research papers as solely text, when research in the real world is becoming more multimedia every day, including photos, graphics, animation, sound, and video?

But here's the *really* blasphemous thing. Over the past year, I have come to realize that I may *never set foot in a library again*. As professional reader, writer, and researcher, I can find almost everything I need, and find it faster, on-line than in any library. The book I need is never out, in the hands of another user for two weeks. I never hear, "Sorry, that item is not in our collection." Indeed, except for historic texts, artworks, rare books, or (ironically) fiction, everything I need is immediately at hand.

No, Della, I'm not trying to keep the kids out of your library. And no, I'm not saying that technology is an unmitigated blessing to our budding young researchers. For sure, it brings new problems even as it solves old ones. With the Internet, it's so easy for kids to find and clip information (without even getting a cramp in their wrists) that they tend to gather way too much material, often completely indiscriminately.

Half the time the kids don't even read what they clip. When we were in high school plagiarizing our research papers from the World Book, at least we had to copy all the words by hand! Harumph! And while we were copying the information about the exports of Uruguay we at least had to *read* the information. Kids today can electronically cut and paste an article into a paper without ever reading it.

So: making it easier to gather information doesn't make it easier to evaluate, sift, judge, weigh, or assess it. This is the same problem we always have with those note cards kids dutifully copy from whatever sources: which cards contain relevant, useful, valuable information and which ones are useless? No matter how the information is collected, we still must teach kids to determine its value—and so far, nothing I've seen on the Internet helps with this high-order thinking skill one bit. We'll still have to teach that one by hand.

So are there still some reasons for marching our kids through a traditional term-paper assignment, the old-fashioned way? We might say: it will get them ready for college. Well, at most of the colleges our kids will attend, there will be even better technology facilities than we have at BPHS. They will have computers in their dorm rooms with fast Internet access—and they'll need to know how to use it. Well, maybe the old-fashioned research paper process, with all of its laborious steps, builds character. That's a better argument, but I still worry about anything that distorts or misrepresents the writing process for students. I keep coming back to the idea that the more congruent our teaching can be with the way real people operate in the real world, the better off the kids we will be.

Whew! We have a lot to weigh—and a lot to learn ourselves. Let's keep this conversation going.

As great as computers are, they are not the only valuable form of instructional technology. At BPHS, video has been a very important tool as well. Our ongoing partnerships with several video-oriented organizations, including Chicago Community Television Network, Street-Level Video, and the Museum of Broadcast Communications, have involved scores of our students in video production and editing, leading to career aspirations for many and part-time and summer jobs for several. In these weekly internships and after-school projects, many of our kids have been producers of programs, on-camera talent, technical crew, and editors. Back in the classroom, our teachers encourage students to make video presentations and reports in place of the traditional written papers. And as our first class graduated in June 2000, they produced our first-ever BPHS video yearbook. Throughout, we have noticed that certain kids express themselves much more fully and reveal their special insights when they get behind a camera, showing a type of intelligence that doesn't always manifest itself in traditional classroom discussions or written homework.

TEXTBOOKS

The backpack has become the symbol of American studenthood. Every morning, about fifty million young people trudge off to school toting these ubiquitous carryalls, mostly made by Eddie Bauer—and apparently, only in dark green. So what do our children carry in those backpacks? Well, textbooks, of course—math, English, history, science, foreign language, home economics, art, and others—perhaps along with a couple of spiral notebooks, some pencils, pens, and gum they're not supposed to chew.

Some of us remember going to school carrying our books under our arms. In those days, using a container of any kind, like a briefcase, would have been both unnecessary and unspeakably geeky. But today, with the vastly expanded size of the average high school textbook, the casual underarm grip will no longer suffice. Luggage is required. Indeed, orthopedic surgery conventions now feature sessions on backpack syndrome—teenagers and young children being treated for spinal injuries caused by the ponderous loads of today's textbooks. The backpack industry, which apparently tracks both educational and medical trends, has begun introducing rolling backpacks, much like flight-attendant suitcases, that allow kids to drag rather than shoulder their book burden.

Harvey remembers his daughter's first visit to the high school bookstore, just before freshman year. This errand resulted in a stack of seventeen books and a $300 bill. When we got home, we put the books on the bathroom scale, just out of scientific curiosity: forty pounds. Forty pounds! Just about the same weight, Harvey thought, as a bag of sand you'd buy at the hardware store—the one you'd better hoist very gingerly into the trunk unless you want to spend a week flat on your back. Just about the same weight, Marny's Mom remembered, as a three-year-old child, the age when they are getting too heavy to carry around.

Marny's allocation of books wouldn't fit in a single backpack, no matter how we tried to pack and repack them. She was worried. She had heard ominous rumors: you get a Saturday "breakfast club" if a teacher catches you without all your books. Finally, she reluctantly agreed to leave a couple of obscure workbooks home, and at last the zipper turned the final corner. Ready for school!

After her first day, Marny came home and gratefully threw down her backpack. How'd it go? She'd survived, in spite of the long and steamy hike between some classes. She'd shouldered her burden successfully—as a strong, six-foot-tall girl, she could handle it. But some of the smaller kids would simply tip over when they put on their backpacks. This became especially problematic in the stairwells. If it weren't for the closely packed crush of traffic, Marny reported, all these unbalanced teenagers would have tumbled backward into a pileup of people and bookbags.

So the question is: forty pounds of *what*? For what are we risking the spines and safety of our teens? The centrality of textbooks in American education would be hard to overestimate. For many classes and teachers, the textbook is the basis, the core, and the Bible. It is the source of the content to be learned in a given class and may also provide drills, exercises, homework assignments, and tests—as well as detailed plans for what the teacher might say and do. Though most high schools have their own curriculum guides specifying the content of every course, these are often copied from the table of contents of whatever textbook the school previously adopted. Textbooks are even legally exalted in states like Texas and California, where elaborate adoption hearings spawn politics, pandering, the exchange of big bucks, and rumors of who knows what other kinds of favors. In our home state of Illinois, every school gets a yearly allocation of funds for books—but only for official textbooks. It's illegal to use the funds for sets of novels or nonfiction books.

So what exactly are these weighty, powerful, iconic ingredients of school? Textbooks are mainly storage systems for knowledge, repositories of information. Their job is to contain, in some organized fashion, the content or the body of knowledge that is calculus, British literature, or health. As a type of written language, a textbook is very different from a novel, biography, or magazine article. Because of the overarching need to pack in a huge amount of information, the content load in textbooks is far higher per sentence, per paragraph, per page than other kinds of language that occur out in the world. Textbooks also typically make fewer concessions to engaging or entertaining the reader. Algebra textbooks have no story with a beginning, middle, and end, no narrative thread that holds the text together and pulls a reader through.

School textbooks are a different kind of writing. In the nonschool world, authors of normal nonfiction, whether the topic is pollution, asteroids, or marriage, typically make many efforts to hook, engage, and entertain their readers. The first thing they do, of course, is narrow the topic—setting reasonable limits for what a reader might be expected to take away from any given chunk of text. Then the authors pace their information, slow things down, offer comparisons, metaphors, and connections, to make sure the reader gets it. Though school textbooks of course make some efforts to connect with their kid audience, this goal is always secondary to packing in the information.

In other words, *school textbooks are not like normal books*. Their "content overloaded" style makes for very, very tough reading. Kids who can effortlessly understand and enjoy novels written at their grade level or magazine articles about their favorite hobby may have enormous difficulty comprehending material in a textbook designed for the same grade level. This isn't just the kid's fault. Indeed, we adults should take an honest look at a high school textbook, read one page, and then quiz ourselves: how much do I understand and remember? Sometimes in workshops, we have had teachers bring in their own textbooks and exchange them with teachers in other disciplines, taking a few minutes to read some of the material that students are expected to understand. It is often an eye-opening experience to hear that the text we find so clear and accessible in our own teaching field is utterly confounding to another educated adult.

There is absolutely nothing inherently wrong with textbooks. As storage systems for information, they can be tremendously useful. The trouble comes from how we use them. In American schools, we have a long history of using them wrong, and the single most prevalent misuse is memorization. In the real world, even experts do not commit all information in their field to memory; they learn where to find information when needed, and it collects in their memory as they use it. Textbooks, properly used, are a wonderful resource—a place to look up information when we need it. Indeed, teachers who conduct "open-book" tests are actually teaching students a much more appropriate, reality-based use of textbooks.

Of course, textbook publishers are far from innocent in the ongoing misuse of their products. They encourage lower-order thinking by including factual recall questions at the end of each chapter, and offering teachers handy quizzes and tests that stress memorization of details over the understanding and application of key concepts. In their defense, publishers argue that they are only giving the teachers what they want—and that more progressive texts don't sell as well as the traditional ones.

Obviously, textbooks are very firmly entrenched in American education and will remain part of the high school scene for years—probably generations—to come. The industry is powerful; textbooks are institutionalized in many ways. Teachers have become dependent on them, some even living out their whole careers teaching from a single textbook and its succeeding, thicker and thicker editions. As a result, these teachers literally do not know how to teach without this encyclopedic prop—or don't want to. So does this mean that high school curriculum will remain a captive to textbooks and their makers?

Fortunately plenty of teachers have found ways to broaden their kids' reading lists and roam far beyond the textbook. A dedicated student teacher like Michelle Weitz can show us how—and why—to step away from the lock-step memorization curriculum. Working with cooperating teacher Melinda Zibart at Sunset Ridge School in Northfield, Illinois, Michelle was eager to design a unit on the Holocaust around the classic *Anne Frank: The Diary of a Young Girl*. Before assigning the book, she wanted the kids to deeply understand the period, the place, and the context of Anne Frank's powerful story. But she was disappointed by the adopted history textbook's shallow coverage. While it spent seven pages on the events leading up to the "Final Solution," the text failed to convey either the actuality or the horror of these events. Michelle explains:

As I looked through available resources, including both our Social Studies and Language Arts textbooks, I couldn't find anything that was both accurate and engaging. So I went back to Anne Frank's diary for ideas. In the first ten pages of the book, Anne talks about the world she knows and how it is changing: "The anti-Jewish decrees follow in quick succession. So we could not do this and were forbidden to do that. But life went on in spite of it all."

I thought to myself, "Wouldn't it be valuable to explore these laws? I'm certain that there must be a list of these anti-Jewish decrees somewhere, but there was no complete listing of them in any social studies textbook or Anne Frank unit I could find. Gradually, I was able to assemble bits and pieces in different places, often mixed with other military or political events. I decided it would be most powerful to combine the anti-Jewish restrictions and laws into a single timeline. This was painstaking work—it took hours of research to create this document.

Timeline of Anti-Jewish Legislation

Jan. 30, 1933—Adolf Hitler is appointed Chancellor of Germany: a nation with a Jewish population of 566,000.

Apr. 1, 1933—Nazis stage boycott of Jewish shops and businesses.

Apr. 11, 1933—Nazis issue a decree defining a non-Aryan as "anyone descended from non-Aryan, especially Jewish, parents or grandparents. One parent or grandparent classifies the descendant as non-Aryan . . . especially if one parent or grandparent was of the Jewish faith."

Sept. 1933—Nazis establish Reich Chamber of Culture, exclude Jews from the arts.

Sept. 29, 1933—Nazis prohibit Jews from owning land.

Oct. 4, 1933—Jews are prohibited from being newspaper editors.

Jan. 24, 1934—Jews are banned from the German Labor Front.

May 17, 1934—Jews not allowed national health insurance.

May 31, 1935—Nazis ban Jews from serving in the military.

Aug. 6, 1935—Nazis force Jewish performers/artists to join Jewish Cultural Unions.

Sept. 15, 1935—Nuremberg Race Laws against Jews decreed, including the following:

1. Marriages between Jews and subjects of the state of Germany are forbidden.
2. Jews may not employ in their households female subjects of the state of Germany who are under 45 years old.
3. Jews are forbidden to fly the Reich or National flag or to display the Reich colors.

Nov. 14, 1935—Citizenship Law

1. A Jew cannot be a Reich citizen. He has no voting rights in political matters; he cannot occupy a public office.

2. a. A Jew is a person descended from at least three grandparents who are full Jews by race.

   b. A Mischling (mixed race) who is a subject of the state is also considered a Jew if he is descended from two full Jewish grandparents; and was a member of the Jewish Religious Community at the time of this law; who was married to a Jew at the time of this law; who was born from a relationship (marital or extramarital) with a Jew.

Jan. 1937—Jews are banned from many professional occupations, including teaching Germans, and from being accountants or dentists. They are also denied tax reductions and child allowances.

Apr. 22, 1938—Nazis prohibit Aryan "front-ownership" of Jewish businesses.

Apr. 26, 1938—Nazis order Jews to register wealth and property.

June 14, 1938—Nazis order Jewish-owned businesses to register.

July 6, 1938—Nazis prohibit Jews from trading and providing a variety of specified commercial services.

July 23, 1938—Nazis order Jews over age 15 to apply for identity cards from the police, to be shown on demand to any police officer.

July 25, 1938—Jewish doctors prohibited by law from practicing medicine.

Aug. 11, 1938—Nazis destroy the synagogue in Nuremberg.

Aug. 17, 1938—Nazis require Jewish women to add Sarah and men to add Israel to their names on all legal documents including passports.

Sept. 27, 1938—Jews are prohibited from all legal practices.

Oct. 5, 1938—Law requires Jewish passports to be stamped with a large red "J."

Nov. 15, 1938—Jewish pupils are expelled from all non-Jewish German schools.

Dec. 3, 1938—Law for compulsory Aryanization of all Jewish businesses.

Jan. 30, 1939—Hitler threatens Jews during Reichstag speech.

Feb. 21, 1939—Nazis force Jews to hand over all gold and silver items.

Apr. 30, 1939—Jews lose rights as tenants and are relocated into Jewish houses.

July 4, 1939—German Jews denied the right to hold government jobs.

Sept. 1, 1939—Jews in Germany are forbidden to be outdoors after 8 P.M. in winter and 9 P.M. in summer.

Sept. 23, 1939—German Jews are forbidden to own wireless (radio) sets.

Oct. 6, 1939—Proclamation by Hitler on the isolation of Jews.

I wanted students to understand that this series of anti-Jewish laws affected different people and families in different ways. I thought perhaps a role-play might enable the students to enter the timeline and really feel its impact. I designed fictional "families" that would work together to review the timeline and evaluate the laws and restrictions. Sample roles included:

You are part of family A. You are the father in the family. You have a wife and two children. You are Jewish, but your wife is not.

You are a member of family B. You are a religious Jewish family. You are the mother in the family, and suffering from several serious medical conditions for which you rely upon your husband's veteran status to receive state-sponsored health insurance.

You are a member of family C. You are not Jewish. You are the mother in the family. Your husband owns and operates several businesses that are managed by Jews and that offer services to the Jewish community. Your best friend, Liesel, is Jewish.

You are a member of family D. You are Jewish. You are a prominent, well-recognized physician in the community who has both Jewish and non-Jewish patients. You also own several highly valuable pieces of real estate in Germany.

You are the editor of a liberal local newspaper. You are a Jewish man, currently engaged to a non-Jewish woman.

You are an extremely patriotic German Jew. You firmly believe in the country, the government, and all that Germany has to offer.

I handed out the timeline of events to each student, and asked them to read quietly through the list. Then I asked each group to move to a quiet location around the room and gave each one their "family" to role-play. The instructions suggested: As a group, decide which law would have the greatest impact on you and your family. Would a different law have a greater impact on you if you were alone? Which law most severely restricts individual freedoms? As a group, you must reach a consensus.

In all honesty, I was shocked at how involved and interested all of the students were in the activity. They really considered their options, debated pros and cons within the group, and came up with well-supported reasoning. What I (and I think the students) found most fascinating was when we reconvened as a large group, we all had focused on different laws and different reasoning. Now, I expected this in some circumstances, but to hear the students clearly articulate the importance of health over money, or together-ness over separating a family, was both wonderful and so rewarding.

Michelle's Holocaust unit is an admirable example of how a teacher can go beyond the textbook to use multiple and primary sources. It also shows a teacher becoming a real researcher herself as she creates materials for her students. This story also shows how much extra time and effort it takes to replace traditional textbooks with more balanced, richer, and more engaging materials. Workaday teachers cannot be expected to make such extraordinary out-of-school efforts every day; after all, who's going to coach softball and who's going to make dinner at home? It takes years of a career to assemble such materials, and it takes teams of colleagues working together inside of and across departments to gradually acquire books, articles, files, folders, documents, pages, shelves of better materials.

How to Use a Textbook

Until all teachers possess these rich sets of hands-on materials, the traditional slick-covered, seven-pound textbooks will still have an important role to play in our high schools. How they are used makes a big difference. Here's what we've learned so far about using textbooks more wisely and effectively:

1. *Use textbooks less.* Dependence on single sources of information misrepresents the way scholars and experts in most fields actually operate. Real experts draw on a wide range of sources to understand their field, and we should start modeling this intellectual reality in school. Respect the enormous difficulty of typical textbook material by assigning short, critical passages only. Spend time on the truly important sections and omit chaff.

2. *Slow down.* If you're going to use textbook selections, allow enough time for students to build comprehension, not just skim. Of course, slowing down necessarily goes with the idea of assigning selected chunks, not the whole book.

3. *Substitute with real, readable sources in place of content-overloaded textbooks.* Build an inventory of other materials: magazine and newspaper articles, graphs and charts, historical novels, primary source documents, biographies of historical figures.

4. *Teach kids the specific reading skills they need to cope with dense nonfiction text.* If you are in a situation where you must stick to a

textbook, remember: students will learn and remember information best when they *act upon the material*. That means teachers must employ before-reading, during-reading, and after-reading activities that help kids activate prior knowledge, set purposes for reading, monitor their comprehension, and actively construct meaning.

5. *Jigsaw textbook assignments*. Everybody does not need to read everything! Have different kids read different sections and then put them together.

6. *Give students choices*. As you become more selective about what sections of a textbook you assign, invite students to follow your model by selecting their own readings when appropriate.

7. *Make reading more social and collaborative*. Use pairs, partners, groups, or teams at all stages of the reading process.

8. *Do more reading during class time*. If the text is really important, but kids can't dig out the meaning on their own, then we must provide time and support to make sure they succeed. Cover less material more thoroughly.

9. *Read aloud to introduce selections*. This helps build interest and momentum.

10. *Provide for real applications*. Help students find meaningful connections in the real world—not just take quizzes on the information.

11. *Avoid the read-test trap*. Don't test only for factual recall. Let students approach textbooks like everyday reading, seeking the main themes and the big ideas.

12. *Don't give lectures that duplicate the textbook*. Create activities that help students process and analyze information instead.

13. *Work to change your school's textbook-driven curriculum*. Lobby for one that includes a wide range of real literature—novels, autobiographies, essays, journalism, research reports, primary sources in all content areas.

FINDING YOUR NEXT STEPS

Surf the Internet: Browse through the staggering and entertaining variety of high school websites from around the country. The search term "high school" will get thousands of hits. No matter how good your own school's website may already be, you'll discover plenty of exciting ideas to steal and adapt.

Bookmark the most interesting sites and feed them to your school's website designers (let's hope some of these will be students, who will know more and be more adept than any grown-up in the building).

Study: All schools that enjoy the government's "e-rate" for Internet access must prepare and update a "technology plan," detailing current and future uses of technology in the school. If your school's tech plan isn't already in wide circulation, make copies and share it with interested staff, kids, and parents. Convene a discussion of the document, asking how well it matches the goals and needs of everyone concerned. Your group could volunteer to write an addendum to the tech plan, submitting it to school officials.

Chart: Make a map, a visual representation of the ways technology is currently being used across the curriculum in your school, to find strengths, gaps, and opportunities for growth. You might seek this information from interviews with faculty, looking at old computer lab schedules, and checking with department heads.

Read and Discuss: Gather a group of faculty members from a broad range of disciplines. Exchange textbooks with each other, so that everyone receives a textbook from outside his or her own field. Then go home and read the textbook for one hour. Make notes on the experience: How did you feel as a reader? How would you expect students to experience this text? What made the textbook hard or easy to understand? What suggestions might you offer to the textbook writers if you could advise them? How did this textbook compare to the ones you routinely use in your own teaching field? Meet with colleagues to share impressions. To spur discussion, you might use the "How to Use a Textbook" tips on pages 214–215. Which of these suggestions seem applicable to your school or subject areas?

Try Out: To help students better understand the material in textbooks or other nonfiction materials, read Stephanie Harvey and Anne Goudvis' *Strategies That Work: Teaching Comprehension to Enhance Understanding*, which uses short pieces of nonfiction text to teach kids how to visualize, infer, analyze, question, and remember what they read. Then meet with a group of colleagues to try out some of these practical strategies yourselves, using some pieces of text from your own curriculum. Next, select the most promising activities and implement them in your own classrooms. Finally, meet again with colleagues to compare notes, adjust and adapt, and select another strategy to try in the classroom.

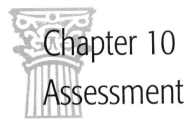

Chapter 10
Assessment

Teachers help students monitor, evaluate,
and guide their own thinking.

A rt teacher Aiko Boyce holds up a handful of photos of students'
art projects. Laura Linhart shows a handful of artifacts from her
students' excursion to an Hispanic neighborhood. Tom McDougal waves his latest math assessment rubric in the air. French teacher
Theresa Hernandez displays a stack of large vocabulary roots and endings posted on notecards. Marilyn and Steve are leading the Best Practice
faculty through a short workshop on portfolio assessment, and to illus-
trate how it works, teachers are sharing in the start to their own professional portfolios.

Teachers find that many students have little experience with reflection, and that for portfolios to be worthwhile, students need to work on
the reflective process. So each teacher has brought something that exem-
plifies high quality in his or her own instructional program: student
work, pictures, plans, and other artifacts. After each teacher describes
the artifact to the group, we brainstorm ways they might write a reflection about it. The teachers draft their reflective pieces, contextualizing
the artifact and explaining its significance. As they share their reflections
with a partner, the room becomes electric with animated conversation. It
is easy to observe that powerful dialogues have been ignited.

Steve then asks the teachers a simple question: "If someone were to
look at your artifact alone, to what extent would they understand your
achievement? And how much would they learn from the reflection? Take
a guess at the percentages." The teachers estimate: some think there
would be a 30 percent understanding with just the artifact and 70

percent would come from the reflection. Others figure only 10 percent of the value could be seen in the artifact alone and 90 percent would appear in the reflection. The point is clear: the reflective process is key to developing a portfolio and gives both teacher and student crucial information for assessing learning.

This workshop took place, not as we started the school, but in the spring of our fourth year. Why did it take so long for us to get to working on assessment? As we dreamed and planned the school, meeting together around Tom and Kathy's dining room table, reading books and articles and sharing them with each other, and visiting powerful new, small high schools, we were overwhelmed with the sheer quantity of decisions to be made. Gradually, however, our planning process led to a list of design features that we could all agree upon. We wanted our new school to have:

- small total size
- heterogeneous student body
- teacher decision making
- student-centered instruction featuring reading-writing workshop
- student choice during part of the weekly schedule
- inclusion of special education in regular classrooms
- daily advisory
- some form of block scheduling
- technology-rich instruction
- service learning
- parent involvement
- community partnerships
- a caring environment
- authentic assessment.

At the very bottom of the list was authentic assessment. We all knew that we hated the way assessment is handled in schools, and we wanted something better—but what? In some of our visits, we saw schools that had started with a design for assessment and worked backward to curriculum and instruction. Often, this seemed to create a solitary senior experience in which students worked alone on required graduation portfolios. This didn't jibe with the student-centered, authentic, and collaborative experiences that we were convinced would bring power and substance to the lives of young people.

But as our list of design features kept growing and started to include items like "order chairs" and "hire PE teacher," assessment always lingered at the bottom. With the luxury of hindsight, we have to admit that we also suffered from "assessment aversion." The toxic effects of grading and testing on our own lives, the lives of our sons and daughters, and many of our students left us reluctant to specifically and programatically address this very slippery aspect of schooling.

Of course we had opinions and vague visions. We knew we wanted to avoid using tests as much as possible and substitute projects as the primary way that students would demonstrate what they knew and could do. We were opposed to letter grades that had little detail and significance, and we wanted students to become self-evaluators, taking charge of their own learning. We knew that portfolios were an excellent way of showcasing student growth across time. But the procedural questions remained: How would we evaluate? When would we evaluate? Why would we evaluate? Who would evaluate?

But since we all tended to avoid the subject, the early BPHS teachers, even with their hearts in the right places, were pretty much left on their own in designing assessment procedures. While some experimented with rubrics, others with portfolios, and others with self-evaluation, traditional homework points, tests, and grades also remained the norm. It was not until our fourth year that we carved out the time and mental energy to give assessment the attention we knew it and our students deserved.

Of all the elements of BPHS, our approach to assessment is probably our most traditional, our least innovative feature. Our portfolio assessment process is in its infancy, and students and teachers alike are working to refine it. So ours is certainly not the definitive story on alternative assessment. Instead we are a work in progress, trying to catch up with the thinking of other schools that can help us to learn and grow.

WHAT IS GOOD ASSESSMENT?

How *do* good teachers and smart schools make assessment more meaningful and ensure that it creates improved learning for kids? Not long ago, we heard a high-ranking school administrator, in defending his system's many-layered, time-consuming standardized test program ask, "If we don't teach to the test, what do we teach to?" Well, how about teaching to the students? This simple rhetorical switch helps us place the emphasis where it belongs—on student learning. Teachers at all grade levels can view every part of the teaching role, even designing assessments, as part of facilitating student learning. In practice, teachers can achieve this with assessment in the following ways:

1. Assessment should reflect, encourage, and *become an integral part of good instruction*. While many traditional measures occur separate from or after teaching, the most powerful assessment activities—such as conferences, analytic scoring scales, and portfolios—can be made ingredients of good instruction.

2. Powerful evaluation efforts focus on the major, *whole outcomes* valued in the curriculum: real, complex performances of writing, researching, reading, experimenting, problem solving, creating, speaking, and so on.

3. Most school assessment activities should be *formative*. This means that we assess primarily to ensure that students learn better and teachers teach more effectively.

4. Constructive programs increasingly rely on *self-referenced growth measures*. Traditional norm-referenced competitive measures that rank students against each other (such as letter grades and numerically scored tests) provide little helpful formative assessment and tend to undermine progressive instruction.

5. Effective thinkers, writers, problem solvers, readers, and researchers constantly *self-monitor and self-evaluate*. A solid assessment program must help students to take responsibility for their own record keeping and self-reflection.

6. Skillful and experienced evaluators take a *developmental perspective*. Rather than checking students against arbitrary age- or grade-level targets, teachers track the story of each child's individual growth through developmental phases.

7. Teachers need a *rich repertoire of assessment strategies* in designing sensitive, *appropriate evaluation* activities for particular curriculum areas. Among these are anecdotal/observational records, checklists, interviews, portfolios, performance assessments, and classroom tests.

8. We now use *multiple measures* for assessment, examining students' growth from several different perspectives. It is never enough to look at learning events from only one angle.

9. Teachers need to *reallocate the considerable time they spend on assessment*, record keeping, and grading. They need to spend less time scoring and more time saving and documenting student work. New assessment procedures should not require any more time of teachers than the old ways.

10. Sound evaluation programs provide, where necessary, a data base for deriving *legitimate, defensible student grades*, though at the same time teachers and schools must work to de-emphasize and replace norm-referenced grading.

11. It takes *many different people working cooperatively* to effectively evaluate student growth and learning. There should be a balance between external assessment such as standardized tests, teacher-run evaluation, student self-evaluation, parent involvement in assessment, and collaborative assessments involving these parties.

12. Teachers should *show colleagues, parents, and administrators the more sophisticated, detailed, accurate, and meaningful assessments* they have developed for their own classrooms. This can help de-emphasize the currently available standardized tests that yield an exceedingly narrow and unreliable picture of student achievement.

(Adapted from Daniels and Bizar 1998)

PORTFOLIOS

One of the most effective ways to enact many of these principles is to use portfolios to provide a record of growth, thinking, self-reflection, and goal setting as the student progresses through his or her high school career. Portfolios can represent the learning in individual content classes, achievement in particular integrated study units, or growth across content areas over a four-year period.

Many high school teachers who use portfolios ask students to *collect* samples in working folders—rough and polished; written, drawn, acted, and painted; individual and collaborative. Students may include videotapes, records of experiments, graphs, narratives of research and inquiry projects, photographs, essays, poetry, artifacts, and other representations of learning that we haven't even thought of. From the large collection in their working folders, they *select* important pieces to be included in their portfolios. Items are chosen for various reasons: best work, examples of growth, display of genres covered, artistic merit, demonstration of particular skills such as use of detail, to name a few. As pieces are selected, students are given time to *reflect* upon the work and the reasons it was chosen to be included. This reflective process includes a whole range of important learning activities for students:

- becoming aware of what one has learned and achieved
- evaluating one's own strengths and weaknesses
- identifying strategies used successfully and others that may help in doing better
- setting goals for the next unit of study.

It's important to understand that there are several very different approaches to portfolios. One kind of portfolio is a record of a student's work and reflection over a period of time such as a quarter or semester. It may include first drafts, earlier less-successful projects, and the student's thoughts on how he or she is improving or might do better. It is, in other words, a longitudinal record of the student's learning. By another definition, a portfolio is a display of the student's best work, a final, grand presentation that includes a variety of projects and outcomes. Its focus is on assessment of prepared performance, rather than a history of learning. Let's look at an example of each one.

The Portfolio as a Record of Growth

At BPHS, portfolios are used to provide students, teachers, and parents a sense of the student's growth throughout their high school careers. The process itself is still evolving, and teachers are working to implement and refine it. Students develop their portfolios by placing one piece from each subject into the showcase portfolio at the end of each marking period. Students write reflections for each item explaining to the reader the rationale for including the piece.

The portfolios stay with each student's advisory teacher, and at the end of each quarter, students spend a week in advisory, reading and responding to their peers' portfolios. Student portfolios are shared with parents at the time of report-card pickup (in Chicago, parents must come to school to obtain students' report cards). An upcoming further step at Best Practice will involve student-led conferences, where students guide their parents through their portfolios, and the teachers are present to answer questions and pour coffee. In this approach, the teacher becomes an event facilitator, while students are the main attraction, sharing their portfolios and explaining their work. Another goal we've just begun working on: helping students to digitize their portfolios, moving toward websites as a final form of portfolio publication.

The Portfolio as a Final Presentation

Like many members of the Coalition of Essential Schools, Central Park East Secondary School in New York City employs portfolios as a series of final performances required of seniors for graduation. Students in the Senior Institute graduate by completing fourteen separate portfolio requirements designed to reflect cumulative knowledge and skill in each subject and to demonstrate the "habits of mind and work" that are stressed throughout the school. Following are the fourteen portfolio areas:

1. Postgraduate Plan
2. Science/Technology*
3. Mathematics*
4. Literature*
5. History and Social Studies*
6. Autobiography
7. School and Community Service and Internship
8. Ethics and Social Issues
9. Fine Arts/Aesthetics
10. Practical Skills
11. Media
12. Geography
13. Language Other Than English
14. Physical Challenge.

The majority of the work displayed in a portfolio is the outcome of the courses, seminars, internships, and independent study that a student has engaged in during the normal course of her two Senior Institute years. Included in these fourteen areas are seven "majors" and seven "minors." Students are encouraged to be creative, as there is no one way to complete the portfolios and no one way to present them.

Each student must make a major presentation in seven areas, including the four starred subjects and three others chosen in cooperation with his/her advisor. Passing is upon recommendation of the advisor and approval of a committee of teachers and outside community members. Portfolios are evaluated on quality and depth of understanding, good use of the habits of mind, and the capacity to present competent and convincing evidence of mastery of the subject matter. Both substance and style are important; here are the items in the scoring rubric that is used:

- viewpoint
- evidence
- connections
- voice
- conventions.

Central Park East Secondary School considers student portfolios to be the product of the curriculum and the culmination of the entire school experience.

GRADING

Even when they follow a more meaningful process for assessing student work, most teachers in high schools across the country still have to boil the results down to a single grade for the semester. This raises a complex and difficult question: what and whom are grades for, and why do we give them? One of the insidious aspects of grading is that while assigning a letter grade can look simple, when we look deeper, there are disturbing complexities. For example, for whom do we give the grade? If it were only for the student and her parents, why not give two grades, one for effort and one for understanding, a practice adopted by many elementary schools? But at the high school level, grades also feed the competitive race for college admissions, and so we reduce students' efforts and accomplishments into one letter grade, something that ranks kids but communicates little significant information about them.

But it's still more contradictory than that. Even if the grade is given to communicate with the student, what do we hope it will accomplish? Is it given to motivate (Alfie Kohn, the articulate critic of behaviorism, would definitely have problems with this), to help the student understand and set goals, or perhaps to reward or punish? It's nearly impossible for a teacher to do one of these without undermining the others. Concerned teachers struggle with these serious questions every time they sit down to reduce a student to a single letter or number.

Still, one of the most universal—indeed, defining—ingredients of American public high schools is their function in comparing and ranking students. The following grading chart, used at a suburban high school, is fairly typical—and shows how tortured and technical this preoccupation can become, especially when students are categorized into five "ability levels."

Grade Weights as of 1999–2000

Ability Level:	1	2*	3	4	5
A	3.33	4.00	4.67	5.33	5.67
A–	3.00	3.67	4.33	5.00	5.33
B+	2.67	3.33	4.00	4.67	5.00
B	2.33	3.00	3.67	4.33	4.67
B–	2.00	2.67	3.33	4.00	4.33
C+	1.67	2.33	3.00	3.67	4.00
C	1.33	2.00	2.67	3.33	3.67
C–	1.00	1.67	2.33	3.00	3.33
D+	.67	1.33	2.00	2.33	2.67
D	.33	1.00	1.33	1.67	2.00
D–	.33	.33	.67	1.00	1.33
F	0	0	0	0	0

*This column is used when computing unweighted averages.

An immediately evident peculiarity is that some students can graduate with a 5.67 GPA on a scale where the standard "unweighted" maximum is 4.0. The astute reader of this matrix will also note that a student getting all A's in the lowest-track courses simply cannot achieve a 4.0 GPA. Conversely, a student who earns a C in a level-5 course gets more points than the basic-track kid earning an A. A level-5 slacker who slides by with a D gets the same GPA points as a low-track kid fighting for a B–. And so on.

Grading systems like these obviously obstruct learning and distort everyone's behavior. For highly competitive kids fighting for top class rank and elite college admissions, such elaborate grading systems spawn a complex game of course selection by point calculation. Why not take a level-5 course instead of a level-4? Even if I coast a bit with a B, it is still worth the same as an A in the middle track. One young friend of ours who was in the running for valedictorian in his senior year had to make an agonizing choice. Unless he selected all top-level classes, with their bonus GPA points, he couldn't win the valedictorian race. But one of the courses he wanted to take—photography—didn't have an AP section, so even an A in the class would drag down his GPA. To Jerry's credit, he took the photography and stepped out of the race.

We're now seeing evidence that grades actually have a negative effect on student learning. In a talk at the January 2000 annual meeting of the Principal

Investigators for Local Systemic Change, Paul Black described how the research of Israeli Ruth Butler raises this concern. Butler divided 132 eleven- and twelve-year-olds into three groups: A, B, and C. All the kids experienced the same teaching by two instructors who communicated the same aims and criteria to all classes. All students were asked to produce the same work to be graded. The three groups were given feedback in different ways: Group A was given only comments on their work, with no grades. Group B was given only grades, unaccompanied by comments. Group C was given grades and comments. Group A showed 30 percent gain in learning, and Groups B and C showed no gain in learning. Black concludes "the first two groups showed that comments help and grades do not. This third group shows that if you give both together, the grades wipe out the positive effects of the comments."

Of course, high school grading, with all of its hurts, inequities, and inconsistencies, is nothing new. Secondary schools long ago assumed the role of screening, labeling, and classifying young people—and became a key institution in allocating students to future life opportunities. Get good grades, and you go to a nice college; do poorly, and you start work at graduation. Get really bad grades, and you'll be held back, or pushed out without even a high school diploma to show the boss at your prospective minimum-wage job.

The adverse—some say catastrophic—effect of grades on learning has been documented and decried by many experts before us. Almost every major school reformer of the past century has argued that grades stand between young people and their education. In general the critique holds that the grading system in schools serves to prop up the existing social order, validating the offspring of the privileged. If you look at the correlation between school grades, test scores, and family income, this inequity is hard to deny.

But just when we start thinking it is impossible to ever deal with the grading problem, we hear about a hopeful development like the one taking place at Highland Park High School. Located in one of Chicago's most elite lakeside suburbs, Highland Park has long been noted for its powerful parent community, which is fiercely focused on top-rank college admissions for their offspring. So when four teachers, with the full support of Superintendent Linda Hanson, proposed eliminating all daily, weekly, and midsemester grades from a pilot group of courses, savvy observers predicted a firestorm of parental outrage. This community will never accept "alternative assessment," the reasoning went. They'll demand hard numbers, letter grades, and rankings—not conferences and portfolios with a single end-of-semester grade.

But, for three years now, students and teachers have pursued this experiment with little resistance. And the parents—not a voluntary or handpicked group, but a cross section of the families whose students enrolled in these classes—have bought into the experiment, many of them with enthusiasm. Teachers report that removing the burden (and the threat) of daily grading has opened up and deepened their instruction. Of course, it is a major concession to tradition that each teacher does finally assign a letter grade at the end of the eighteen-week semester. But this grade comes as no surprise when students have been conferring with their teacher and monitoring their own work throughout the term. Whether this experiment will spread further through this or other schools remains to be seen. But it has at least shown us that daily or weekly grades—those long strings of numbers, checks, and letters in the teacher's record book—are in no way necessary to conducting challenging, effective education for teenagers.

Student-Centered Grading: Brainstorming Performance Assessments with Kids

Earlier we said that teachers should make assessment a part of instruction. Well, it sounds good, but putting this attractive idea into action requires deep changes in the way schools work. In most schools and classrooms, assessment is something that very definitely happens *after* instruction—when the teacher puts a grade on a finished research paper or science project. But when we assess a kid's term paper with a B–, in what sense is this instructional? How does this instruct the kid about writing term papers? What does it explain about the strengths and weaknesses of his effort? How does it help the student to do better next time? Obviously, the function and intention of such assessment isn't instructional at all; instead it is a summative assessment, used for reporting to some outside entity (parents, the state, etc.) about how the kid did compared to some others.

The procedure we are about to describe is the closest we've come to bridging the gap between meaningful assessment and narrower grading in schools where teachers are still required to give grades. While this process can yield a traditional numerical or letter grade, it also gives students a voice in setting the criteria for evaluation and may actually help them achieve goals that they have set for themselves. The basic idea is to develop and use performance assessment scoring rubrics, charts that break complex performances into multiple criteria with a numerical scale for each.

Such analytic scoring scales are quite common in educational literature—they have been used for rating essays, speeches, and work samples for decades. For example, here in Illinois, our state board of education decided that a successful piece of writing had four equally important traits—focus, support, organization, and conventions—across all genres of text. You might want to quibble with their formula, but if you are a teacher in this state, you'd better be sure that your kids can manifest those elements in their writing. Interestingly, when teachers started explicitly teaching these four key concepts, like supporting your position in a piece of writing, their students' writing actually got better. We were finally living the alternative assessor's dream—assessment was actually becoming part of instruction, a helpful and positive part.

But instead of letting the state do it, students can cocreate these rubrics with teachers, so they both own and understand the criteria. We learned about this from our work with literature circles, which are the school version of adult book clubs. When teachers began devoting classroom time to student-led book discussion groups, they began to worry about justifying this time expenditure with some kind of grade (just think how long an adult book club would last if one member gave out grades just before people put on their coats to go home!). We hit on the idea of having students try out the activity a few times and then define for themselves the criteria for evaluation. We figured that students would probably come up with just as meaningful and accurate evaluation criteria as adults—and that they would feel ownership of them to boot.

Our prediction was right. Using the following step-by-step process, kids consistently came up with meaningful scales—ones that largely included the ingredients we adults might have imposed upon them. But the fun part was that kids came up with scoring scales that were much more complex, idiosyncratic, and playful than anything we grown-ups would have devised. One of our favorite scoring guides for book clubs was created by a fifth-grade class—it listed thirteen different ingredients ranging from coming to class prepared (10 points), to having original ideas (22 points), to being well dressed for literature circle meetings (3 points).

Student-Created Assessment Rubrics

1. *The class identifies the performance to be assessed*—giving an informational speech, conducting a laboratory experiment, writing a sonnet, developing a website. In other words, what ability, project, activity, or chunk of curriculum do we need to assess?
2. After reading or observing several samples of the performance (samples should show various levels of success or ways of accomplishing the tasks), *individual students write down a list of words or phrases* associated with successful performance of the task at

hand (e.g., list some ingredients of a successful research paper, traits of an effective member of a collaborative group, etc.).

3. *The whole class shares and develops a list of these traits and ingredients* as the teacher jots them on a board or overhead screen.

4. Probably there will be dozens of widely assorted ingredients on the list. Now, *students in small groups categorize or group the list* into a smaller number of related items. Sometimes we press kids to group them into no more than three to five entries, even if this means leaving some minor ingredients out. After all, we don't have to evaluate everything all the time!

5. *Next comes the winnowing process.* We go through the items that kids came up with. Groups take turns proposing one element at a time. If one or more other groups have the same criterion, we star it as a possible "finalist." If groups have the same basic criterion under a different name (e.g., "supporting your argument" and "giving lots of examples"), we surface the commonality and agree on one name.

6. Now that we have arrived at a list of criteria—which is to say, we have broken down a successful performance in the target activity into four or five component ingredients—*the class figures out the relative importance of each criterion.* Is correct spelling as important as good organization in a piece of writing? If not, how much does each contribute to the overall quality? For this step, we give students a blank assessment rubric and a bank of 100 points to work with, and send them back to their small groups to determine point allocations for each of the agreed-upon criteria and fill in a simple form like this:

Blank Rubric Form

CRITERION   POINTS

1 _____   _____

2 _____   _____

3 _____   _____

4 _____   _____

5 _____   _____

                                              TOTAL_____/100_____

In old-time school, teachers never told kids what lay behind the A or the D we slapped on their papers. Disgruntled students would sometimes gripe that this kind of grading was subjective. More to the point, it was secret. Most good teachers actually did base those grades on a set of criteria that they could justify if pressed. If you asked a teacher to explain a low grade, she could usually mention specific flaws: it was poorly organized, lacked detail, was sloppy, or violated the conventions of standard English—though for many teachers these standards were being enforced unconsciously. The trouble was, most kids wouldn't dare to ask, and so the criteria remained unannounced and unexplained.

Rubrics like those we're proposing, on the other hand, are totally explicit. They are much like the scoring systems that food critics use to rate restaurants. One noted Chicago food writer gives 50 percent of his points to food, 20 percent to atmosphere, 20 percent to service, and 10 percent to value. The critic is saying that the single concept we call "good restaurant" actually has four component ingredients (food quality, atmosphere, service, and value). Further, he's said that some ingredients are more important than others, by assigning relative weights to each. The transfer to education is evident: if we can define the components of a successful performance and assign relative values to these components, we can provide an assessment that is far more detailed and meaningful than, say, a grade of C+. Indeed, when we are doing this activity with students, we sometimes start with the restaurant example, having kids come up with their own weighted scale—defending their own scores for McDonald's, Taco Bell, and other dining spots in their own neighborhoods.

At Best Practice High School, Tom McDougal's math students have worked collaboratively to develop rubrics that address four issues: classwork and participation, cooperative learning, mathematical skills, and independent work. The students collaborate with Mac to reach agreement about what is important in mathematics, and both students and teacher fill out the rubric and meet together to discuss the student's work and progress. Three aspects of this process come together to make it a powerful form of evaluation. First, the design of the rubric generates important discussion about what good work in math looks like and what students should be responsible for knowing and doing. Second, since self-evaluation is the most important form of assessment, this process helps to put students in charge of their own learning. And third, assessment becomes more meaningful for the teacher. While Mac still struggles with boiling so many dimensions into a single letter grade, he says, "When I'm sitting at home doing my grades, reading the student rubrics helps me to feel like I'm having a conversation with each student."

Tom McDougal's Math Rubric

Name _____ Date_____

Geometry Grading Rubric
Q4 1999–2000

Using class time to learn

How well do you use class discussions, activities, and presentations to advance your learning?

	F	D	C	B
During class assignments, how much of the time are you working?	50% or when the teacher reminds me	60%	70%	80%
During class discussions, what is your level of participation?	Disruptive (talking) or not paying attention		Mostly listening	
During a discussion or presentation, what do you do if you don't understanding something?	Don't notice, or Let it go		Ask someone at your table.	
What do you do on the openers	Usually don't do	Start, but usually don't finish.	Start when the teacher reminds me	Start right away, finish.
How often do you present?	never	once a quarter	twice a quarter	once per 2 weeks
Classes missed by absence	9 or more	6-8	4-5	3-4
Classes partly missed by tardiness	9 or more	8	6-7	4-5

Comments:

Group success

In which of the following ways do you contribute to the success of your group, and how often?

	Rarely	Sometimes— once a week
Make sure everyone knows what the assignment is		
Read part of an assignment aloud to the group		
Get help from the group before asking the teacher		
Help another group member [whom? _____]		
Encourage a group member ("Good idea," or "You're getting it")		
Discuss someone else's idea		
Remind group members to quiet down		

Other ways you help your group succeed:

Comments:

Independent work

What choices do you make with your own time to advance your own learning?

	F	D	C	B
How many hw assignments did you complete on time?	less than 40%	40-55%	55-75%	75-85%
What do you do when you don't understand part of the homework?	Nothing, or write "I don't understand," or copy off someone	Ask a friend or parent who doesn't know either	Reread it a few times, ask several friends who don't know either; leave it incomplete	[C-level] and: Ask or listen in class and fix
Did you do "Count the Pegs" POW?	No			

Tom McDougal's Math Rubric (continued)

Mathematical skills and understanding

Indicate your level of mastery of each skill or concept.

Skill or concept	Relevant assignments	Confused – Can't generally do it without help			Getting there — Can sometimes do it; a little reminder is all it takes	
Complex problem solving	Bags of Gold POW	0	1	2	3	4
	Count the Pegs POW	0	1	2	3	4
	Bees In-Class Assessment	0	1	2	3	
	Bees Take-Home/Swim Pool	0	1	2	3	
	Presentations					
Communicating a math idea or solution so others can understand.	Bags of Gold POW	0	1	2	3	4
	Count the Pegs POW	0	1	2	3	4
Solve triangles using sin, cos, tan						
Solve triangles using the Pythagorean Thm						
Explain what area, volume, surface area, and lateral surface area mean.						
Use formulas to compute areas of rectangles and triangles.						
Compute areas of regular polygons with 5 or more sides						
Determine surface area and volume of irregular shapes made with blocks						
Determine surface area and volume of boxes						
Solve Mystery Bags problems						
Substitute values and evaluate expressions						

Comments:

Other

What other strengths do you have?

Grade

Give yourself a grade for each category:

Using class time to learn	I give myself a _____	McDougal says:____
Group success	I give myself a _____	McDougal says:____
Independent work	I give myself a _____	McDougal says:____
Math skills and understanding	I give myself a _____	McDougal says:____
Overall grade	I give myself a _____	McDougal says:____

While this rubric process is far superior to the "secret" method of grading, it is important to recognize that it still has some limitations. First, the approach as we've described it allows for no surprises or serendipity. Suppose a student learns or achieves something really powerful that's not on the rubric. Perhaps this can be remedied with additional flexible lines added to the chart. But more problematic, as long as it is still being used to generate single letter grades, even a student-designed assessment rubric may still be feeding an evaluation system that undermines learning and motivation.

THE PROBLEM OF STANDARDIZED TESTS

An article in the *New York Times* (Mosco 2000) raises important questions about New York State's new Regents examination in English language arts and about testing in general. New York, just like most other states, responded to the cry to raise standards by writing an exam so difficult and obtuse that it loses all value. Consider this sentence from one of the passages students had to analyze and write about: "For I should see one stream within a score on me; then the space of two score, no snow would stir; but, after so much quantity of ground, another stream of snow, at the very same time, should be carried likewise, but not equally, for the one would stand still, when the other flew apace and so continue sometime swifter, sometime slower, sometime broader, sometime narrower, as far as I could see." This dense passage was only one example in a test that seemed to be designed to stump and frustrate, rather than assess student knowledge and skill.

We believe that a passage such as the one above would confound a great percentage of the adult population who manage to participate perfectly effectively in everyday life. Shouldn't this be a clue that something is wrong with the test? Not surprisingly, many students did poorly, even those who regularly demonstrated high-quality work. Along with the article, the *New York Times* printed this question:

Comprehensive Examination in English

a. Incomprehensible   c. Sadistic

b. Overly Long   d. Regents

e. All of the above

We choose all of the above.

In Chicago some of the academically elite students who attend Whitney Young, the city's highest-ranked public high school, responded to the ever-widening barrage of standardized tests in a dramatic way. Calling themselves Organized Students of Chicago, they rebelled against what they called a "test-taking frenzy" and deliberately flunked portions of the Illinois Goal Assessment Program (IGAP) exam. Since then, students from high schools across the city have joined the fight (Rhodes 2000).

In a petition the Whitney Young students explained, "We are tired of excessive emphasis on standardized tests—Our schools do have problems, but they can only be solved by actually changing the way students are educated instead of simply giving more tests." In a follow-up letter to Whitney Young principal Joyce Kenner, the students made their most stinging point: the emphasis on standardized testing was encouraging teachers to employ a narrow, programmed curriculum that shortchanged students on substance and challenge.

Nationally, many parents, teachers, principals, and other concerned parties worry that constant testing is forcing schools to dumb down the curriculum and reduce instruction to boring, mechanistic coverage of mandated content. Teachers who believe that students should learn topics in depth—rather than skim superficially over masses of material—feel caught in the middle. It's true that in classrooms where teachers and students explore curriculum relevant to students' lives, where students have choices of inquiry topics, and where they study these topics in depth, students usually do just fine on most of the tests, even when not explicitly prepped for them. But if you are a teacher whose reputation, even your job, depends on test scores, would you dare take the chance on progressive practices?

If one problem with tests is how they can degrade instruction, another is how they can affect students' learning. One of us observed this at a large high school in a Chicago suburb. As a group of students studied together for a history final exam, one of the most common comments was, "We don't have to learn that. It's not going to be on the test." In fact, these kids spent more time arguing about what to learn and what not to learn than actually studying for the test. The students were more invested in not "wasting time" on learning untested material than actually understanding the subject matter.

Which brings us to a third problem with designing good assessment: the unintended lessons that students *do* learn from many tests. Kids discover very quickly what is valued by their teachers and too often conclude that how they do on the test is much more important than the subject they have studied. Students learn that writing short answers, choosing true or false statements, and circling multiple-choice answers is their best shot at accruing the points that will be added together to determine their letter grade. According to George Wood, this kind of evaluation is unique to the school setting:

> Nowhere else in our society will one's worth or abilities be measured by a paper-and-pencil test of short-term memory. Instead we base judgments of competence on actual performance. Those aspiring to be medical doctors do residencies to see if they can do medicine, mechanics actually repair things and, on the basis of their work, hold a job or earn our business; farmers are paid for the crops they deliver, not for how many pages they can write on soil conditions. But in school most kids never produce anything "real," instead spewing back memorized facts to prove what they have learned. (1998, 96)

These are problems that affect all students who take tests. We haven't even touched upon the controversy over whether some tests discriminate against particular groups of students, which it seems entirely evident to us that they do.

Given the political realities of our age, standardized tests, no matter how banal, inaccurate, or unfair, will doubtless be part of school life for some time to come. But they needn't be our principal means of monitoring student learning or shaping instruction. The curriculum in our high schools can be far better evaluated in challenging and authentic ways. When we give students a multiple-choice test, what we learn is what they don't know, but when we ask kids to demonstrate their learning in a project, we find out what they know and what they can do. Authentic assessments can include performances such as essays, videotapes, drama and art, learning fairs, projects, and portfolios that demonstrate student growth. Such products and events are part of the curriculum, not merely add-ons, and they place responsibility for the work on the student rather than the teacher.

Authentic assessment measures communicate to the students what is important about learning and what we value. When we administer multiple-choice tests, we tell students that we value the memorization of facts. When we ask students to create a project that shows what they have learned, we tell students that we want them to think, learn content in depth, and demonstrate their learning in a way that is meaningful and useful to them as citizens of the school community and, eventually, citizens of the world.

Alternative approaches to assessment also enhance instruction by encouraging teachers to think more deeply about their objectives, methods, and results and promote a curriculum that aligns assessment with educational values, goals, and practices (Darling-Hammond, Ancess, and Falk 1995). Authentic strategies for assessment are gaining ground in many high schools because they give students choices and they allow them to demonstrate competence by "doing." Many supporters of traditional methods argue that alternatives to multiple-choice assessments are more costly and time-consuming to develop, administer, and score. This may be true, but the time and effort are well worth it. Authentic assessments can be made a seamless part of the curriculum that helps us to look at individual student learning without pitting students against each other, without promoting a quest to beat the curve and succeed while others fail.

FINDING YOUR NEXT STEPS

Remember: Think back to your own high school education. What kinds of assessment instruments were used? How were you graded? What was the role of standardized tests? How often were they administered? Did you know the criteria for grades, or were you given letters or point totals without further explanation? Were there opportunities for self-evaluation? How did you respond to tests and grades, and how did they make you feel?

Experiment: Pilot the use of a portfolio for one unit that you teach. Have students *collect* all of their work and projects in a folder. At regular intervals, invite students to *select* examples of their work to be placed in showcase portfolios. Spend time helping students brainstorm the criteria for selection. Allow time for students to review work and projects they've completed, and ask them to *reflect* upon the work and why it was selected. Model for them how you would write a reflection on a piece of your own work. In order to help students understand the reflective process, provide examples of real portfolios, and allow them to read other students' reflections. Ask students if the reflective essays enhanced their understanding of the selected student work.

Team: Using the steps described in this chapter, invite a few fellow teachers to work with students to develop a rubric to evaluate one project. Then meet to share the student-created rubrics and compare their similarities and differences. What does the math rubric have in common with the art rubric? Do we need separate rubrics for each content area, or can they be used across disciplines?

Spread the Word: Invite the parents to a discussion on grading and assessment. Have them reflect upon their own high school experience. Invite them to consider the place of grades in their lives: Did they work for grades or to learn? Did grades stand in the way of their learning? Did grades motivate them to learn? Were grades a source of rewards and/or punishment? When they did work hard and accomplish something, what motivations were involved?

Surf the Web: Search the Internet for schools that have digital portfolios. Many high schools around the country have their own websites with links to the various activities that they sponsor. Best Practice High School's initial attempt can be found at www.bphs.org.

Chapter 11
Professional Development

Teachers are students of instruction, with many opportunities to learn and grow.

O n the steamy morning of August 23, 1996, the day the first fresh-man class arrived at Best Practice High School, the three of us, Steve, Harvey, and Marilyn, were in for a surprise. For two years, we had been creating the school's vision, writing the proposal, finding the site, selecting teachers, and, along with them, planning every-thing necessary to begin a new public high school. That morning, we held an opening ceremony in the auditorium, welcoming the kids and inaugurating the school. The kids were pleasant and curious. We adults were excited, even ecstatic: our dream was coming true. Then, at 10:30 A.M. the 137 students headed upstairs with their teachers.

The three of us stood there and looked at each other, not quite sure what we were supposed to do, where to go. For all of our planning, we had never really figured out what our own role would be, once the school actually began. Until the kids showed up, we had been equals with the teachers, three extra pairs of hands, putting our shoulders to whatever wheel presented itself. Now, with the teachers suddenly in their classrooms, each with twenty-eight kids, there we stood in the empty auditorium, trying to think how to make ourselves useful. We'd never felt more like professors.

Harvey and Marilyn spent the next couple days laminating name tags and CTA bus passes, while Steve carried heavy cartons of books and supplies up the three flights of stairs. We unpacked boxes of books and stacked them up for the librarian to catalog. We hooked up computers and loaded software on hard drives. We read and catalogued kids' writ-

ings from the first days of school ("Couldn't we just have regular high school one day a week?" one young man wanted to know). After a few weeks of these general and unfocused chores, one of our main roles began to emerge: while we would always be three extra pairs of hands, we would especially serve as the school's staff developers.

Our job centers on helping the teachers at Best Practice High School get what they need to learn, grow, and teach even better. Sometimes, this means one of us guiding a lesson in the classroom: after all, someone has to show the teachers how not to teach, we often joke. More helpful are the times when we coteach with faculty members, providing an extra adult helper for a new or complex classroom activity. Sometimes we'll work with the whole faculty or small groups on specific classroom strategies, large projects such as portfolios, or how advisories can best serve kids. We provide teacher retreats for planning, problem solving, and community building. During the winter, we plan a weekend at a conference center, and during the summer, we bring the whole faculty to the Walloon Institute in northern Michigan for an entire week.

Some of our work is more indirect: we write the grant proposals that fund these workshops and retreats. Other grants provide consulting help from other master teachers, real experts, who help BPHS staff right in their classrooms. Finally, we have helped BPHS become a professional-development site for other teachers from Chicago and around the country, organizing visits and conversations with our faculty.

Four years later, when curious visitors or colleagues ask us exactly what we do at the school, we are still a little hesitant and unsure. Sometimes we still stare at each other blankly when that question comes up. Although it should be easy to simply say we are the school's staff developers, the job now seems more complex, subtle, and diffuse than that. Maybe we should just say we are the extra pairs of hands and leave it at that.

SCHOOL REFORM AND TEACHER GROWTH

American public education may now be concluding its second decade of reform, but the teaching in most high schools still looks pretty familiar. After fifteen years and tens of millions of dollars spent on reform, secondary classrooms still look and feel and operate much like the classrooms of the 1970s—or the 1920s. Kids sit in the same desks, in the same rows, in the same lime-green rooms, arranged into the same "ability groups," studying the same state-mandated curriculum, reading from the same textbooks, taking the same tests and quizzes, overseen by teachers who use the same methods.

Why has so little changed where it really matters, in the classroom? After all, if improving student achievement is the ultimate goal of school reform, then empowering teachers would seem to be the crucial, next-to-last step in seeking the payoff of all these reform efforts. We know that teaching is the key to school renewal, not just from our common sense and gut instinct, but also from current educational research. As reported by the National Commission on Teaching and America's Future (NCTAF), teacher expertise has been found to be the most significant determinant of student success (Darling-Hammond 1996). In one study, teacher qualifications (such as scores on a licensing exam, degrees held, and years of experience) accounted for 40 percent of the difference in overall student performance. In other studies reviewed by NCTAF, teacher quality proved to be a more powerful factor in students' learning even than socioeconomic status, showing that superior teaching can overcome serious social disadvantages that some students bring to school (Darling-Hammond 1999).

But while there has been much exhorting, cajoling, and even threatening of teachers to get better, there have been surprisingly few actual resources committed to *helping* them to become more effective and powerful in the lives of children. Instead, we seem to think that teacher growth is some kind of magical by-product of top-down reforms. We assume that if you want to raise children's achievement, what you do is make structural, political, legal, economic, or logistical changes in state or district policies. Pass standards laws. Design new tests. Set official benchmarks. Then sit back and wait for these macro-level changes to trickle down into the system.

You might call this the domino theory of school reform. It assumes that by tipping over the first domino in an assumed chain of causes and effects, you commence an inexorable process through which classroom-level change will eventually occur, the quality of teaching will rise, and student achievement will improve. However, as we've seen quite dramatically across the country, this mechanistic model of school renewal doesn't work. The dominos have not yet toppled over in very many classrooms.

School reform is *not* like dominos. Instead, we've got to walk up to each of these educational dominos and push them over, one at a time. If we want teaching to change in real classrooms, we have to go where teachers are and make it happen. That's where professional development comes in. Some of the broader structural, political, and governance changes have created a climate in which teachers *might* teach better and kids *might* learn more. But now teachers must be helped—not just commanded—to teach in new, different, better ways.

Some have questioned whether today's teachers are worth such an investment, suggesting that the impending wave of baby-boom teacher retirements will soon restock classrooms with younger, better-trained teachers. But the demographics don't compute. Despite the record number of retirements, the majority of today's children will be taught by teachers already in the system. If you have a child entering kindergarten this year, about 85 percent of her teachers will be people who are already trained and on duty now. Each of these teachers will work with children for another ten or twenty or thirty years, and either they will get better, helped by some form of professional development, or they won't. All the reforms we can manage in preservice education, laudable as they may be, will not transform the culture of American teaching for at least fifteen years.

This means that staff development—the name we give to a wide range of professional growth experiences offered to veteran teachers—is the urgent, critically important last step of school reform. Success will depend on old teachers learning new tricks. And, of course, even the newly trained teachers—as brilliant as they may turn out to be—will need career-long support, as do professionals in every other field.

STANDARDS FOR PROFESSIONAL DEVELOPMENT

So what does good staff development look like? To begin with, staff development must be rooted in "best practice," in our best understandings of how kids learn and how teaching works. We outlined these principles in Chapter 1, and they apply as much to the teaching of teachers as they do to educating young people. If we expect teachers to create classrooms that honor our national curriculum standards—by being challenging, authentic, and collaborative—then learning for teachers must have the same characteristics. Just as students learn what they live in classrooms, so too will teachers learn what they live in staff development programs. Teachers must be supported as well as children, with staff development activities that are teacher-centered, challenging, authentic, and collaborative.

There is abundant research literature on the connection between staff development and school change (Wood 1992; Barth 1990; Wasley 1991; Lester and Onore 1990; Livingston 1992; Zemelman, Daniels, and Hyde 1998). Drawing upon these sources, we begin to understand that the most effective professional-development programs are:

Voluntary. While it's tempting to force teachers to change, it doesn't work. Personal choice and control are just as central to the learning process of adults as they are for children. Besides, disgruntled conscripts can quite easily subvert a promising innovation in a school. A better approach is to begin with the willing and work patiently through a faculty, drawing in the more reluctant teachers as they see the successes enjoyed by the early volunteers and excited students.

Peer-Led. Nothing substitutes for the credibility and expertise of fellow teachers who have implemented the practices they are preaching. While outside experts, like college professors, can be useful supplements or can help to train teacher-leaders, teachers' best resources are respected colleagues. In urban schools, it is especially important that peer leaders be from the city, since the teachers there perceive, often accurately, that the issues in their classrooms are different from those faced by rural and suburban teachers.

Curriculum-Centered. Many professional development programs are generic, addressing diffuse issues such as thinking skills or classroom management. However, the most effective programs put content at the center, focusing professional development squarely in the curriculum: on math, science, writing, social studies, or reading. Broader concerns such as thinking skills or classroom management are quite naturally covered in the context of content learning, not vice versa.

Standards-Oriented. Almost all the national curriculum standards reports prescribe best practice teaching, and some—most notably the science and language arts standards—offer detailed pictures of what high-quality, standards-based teaching looks like in their field. It is important for teachers to know that these instructional approaches are not transient fads but rather are enduring, professionally approved, and nationally sanctioned methods.

Lengthy. Helping teachers to change long-standing, cherished classroom practices takes time. The National Writing Project's highly successful staff-development model involves a thirty-hour workshop just for starters, with significant school-based follow-up. To train leaders to deliver this program takes much longer—a multiweek summer leadership institute, often followed by a school-year internship of thirty to sixty hours. Though lengthy and costly, this model works, yielding documented advances in student achievement.

Active. In staff-development programs, advice is not nearly as helpful as direct experience. Teachers need involving demonstrations, not lectures, of the new activities recommended for students. Teachers must not just hear about but personally experience math manipulatives, peer-editing groups, science experiments, dialogue journals, or other new activities themselves in professional development workshops.

Practical. Teachers want specific ideas and examples of how to reorganize time, space, materials, children, and help in their daily schedules. While such concerns are sometimes dismissed as "mere methods," these practical issues are critical to the change process—just as important as teachers buying into the conceptual basis of an innovation. Of course, when programs are led by teacher-consultants who address these management issues in their own classrooms every day, the practical side of change receives plenty of attention.

Open-Ended. While good professional development programs share the best practices embodied in the standards for a given teaching field, they do not mandate how any one teacher must grow. Respecting the diversity of adult learners just as we do that of children, workshops must be structured to provide choices, so that each teacher can find his or her way into new practices. It is vital for professional educators to determine their own next steps and then commit to a sequence of changes they can believe in and sustain.

Long-Term. While initial, intensive programs—like workshops or summer institutes—can get innovation started in a school or district, follow-up is needed to sustain change over the long run. This can take many forms: peer coaching, professional reading, discussion groups, classroom consulting, seminars, retreats, demonstration lessons.

Supported by the Principal. Staff development works best in buildings where the principal takes on the role of instructional leader. That means the principal:

- is a learner joining personally in at least some of the ongoing staff development projects
- involves teachers democratically in planning professional development activities
- gives teachers choices in their professional growth
- finds the funds to bring valuable programs to the school or to send teachers to important professional events outside the building
- encourages change, innovation, and risk taking among faculty

- values professional growth in teacher evaluations and other communications

- nurtures the growth of curricular and instructional leadership within the staff

- develops relationships outside the building, partnerships that can feed the professional growth of teachers.

Part of a Buildingwide Change Process. Professional development works best when it is part of a wider process of school development, gradually drawing in more teachers, kids, parents, administrators, and community members.

A RANGE OF STRATEGIES

What are the structures and activities that can embody these characteristics for staff development in a school? The traditional staff-development day at a high school begins in the auditorium with a short exhortation by the principal or superintendent. A famous education writer gives an entertaining (you hope) talk for an hour. Then it's off to several rounds of smaller, one- or one-and-one-half-hour workshops on a variety of topics of varying quality and practicality, featuring a mix of experts from around the region. If you're lucky, the district serves a nice lunch before one more round of workshop sessions.

But many forward-looking districts have expanded their view of staff development to a much wider and deeper range of strategies more likely to engender real improvement in teaching and learning. One well-used step is to assemble a yearly catalogue of the district-sponsored after-school courses on a variety of topics, during the year and in the summer. Some districts identify a focus for the year—though we prefer to see at least a three-year cycle or longer, so that development doesn't become just a revolving door, and significant changes have time to take root. Other schools go still further, with peer mentoring, or department- or school-level rethinking of curriculum.

The teachers and partners at Best Practice High School have developed their own organic approach to professional growth that has come to include these ingredients:

Out-of-school retreats: Since we university partners sponsor an annual summer five-day residential program, the Walloon Institute, the BPHS faculty began attending before the school even started. The faculty meets on its own, hears from national experts and well-known authors, and exchanges ideas with other teachers from around the country. It's also an excellent way to bring newly hired teachers into the fold. Now we've added a winter two-day getaway for BPHS faculty alone, invaluable for problem solving, refocusing, and renewing our energy.

Whole-school staff-development sessions: By scheduling extra minutes into each school day, our school is able to convert every other Friday to a half-day of school, leaving the afternoon for teachers to meet (a strategy used by many Chicago schools). The teachers plan the topics, varying between presentations by visiting experts or by us university partners and discussions among the teachers themselves.

Professional conferences: Like many districts around the country, Chicago does not strongly support conference attendance by teachers. Nevertheless, our teachers get themselves to many—the meetings of Project Arise (the Physics-First program at Fermilab), the National Council of Teachers of English, the National Council of Teachers of Mathematics, and so forth, both to listen and to present. Speaking at a conference is one of the best ways for a teacher to clarify her own ideas.

Visits to other schools: As we started Best Practice, visits to small schools in New York showed us the many design choices we faced and inspired us to continue our work. We've since gone back, not just to learn about curriculum, but also to see how other professional development groups work with teachers.

Professional books: Like other professionals, teachers need to keep up with crucial developments in their field. Yet it's especially hard for high school teachers, with their large student loads and frantic schedules, to find time to read. So one function for the university partners has been to help our teachers use their limited time well, finding books that address their most immediate needs. One of our favorite uses of grant funds is to pick up the phone to order five copies of a text the teachers have asked about, like Jeff Wilhelm's *You Gotta BE the Book*, and hand it to them two days later while it's fresh in their minds.

One-on-one and in-classroom support: This has grown to be one of our favorite staff development tools at Best Practice—and so we'll discuss it in more depth shortly. The university faculty and several of our full-time demonstration teachers at the Center for City Schools meet with individual teachers and visit their classrooms to help with specific issues, at the teacher's request.

Teachers planning together: Education experts like to be needed. But one of the most important resources for teacher growth is simply time—and a focused purpose—for teachers to work together on their own. At BPHS, teachers meet in grade-level teams on Wednesdays, while their kids are at their half-day school-to-work internships; and department meetings usually occur once a week after school. These sessions focus on curriculum and individual student needs, since procedural matters are usually covered at regular Monday after-school meetings. Research on site-based management suggests that teacher planning time isn't always as productive as educators have hoped. But we think it works at Best Practice for a number of reasons. First, the grade-level teams share the concrete goal of planning integrated study units for each quarter. Second, there are so many other supports for professional development that the teachers always come to the meetings with pressing concerns and issues. And they share enough of a common philosophy that it's usually possible to reach consensus on the solutions.

No one of these strategies suffices on its own. Instead, they build to a critical mass. Some of our favorite moments as university partners occur when we get to school and see this happening. One day, for example, math teacher Tom McDougal stopped Marilyn in the hall. He'd heard about history teacher Mike Myers' successes with simulation activities and wanted to try one. He also knew Mike had struggled with ending the simulation and helping students reflect on it. Marilyn suggested having students jot responses to three questions about the activity that are written on the board. Students then compare their answers in pairs, in small groups, and finally as a whole class. Both teachers resolved to plug this step into their next simulation. It's the endless rounds of interchange like this that move us toward the goal that is Best Practice.

IN-CLASSROOM SUPPORT: PROVIDING PERSONAL HELP

One missing link in many staff-development programs has been the opportunity for teachers to get help right in their own classrooms. The literature on professional growth is thick with examples of how workshops alone can reach only a small percentage of teachers, those who are open to the idea of change and who aren't completely threatened by the notion that what they have been doing for years can and should be changed. Many teachers, even those willing to jump in and try new strategies, make valiant initial attempts, only to encounter problems, give up, and conclude that the strategies were flawed or "didn't work with my kids." The staff-development literature has often called for follow-up to support those teachers who are willing to try new ideas and who usually operate "without a net." We believe that in-class support by demonstration teachers is the kind of follow-up that can provide teachers with that net. Since classroom consulting has seemed so natural a development at Best Practice, we'll focus on how we've learned to make this intensive strategy work.

At the Center for City Schools at National-Louis University, we have gathered a cohort of ten accomplished public school faculty we call demonstration teachers, who lead staff development at Best Practice and at the network of elementary schools feeding into it. Their job is to support individual teachers directly in their classrooms, during recurring two-week residencies. The partnership begins when a classroom teacher requests a demonstration teacher, and the two meet to discuss what strategies the teacher wishes to try. The demonstration teacher comes in for about an hour and a half per day for two weeks, and the two of them work to install or refine the target strategies. During the rest of the day, the demonstration teacher is doing the same work in two or three other classrooms in the building. When the two weeks are over, the demonstration teacher moves on to another school, and then returns two weeks later for another cycle.

This means that the classroom teacher gets on-site assistance for two weeks, followed by two weeks to practice on her own, with the knowledge that the demonstration teacher will return to help with problem solving and next steps. All of our demonstration teachers are classroom veterans, as well as workshop leaders; they've implemented best practice strategies with their own students and helped colleagues to grow and change in many settings. They speak with authority—they know how schools work, are sensitive to the real demands of teaching, and operate with great consideration in other people's space.

In-classroom consulting achieves several aims at once:

- It provides support at the level where new teaching approaches often break down, in actual everyday classroom situations.

- It helps deprivatize practice by pairing teachers in their classrooms, making new teaching practices a more public topic.

- Students can become change agents, asking teachers in other classes to try new activities introduced by demonstration teachers in target classrooms.

Providing in-classroom support is not a one-size-fits-all proposition. What teachers need from a consultant can vary as widely as the classrooms in which they teach. Some teachers need to actually see the strategies being demonstrated while they watch, and others need to have a friendly helper in the classroom who can observe their teaching and provide feedback. Still others prefer to team-teach, using the demonstration teacher as an extra pair of hands. Some teachers merely need some encouragement, or suggestions on management, or ways to move the strategy forward.

Just being invited into a teacher's classroom is in itself a very personal experience. As teachers understand with their hearts and minds, our classrooms are very private domains where we operate in ways that are ours alone. Others who enter these personal domains are rarely there only because they wish to help. Instead, most visitors come to judge what they see and write up the dreaded evaluation. Some teachers have reported to our staff that they have not had a single friendly observer in their classrooms since they student taught. So effective demonstration teachers learn to take plenty of time to build trust and to watch for their client's strengths and sensitivities. They must find ways to help that do not undermine or steal initiative from the classroom teacher, or overwhelm her with too many ideas, too quickly.

Doing this job well is truly an art. One of our demonstration teachers tells of the first day a teacher tried out the simple strategy of pair sharing in response to a short story, "Eleven," by Sandra Cisneros. This very traditional English teacher ran a "tight ship" with students seated in rows, and classroom interaction focused on lecture and teacher-initiated questions. After the reading, she took the risk of inviting the students to talk with partners about what the piece made them think and feel. The short story, about birthdays and growing up, was filled with concepts that moved the kids, who immediately and noisily shoved their desks around to begin animated discussions.

The classroom teacher threw up her hands and told her visitor that this would never work and she'd never get the students "back in control." The demonstration teacher calmly asked her host to walk around the room and listen to the conversations. They found, to the classroom teacher's surprise, that the children were all "on task," talking animatedly about the story. Without this support, the classroom teacher would have given up and returned to her traditional skill-and-drill curriculum.

We are very careful to tell classroom teachers that there are a couple of things demonstration teachers don't do: substitute teach or provide preparation periods. Every one of our consultants can tell a horror story of a teacher who leaves the room when the visitor arrives, hoping for a break from the students. Nevertheless, most teachers find that the presence of someone who truly understands their struggles and the intense demands of their classroom provides a tremendous boost and opens up possibilities they hadn't imagined.

HOW ONE CLASSROOM CONSULTANT OPERATES

Yolanda Simmons, our professional-development coordinator at Best Practice High School, has taught us some effective ways of entering classrooms with respect for teachers, for students, and for the complexities of high school life. Having been a secondary teacher in Chicago for many years, Yolanda understands the issue of classroom territory and the delicate role that an outsider must play. Being in a teacher's classroom is like cooking in another person's kitchen, where you don't know the rules or where things belong. Yolanda offers her services, waits to be invited in, and when she does get in the door, is very good at watching and listening.

Yolanda's work with math teacher Tom McDougal shows just how creative this kind of intervention can be. Tom had been experiencing discipline problems with one of his classes and asked for help. The two had developed a trusting relationship over several years, and so Yolanda decided to try a seemingly unorthodox approach. Instead of offering suggestions to Tom, she took aside two students who seemed to be causing the most trouble and asked them what *they* thought was needed to improve the situation. Following are several letters that were exchanged among this triangle of actors.

Letter from Tom

12/10

Dear Yolanda,

At my invitation, you came to my 7th period Algebra class, with which I have been struggling for most of this year. You pulled two students out of class to talk to privately: Patrice Graft and Toneshia Shepard. Perhaps a week later you, Patrice, and I met together during lunch to talk about Patrice's ideas for making the class better.

Patrice had several comments. As I remember, some of them were: (1) homework was not adequately explained before it was given out; (2) I should let students who understood help those who did not; (3) I lost my temper and yelled at students instead of setting a positive example. She presented these comments very courteously, and we were able to discuss my frustrations as well. (E.g., students not listening when I do try to explain better.)

I showed her what I had planned for an upcoming lesson and invited her input. (It helped that you, Yolanda, had told me over the phone what some of Patrice's comments would be.) She thought it looked pretty good and also seemed pleased to be consulted.

Sitting on the sidelines, you exercised admirable restraint. (smile)

One immediate change that followed this discussion was that Patrice herself was much more engaged in the class. She also encouraged other students to quiet down. The next day or so, after school, I called Patrice into the classroom to ask her about seating. Although I hadn't given a quiz yet, I thought I had a pretty good idea who knew the material and who didn't. She and I worked together to find a new seating arrangement that would place students who needed help at tables with students who could provide it. Patrice was particularly good about identifying which students could sit together and work productively. When I gave the quiz, it corroborated what we had done. I explained to the students the new seating arrangement. With a notable lack of complaining, the students accepted their new seats.

Since then, the chatter in the class has reduced, and Patrice has taken an active role in keeping the class focused. My presentations are shorter and more organized. I am trying to make more positive comments to students. I have (so far) avoided outbursts of temper.

Patrice is enthusiastic about my improvements in the class. From my perspective I have noticed several students working better then they used to, and overall the classroom climate is less contentious. I suspect that Patrice enjoys the class more at least partly because she herself is more engaged, and I worry sometimes that her enthusiasm may cover up (and even discourage) other students who are not engaged or who are not understanding the material. But other students do respect her and take a cue from her, so she has an undeniable positive effect.

I have always been glad, Yolanda, to have your comments, support, and assistance with this and other classes. You have always been careful to respect my position as the teacher. You act as collaborator, as supporting teammate, not as "expert." I never felt as though you were "taking over." Your suggestions and actions have always been helpful. It helps, too, not insignificantly, that you have always found something positive and encouraging to say. We don't get many positive strokes in this business, so the ones we do get mean a lot. Thanks again for your help—past, present, and future.

Tom

Yolanda's Reply

Dear Tom:

Patrice ran up to me, gave me a big hug, and told me that 7th period Algebra is "so much better." Congratulations! I asked Patrice to express her feelings in words and to share them with me. A copy of her letter is attached.

Yo

A Letter from Patrice

7th Period Math Class Since The Meeting: In my opinion, 7th period Algebra has really improved since our meeting. The paper that I wrote contained a few suggestions that I felt would help to improve 7th pd. Algebra.

So far, all of these suggestions have preserved Mr. McDougal from failure. Mr. McDougal used my advice wisely. He took them and expanded them in many ways.

For example, I suggested that he let people who understood what they were doing help others who didn't. Mr. McDougal gave the class a quick quiz just to see where we were in the lesson, and who had the lesson down pat. Mr. McDougal and I placed them in groups where they could help others around them. That has been successful.

In class Mr. McDougal doesn't have to do a lot of yelling because the seats are arranged so that the students can do their work without talking to their friends.

I think if Mrs. Simmons hadn't suggested that I tell Mr. McDougal how I really felt, then I probably wouldn't have been able to share my opinion with Mr. McDougal.

I even heard a few of my friends in 7th period say that Algebra is going better than before. In conclusion, I think that Mr. McDougal's 7th pd. Algebra class has really improved thanks to Mrs. Simmons, Mr. McDougal, and myself.

Patrice Graft

This kind of deep and subtle staff development evolves only through the gradual development of trust and collaboration between teachers and external partners. It also requires a combination of other supportive conditions—a general atmosphere that encourages risk taking and safety to discuss our struggles; lots of shared planning time when teachers learn from one another;

ideas from experts like Jim Beane and Barbara Brodhagen on negotiated curriculum, Nancy Doda on interdisciplinary teaming, Lucy Calkins on teaching reading and writing, Alfie Kohn on providing choice and reducing competition among students, Jeff Wilhelm on teaching reading, and others. When all these forces combine, we realize that as university partners, we do only a small proportion of the work of providing support. Instead, a structure has grown up in which help and encouragement come from many directions, and we watch with fascination as new developments spring up almost every time we walk in the door.

BEST PRACTICE HIGH SCHOOL AS A PROFESSIONAL-DEVELOPMENT SITE

Experts on teacher education have extolled the benefits of Professional Development Schools, sites where visiting educators and education students come to observe, to study, to intern, and to teach collaboratively for periods of time. As of 1995 there were approximately three hundred such schools/partnerships nationwide (Fullan 1995). While little research has been done on the effectiveness of these schools, our own experience shows us they can work powerfully to help new teachers to get a good start and experienced teachers to change.

 So when we started the Best Practice High School as a regular, small, Chicago public school, we promised the central administration that in addition to eventually serving 440 youngsters, we would create a site where teachers from around the city could come and see Best Practice in action. After our first year, as we hired the new teachers for the incoming class we also assigned a professional-development coordinator from our Center staff, using grant funds. In addition to her classroom consulting duties, Yolanda Simmons provides visitation days and residencies for Chicago teachers and visitors from around the country.

Teachers, usually in school teams, come for whole days, and after they learn a little about the school, they spend the morning visiting classrooms. The visitors are especially encouraged to talk to the students, so they can evaluate the quality of the teaching methods from the student point of view. In addition to thinking about the specific classroom strategies they see, the visitors often hone in on other features of the school. Many immediately notice there are no bells, and students still manage to get to classes on time. Teachers often want to see how the block schedule works. How does a teacher effectively use one hundred three minutes? Teachers who come from large high schools are interested in ways to make their schools feel smaller.

At noon, visitors and BPHS teachers sit down for a "power lunch" to discuss the classroom activities that were observed. Teachers get answers to dozens of questions on the many concrete details that make specific strategies work: How were the kids trained or prepped for the activity? How large should the groups be? What if someone hasn't read the material, or was absent the day before? Does this activity cover topics on the state test? How will the project be assessed when it's finished? In the afternoon, the visiting teachers meet together and each chooses one idea he or she wishes to adopt—integration, collaboration, simulations, team-teaching, block scheduling, peer mediation. The teachers then work in teams to plan how they'll transport the ideas to their home schools.

Visiting teachers obviously don't copy everything they see: their own school situations may make some approaches impossible. Nevertheless, when visitors see teachers like themselves using new strategies, and when they see ordinary students energized by these strategies, they can be inspired to try something new. At first, we thought this process would be relevant only for other high school teachers and perhaps middle school faculty. But we began including elementary teachers from our feeder schools and found that the observations were just as productive for them.

The BPHS teachers have also come to value the opportunity to share their practice with others. We were fascinated to discover that the more our teachers talk about what they do and why they do it, the more articulate and committed they become. Along with increasing experience in using best practice strategies, talking about their work with visiting teachers helps them clarify their own ideas.

Visitors' comments about the observations and conversations show us not only what they have learned, but what it takes to gain credibility with a teacher who is being invited to change. A few examples:

Today at Best Practice High School, I saw something I never thought I would see, something I had never even considered. As I entered Mr. C's (I regret that I don't know his name) freshman English class, I saw children engaged in various "center" activities. Now, I use centers in my first-grade class every week and have the children rotate around to different activities every twenty minutes, but I had no idea that there were high school teachers who use centers as well.

It didn't take long to figure out that these centers were based on the multiple intelligences. In fact, the sheet given to students listing the stations also gave information on which intelligence(s) would be used: linguistic, spatial, musical, interpersonal, logical, etc. One way or another, each of the students in this freshman English class was going to come away with a deeper understanding of the concept being taught, which was setting in a story.

I am very glad that we decided to do this trip. It was nice to see a different school atmosphere. Everyone was very helpful and open with us. I did not feel as if I was interrupting, or was in the way of the learning that was taking place. It said a lot that these teachers were willing to have anyone stop by at any time. It showed that they were very confident in what they were doing at all times.

Other comments are more critical, sometimes reflecting real struggles that the Best Practice teachers still have, sometimes musing on the trade-offs involved in our particular choice of structures, and sometimes reflecting the observer's own preconceptions:

Some things that I saw surprised me. I'm not saying that they were good or bad, I was just surprised to see them. I saw a lot of free time. The day that we observed they followed a block schedule. One hour and forty-five minutes is quite a long time in each classroom, so free time would be necessary. I felt, however, that some time was wasted in certain classes. I would find it hard to teach when students are having their own conversations. I also found the phones in each classroom to be a disturbance. I noticed that in one class the teacher was teaching, and a mother called to talk to her daughter. There was a definite feeling of freedom, and I'm not sure how I feel about this.

I did not care for the block scheduling that the school follows. The time period would be too long for some art projects, but for others it would be helpful to not stop a project that was time-consuming. I would also not like only seeing the students three days a week. Students might lose interest in a project if not working daily on it.

Yet even when visitors don't endorse everything they see, a well-structured visit helps them think anew about educational options. Back when we started Best Practice, when we visited many small, innovative high schools in New York, we stole half of what we saw and rejected the other half. Any schools that accept visitors regularly to share their practice inevitably open their doors to both praise and criticism. This is just one part of the process of change.

So we continue to remind ourselves that serving as a Professional Development School does not mean that Best Practice is perfect, only that it's a work-in-progress. Therefore, we end this chapter with a story of classroom consulting, teacher change, and student initiative that shows how growth occurs as all of these interact. The story tells itself through the journals of demonstration teacher Yolanda Simmons, English teacher Jenny Cornbleet, and poems written by two students.

Yolanda's Journal

Jenny was working with her ninth graders on a Who Am I? unit. Since it was an integrated unit, the students would remain in Jenny's classroom for the entire day and for two hours the following day. Her plan was to help the students examine their many different selves through poetry writing. . . .

Jenny invited the kids to relax, clear their minds, and close their eyes as she utilized guided imagery to help them communicate with their "silent selves." I joined them. When we opened our eyes, Jenny invited us to record our discoveries. We wrote in our journals for two minutes, and Jenny asked us to scan our journal entries, make a list of the many different selves we had identified, and circle the one we wanted to write about. After we made our selections, Jenny invited us to further explore this part of ourselves by celebrating it in a poem. When we completed our poems, Jenny moved on to the next assignment.

I was feeling a bit uneasy, but it was important that I not show it. We had been writing and exploring our many *selves* for over an hour, and had not been given any opportunity to share our responses with each other. . . .

What could I do to help Jenny understand that the students were restless—that I was restless—because she had empowered us to empower ourselves with fresh visions and newly acquired awareness and knowledge of self, and that we would soon explode if not given an opportunity to share it?

Sure, it would be easy to simply pull her to the side and suggest *pair sharing*. But every consultant worth her salt knows that "telling" is not a best practice. Teacher space must be honored. No matter how often we consultants try to convince ourselves to the contrary, the simple truth is this: *the most important and potentially effective adult in the classroom is the classroom teacher, not the consultant.* . . .

I noticed an empty seat at a table in the front of the room. I walked over to it, told the students that I'd grown tired of standing, and asked if it would be okay for me to sit in the unoccupied chair. They nodded approval and I sat down. . . .

After about two minutes, the student sitting next to me passed me her journal. She didn't utter one word, but pointed to the section she wanted me to respond to. Jenny had required that we remain silent while writing, so I could not engage in a verbal dialogue with the student. So I read her journal entry, wrote a response on a yellow Post-it, attached it to her piece, and passed it back to her. She read my response, reached over and took a couple of slips from the stack of Post-it notes, and wrote me back.

Meanwhile, three other students at the table snatched a Post-it note from the stack, attached it to a personal entry to which they wished me to respond, and stacked up their journals in front of me. I asked the kids if it would be okay for them to exchange journals and respond to their peers. They said it would. So they did. And they did it without making a sound.

Jenny walked over and observed that the students wanted to share their thoughts. She looked at me, smiled, and said, "This is a great idea! I think we should give all the students an opportunity to talk about what they've written." Jenny went to the storage cabinet, took out a stack of multicolored Post-it Notes and asked me to show the other students how to respond to each other's work. I did.

Within five minutes the class was humming, kids were honoring one another's writings with serious response. Some kids were so impressed with themselves that they took turns standing before small groups to share their writings. Each group member offered a written response.

Most kids were smiling, but one was crying. Her exploration of self had brought her to the realization that it was time to dispose of *the angry-daughter part of her self.* The part that hated her father for abandoning her when she was a child. The part that wouldn't allow her to talk to him on the phone without revealing her anger. She had decided that it was time to move on now. . . .

Since Jenny's students were engaged in responding to one another's writings, I quietly slipped out and went next door to visit Tom and his students. Tom is the ninth-grade math teacher. . . . I noticed a tall, dark, robust girl with thick black hair attempting to make eye contact with me. Her eyes told me that she had something to say. I walked over to her table, smiled at her, and gently touched her shoulder. She whispered, "I hear you've been next door working with students on poetry. Here. Take this," she demanded, as she shoved a crinkled piece of folded paper into my hand. I eased my way out of the classroom so I could read her note in private. This is what she had written:

A POEM FOR THOUGHT

Lord, Lord
Why did you make me Black?
Why did you make me someone
The world wants to hold back?

Black is the color of dirty clothes,
The color of grimy hands and feet.
Black is the color of darkness,
The color of tire-beaten streets,

Why did you give me thick lips,
A broad nose and kinky hair?
Why did you make me someone
Who receives the hated stare?

Black is the color of the bruised eye
When someone gets hurt.
Black is the color of darkness,
The color of dirt.

How come my bone structures so thick,
My hips and cheeks are high?
How come my eyes are brown and not the color
Of the daylight sky?
Why do people think I'm hopeless?
Lord, Lord

Why did You make me Black?

I rushed back over to Jenny's room. The students were still busy sharing their ideas, finding their voices. I walked over to the window and leaned against the ledge. I attempted to establish eye contact with the student with whom I had conferenced about releasing her *angry-daughter self*. She caught my eye and smiled at me. I walked over to her and put the poem I had just read into her hand. . . .

Five minutes later, she approached me, requested I read her response, and take it next door to the author. She wrote:

WHY I WANT TO BE BLACK

BLACK is a powerful word

That I am proud to call my *self*.

We might not have a perfect feature or body,
But I'm
Proud to be called BLACK.

BLACK has meaning to it.

B = BEAUTIFUL
L = LOVING
A = APPRECIATED in every manner
C = COULD DO anything you put your mind to
K = KIND

BLACK has a meaning, and
I'm glad
I'm in a place
That I can be called
BLACK.

I took the response to the author and asked her if she'd like to meet the writer. I introduced them and encouraged them to continue their dialogue.

Jenny's Journal

In past experiences of teaching peer review and revision, I had met with a lot of resistance from students: "I don't want anyone seeing my work. My work is finished. It doesn't need any help. I'm tired of writing this, why do I have to revise it?" Peer review was often seen as a threatening invasion, revision as an onerous chore. . . .

I went to Yolanda for suggestions, and she had a brilliant, yet simple idea that tempted me to throw out every cumbersome revision worksheet I had ever devised: put a pile of Post-its on each table. Ask the students to paste a Post-it to their poem, and then hand it to another student, any other student, so that he or she can respond. Responders: say something support-ive to that person—they put themselves on the line for your opinion! Empathize with them, tell them how the poem made you feel, and encourage them. Instead of criticizing, ask them a question. That was the formula, words of support plus a question.

It spread like wildfire. At first there was a shyness, a few students coming hesitatingly up to Yolanda or me with one blank Post-it attached to their poem. I would smile at the students and then write my responses. The students would usually take their poems back with a solemn and slightly anxious look, but then, as they read the encouraging response, break into a big grin. Then an energy of mischievous delight began to pervade the room, and soon we couldn't keep up with the number of kids bringing us their poems. The kids began venturing out to their friends, and then even to people they didn't know. Soon it became an honor to have a poem covered with notes! . . .

Jenny

FINDING YOUR NEXT STEPS

Form a professional development book study group: Bring together a like-minded group of teacher-colleagues interested in a particular educational concern. Invite the group to choose a professional book focused on this concern to read and discuss together, over a series of sessions. Be sure to make the setting comfortable and convenient—at a nearby restaurant, in various people's living rooms, or if it's more convenient, the teachers' lounge at school. As the group discusses the book, a few chapters at a time, it can also reflect on the ways the ideas are influencing the members' teaching. Or if the focus is on a larger issue (such as tracking or school violence), discuss what steps toward change the group might initiate. And what are the ways that more teachers in the school can be productively involved in this dialogue?

Some possible texts:

on size: *The Power of Their Ideas: Lessons for America from a Small School in Harlem* by Deborah Meier

on size: *A Simple Justice: The Challenge of Small Schools* by W. Ayers, M. Klonsky, and G. Lyon

on tracking: *Crossing the Tracks* by Anne Wheelock

on curriculum: *Best Practice: New Standards for Teaching and Learning in America's Schools* by Steven Zemelman, Harvey Daniels, and Arthur Hyde

on teaching: *Methods That Matter: Six Structures for Best Practice Classrooms* by Harvey Daniels and Marilyn Bizar

on teaching: *In the Middle: New Understandings About Writing, Reading, and Learning* by Nancie Atwell

on teaching reading: *You Gotta BE the Book* by Jeff Wilhelm
on democracy in schools: *A Time to Learn* by George Wood
on portfolios and assessment: *The Portfolio as a Learning Strategy* by Carol
 Porter and Janell Cleland.

Create staff-development guidelines: Form a faculty committee to develop guidelines for effective staff development in your school. Be sure to include representatives of various key departments and constituencies. Administrators should be involved, since their support will be needed to put the guidelines into practice. Some possible guidelines:

fewer whole-faculty workshops
fewer top-down decisions about the content and process of professional development
less lecture
less summative evaluation of teachers

more faculty input
more flexible grouping of teachers in interest groups
more in-classroom support
more opportunities to visit other teachers' classrooms
more visits to other schools
more peer coaching.

The committee may also wish to propose some systematic programs for staff development that go beyond the traditional in service day or summer workshop. Some examples:

- Work with a university or school-reform group to hire a full-time consultant or demonstration teacher.

- Organize a program to exchange visits with teachers from other schools in the area.

- Plan a teacher study program around review of student work and assignments, to analyze what students are learning and what needs they have.

Chapter 12
Relationships

The school works closely with parents, community organizations, and educational institutions.

S teve and his wife, Susan, are wandering the aisles at an auction of *old kitsch pulled from people's basements, held one evening at a church on the north side of Chicago, near the lake. They place bids on several rococo knickknacks they don't want and could never use. They chat with the organizers and the local alderman who has dropped by. Later they'll sit in a local gyro restaurant, drink coffee, and gossip with several of the neighborhood leaders. What's going on?*

This was just one of many scenes that took place as we worked to start Best Practice High School. We often think back to that struggle and what it takes to get a new school started. One of the toughest challenges was not about education at all but about finding a suitable space. An early possibility for us was a school in a lovely neighborhood of brownstone homes on the north side of the city, near the lake—prime property. An elementary school filled less than half the building, while the rest stood empty. Steve spent night after night at meetings wooing the teachers, the Local School Council, the neighborhood residents. But real estate, we quickly learned, is just about the most sensitive, politically charged issue in a city like Chicago. Step by step, the neighborhood turned against us, as people grew nervous about their property values. An ugly slogan sprang up: "Little kids, little problems. Big kids, big problems." We realized that we had few friends working for us and withdrew our bid. Indeed, why would a neighborhood welcome us when we had no history together to build trust and mutual understanding?

We now understood we couldn't do this job alone, and our next try was very different. We'd developed alliances, particularly with two activist groups that had taken a special interest in promoting small schools. One was Leadership for Quality Education, a business-sponsored organization, and another was Business and Professional People in the Public Interest, a nonprofit lawyers' group focused mainly on issues of fair housing and neighborhood redevelopment. They recognized that improving schools would be essential to the renewing of neighborhoods where old high-rise projects were coming down. The Small Schools Workshop at the University of Illinois at Chicago joined these two groups to form the Small Schools Coalition. When the heads of these organizations called the superintendent's office or the mayor's policy people, they could at least obtain a hearing. And ultimately their continued, well-organized campaigning convinced school leaders to support a broader small-schools initiative and then to give us the space to create Best Practice.

John Ayers, director of Leadership for Quality Education, gleefully recalls the moment he convinced Chicago Schools CEO Paul Vallas to make available the handsome building that now houses Best Practice High School. It had been closed the previous spring, and the last-minute program that was meant to bring the overflow there from overcrowded schools in another neighborhood had flopped. The Democratic convention was coming up at the United Center, and (we guessed) the administration didn't want a high school building empty and decaying right across the parking lot. "He called me on his cell phone from his car," John chuckles.

We learned a great deal about the value of community support in our long effort to create the Best Practice High School, and the many sorts of partnerships that are needed. Along with business and community support, a second major partnership is with parents. A third brings together groups of schools. And finally, there are universities and colleges with expertise and energy to help. Let's examine all four, looking not just at Best Practice but at some of the other partnerships active around the country. After all, each community has its own structure of businesses, organizations, and centers of influence, and the process of bringing them into a relationship with schools will be highly idiosyncratic. But finding partners is worth the effort.

DATA ON THE EFFECTIVENESS OF PARTNERSHIPS

While there is as yet little statistical research that directly links business-school partnerships with higher student achievement, more positive student attitudes, or lower dropout rates, numerous individual success stories abound. At Roosevelt High School, in Dallas, Texas, for instance, a community partnership and parent involvement program initiated curricular and structural reforms that led to striking increases in student achievement. Between 1992 and 1996, Roosevelt students improved on state tests from fortieth to eighty-first percentile in reading and from sixteenth to seventieth percentile in math, and attendance improved by 11 percent.

This was not just the result of a small parent group meeting after school to sell cookies. The Dallas Area Interfaith and the Texas Industrial Areas Foundation joined with the Texas Education Agency to form the Alliance Schools Initiative. They mobilized parents using the IAF's highly developed approach to community activism and cooperation. "Core teams" of administrators, teachers, staff, parents, and community leaders were trained and then conducted a "Neighborhood Walk for Success." Parents were encouraged to take classes, to help their kids with homework, and to acquire practical skills themselves. The core teams worked on curriculum and structural reform. Parents secured a waiver from the state for block scheduling. Staff helped the feeder elementary schools strengthen incoming high school students' skills and family support.

Now, a parent liaison calls parents about meetings and discusses their children's academic progress. Report cards for students with failing grades are hand-delivered to their homes. Parents, teachers, and students sign an annual compact assuring good communication, parent involvement in decisions about their children's education, and flexible scheduling of parent-teacher meetings. Ongoing parent training includes how to help with students' college applications and how to prepare students for the state tests. The parent presence helps decrease discipline problems. As one parent remarked, kids "know that even if their parents are not there, there are parents there that care about them and will correct them" (Funkhouser and Gonzales 1997).

An example of a broader partnership can be found in Denver, Colorado. The Public Education and Business Coalition (PEBC) there has worked with fifty-six schools in six districts on curriculum, staff development, and school-to-career partnerships. One project, a new curriculum for reading comprehension, yielded a 16 percent increase in the number of students reading at or above proficient levels. PEBC trained 49 staff developers, who worked with

920 teachers in the participating schools on literacy, math, and technology. This organization recruited over 150 volunteers to work with 600 high school students. It provided job-shadowing experiences for over 1,000 high school students, and placed over 200 at-risk teenagers in paid summer business internships.

A different kind of partnership, the Industry Initiatives for Science and Math Education in the San Francisco Bay area, works solely with teachers. After attending scientific work experiences, participants used new teaching strategies in their classrooms, adopted teamwork approaches they'd learned in business settings, and approached science learning more as an inquiry-based, problem-solving process (Kubota 1993).

An example of a very large partnership is New Visions for Public Education, in New York City. With an annual budget of over $9 million and a staff of forty-plus, New Visions has helped create dozens of new, small, theme-based schools in New York City. For ongoing support, it provides professional development, helps improve school libraries, creates new media centers, increases college-bound guidance capacity, publishes reports and videos, and helps schools to address state standards. As its annual report states, "New Visions invests in good ideas and individual initiative by supporting New York City teachers who venture beyond the textbook and blackboard to design interdisciplinary projects that make learning exciting." While schools in other places cannot necessarily obtain this level of backing, New Visions shows that it's possible to mobilize massive community support for progressive approaches to school renewal.

While no catalogue or evaluation of partnerships around the country yet exists, their growing number and variety is heartening. Businesses, community organizations, parent groups, and individuals are actively involved in most major American cities. Whatever the test-score increases that may result, this involvement can only signal to kids and teachers that people care about them and the success of their endeavor.

When we turn to the question of the influence of parent/family involvement on children's education, the value seems self-evident. Still, it's worth looking at the data. One review of national test scores indicates that nearly 90 percent of the difference in eighth-grade students' mathematics scores is attributable to factors connected with home, such as absenteeism and variety of reading materials in the house (Barton and Coley 1992). A study of the effectiveness of workshops for parents at one school in Milwaukee found that school suspensions for children of participants dropped by 66 percent, behavior-problem referrals by 82 percent, and tardiness from 110 incidents during a first marking period to 28 in the period following completion of the program (Vopat 1994). Interestingly, one study suggests that schools' encouragement of parent participation is more influential than family characteristics such as parental education or socioeconomic level, in determining whether parents actually become involved (Dauber and Epstein 1993).

As for partnerships among schools, an extensive study has just been completed by the Consortium on Chicago School Research, on the many networks developed under Chicago Annenberg Challenge grants over a five-year period. Forty-seven networks formed, involving 220 of Chicago's 560-plus schools, through this project. Each had an external partner, such as a university, museum, or school reform group. Best Practice High School has participated with National-Louis University's Center for City Schools in one of these networks.

Preliminary information on the overall outcome in Chicago indicates that the level of teachers' professional development and of students' intellectual work has improved in network schools. Nevertheless, the results appear to be mixed. Some critics believe more funds should have been focused on a smaller number of networks. Bill Ayers, at the University of Illinois at Chicago, one of the original organizers of the program, states that the Annenberg effort " 'played a big role' in fostering smaller, more intimate, less anonymous learning environments. But . . . the goal of making teaching more of a profession 'is a goal yet to be realized' " (In Richards 2000, 7).

CHARACTERISTICS OF GOOD BUSINESS AND ORGANIZATIONAL PARTNERSHIPS

Many people have traditionally thought of school-business partnerships as primarily a corporate community service activity. A business offers to donate uniforms or computers to a school. Or it encourages employees to become tutors. Or it brings students for a tour of the company, or hires a few kids for summer internships. Some businesses or their wealthy leaders have gone a step further to "adopt" a school, or a group of students, promising college scholarships to those kids who do well. Businesses provide school-to-work internships, as we've described for Best Practice in Chapter 7 of this book. Over the past two decades, however, some much deeper relationships have developed in many communities, aimed at larger structural improvements in the schools. These have not only helped the schools themselves, but have also increased the business participants' understanding of public education and its challenges.

What are the advantages of creating a business- or community-school partnership? Obviously, if you are a citizen wishing to improve school quality in your community, organizing people to work together will be more effective than going in alone to pound on the principal's desk. Businesses recognize that helping schools promotes economic development in their communities and improves the abilities of their entry-level employees. Higher education levels mean lower crime statistics, and thus a lower tax burden. Supporting schools also, of course, enhances a company's corporate image.

However, if you are a school administrator, a partnership may not intuitively seem as good an idea. While additional resources are welcome, a partnership means someone else is looking over your shoulder, someone to whom you will need to devote precious time and attention. However, partner organizations can bring not only new resources but political clout, community support for major changes, and the extra energy needed to overcome the inertia of a school bureaucracy. Accountability measures employed by state legislatures and boards of education so often approach improvement as a punitive process that undermines staff morale; a community partnership, on the other hand, can build people's understanding of the challenges that schools face and deepen support for the teachers who are being asked to do the hard work of reform.

In a study on community-school partnerships, Kathleen Garcia outlines a series of tasks and conditions needed to make a partnership successful:

- Ensure strong commitment of organizational leaders at the highest level: school superintendents, corporate CEOs, directors of involved community organizations.
- Clearly define goals that involve efforts and contributions from all parties.
- Clarify the roles for all involved parties—which can take time as the partners get to know one another and to understand how they can best contribute to the effort. For an organization to simply send an expert in to deliver some kind of help that is received passively by the school is not a formula likely to succeed.
- Develop mutual trust through shared experiences, planning sessions, and visits to one another's sites.
- Provide training, to acquaint both educators and external partners with one another's expertise, needs, and concerns.
- Evaluate and document results to demonstrate to the partners, as well as to the outside world, the accomplishments achieved. (Garcia 1994)

Garcia cautions partners to think carefully about their aims, activities, and relationships. Focus on one special project may seem exciting but may not bring about significant, long-lasting improvement in the school. But once a focus has been chosen, there's still more to do to cement the relationship. Partnerships often bring together people with varying perspectives, who will need to negotiate differences. Then, as understanding grows, people need occasions to celebrate achievements and to refocus energy on the challenges that remain. It's not easy to maintain enthusiasm over the extended time it may take to achieve a goal.

How does a school (or an external partner) initiate, develop, and maintain partnerships like these? At Best Practice High School we have focused primarily on our school-to-work partnerships with businesses, community organizations, and elementary schools, which we've described from the learner's point of view in Chapter 7. Recruiting and maintaining strong relationships with our partners is a massive job. Every week, 440 students go out to the seventy sites around the city. It's asking a lot to require people to take time from their normal work to supervise and mentor the kids at the sites. Some sites prove to be more educational and supportive of the students than others. And, inevitably, some problems develop. Internship coordinator Carolyn Smith explains the process of steering this huge effort:

> For recruiting sites, luck helps. It's best if you have a name of someone to talk to at the company. And you make lots and lots of phone calls—every hospital in the city, for example. You tell them how great the kids are. They need plenty of information—the goals of the program, the time involved, how the program works. We have a PR packet we send out that describes the school, the mission of the internship program, how it works, the time involved. It also includes a list of all the other partners, and quotes from them and from our students.
>
> Then, to keep a partner on track requires plenty of communication. We make sure everyone's expectations are clear. Naturally, there will be problems, with 440 kids out there every week. The important thing is to be honest and keep the communication going. Talk to the kid, talk to the supervisor at the site. The students' journals help to clarify what's really happening, because sometimes the kids will write things that they don't say verbally. Making site visits shows your concern. I wish I had time for more of them. And it's important for the partners to evaluate the program, so they feel part of the process.

While many sites have been loyal supporters for all four years of our existence, some don't work out and either choose to withdraw or are advised to end the relationship. Many improve with experience. At Illinois Masonic Hospital, for instance, when Best Practice students complained that they were learning nothing from their clerical filing jobs, their supervisor, Sandy Rowe, met with Carolyn Smith to solve the problem. In a creative twist, they realized that students could be paired with adult volunteers, opening up a wide variety of tasks for the kids. In addition, our students would be rotated through a number of different departments at the hospital.

Since we've already described the Best Practice school-to-work partnership quite extensively, we'll conclude with an outstanding example from another location, Brighton High School, in Boston. Brighton is a moderate-sized school of just under one thousand students with a 93 percent minority population. It features a hybrid structure with traditional departments for core subjects, elective courses for interests such as art, music, dance, or world languages, and five small learning communities focused on particular career pathways. The five pathways, developed gradually over a nine-year period, are:

- The School of Business and Technology
- The School of Health Professions
- The School of Law, Government, and Public Service
- The School of Media, Arts, and Communication
- The TeachBoston Academy.

Partnerships that support these career programs include St. Elizabeth's Medical Center, WGBH Public Radio and Television, Genzyme Inc. (medical genetics, equipment, and pharmaceutical producer), Allston-Brighton Healthy Boston, Burns and Levinson law firm, Boston University, Boston College, and Mt. Ida College. Courses in career areas feature field trips, guest speakers, community service, and "externships" with appropriate partners. Professional development for faculty has included visits to the pathways externship sites. Components of the Health Professions program, for instance, include

- college courses
- Project ProTech, a program involving junior and senior years, plus two years postsecondary training with clinical rotations in hospitals, part-time employment during the school year, and full-time jobs in the summer
- nursing assistance training at St. Elizabeth's Hospital for interested seniors

- summer jobs and internships through the Boston Private Industry Council.

Comments one teacher, "Learning does not begin and end in the classroom. I have not changed my methods of teaching but have expanded them." As reported by visitors from the American Youth Policy Forum, this teacher "now conducts project-based lessons, follows the students on the job, and tailors her biology and chemistry classes to their hospital work experiences and expectations" (Partee 1997).

Parent Partnerships

Best Practice Students Speak Out on Parent Involvement

The school connects with my family a lot. The grades I get my parents have to look at. And if there's a problem with them, there has to be a connection between the school and my parents. The relationship between them should be nothing but respect for both of them, and communication. Because if there's neither one of those, how could they possibly talk about me?

Parents stay at home. Teachers stay at school. They don't need to *ever* mix.

This school really does try to connect parents with the school. . . . My mom knows all my teachers and gets along with most of them. High school teachers and students should have a professional relationship like my mom has with the teachers.

My school doesn't connect with my family at all, unless my mother comes up to school.

The school has easy access to my parents. It keeps me on top of my work and book smart. Parents should be more involved with students' school life because if the parents aren't involved, the students won't care.

There are many ways that parental involvement can influence and strengthen a school, none of course being mutually exclusive:

- Schools can organize parent workshops—ongoing groups that identify various needs, gather information on issues they identify, whether curriculum or safety or upgrading computers. Such groups often have the broader goal of helping parents become an integral part of the school community.

- Parents can sit on committees that plan for school change.
- Parent volunteers can provide tutoring, conduct special projects, or raise funds for particular needs at the school.
- Parents can undertake lobbying campaigns to obtain resources for the school to build a new gym, rehab crumbling infrastructure, and so on.
- Schools can offer specific courses for parents, for example, how to support students at home and developing their own skills in areas like computers or written communication.

Enacting any of these requires that schools take active measures to build bridges to parents and families. This applies especially to high schools, since teenagers have such a strong need to separate from parents and develop their own sense of independence. As Jennifer Ballen and Oliver Moles observe, in *Strong Families, Strong Schools*:

> While many parents have strong feelings of support for the schools their children actually attend, with 70 percent of all public school parents giving their children's school a grade of A or B, there still is a strong feeling of disconnection with public education in general (Elam, Lowell, and Gallup 1994). Many families feel that their interests are not fully taken into account by educators. At times, parents feel that educators talk down to them or speak in educational jargon they do not understand, while the majority of teachers feel that parents need to be more engaged in the education of their child (Peter D. Hart 1994). Educators need to be willing to recognize the extent of this disconnection as a precondition for involving families in their children's education. (Ballen and Moles 1995, Chap. 2, p. 3 of website version)

Ballen and Moles propose the following strategies to help schools connect more effectively with parents:

- Train teachers to work with parents.
- Reduce cultural barriers and language barriers.
- Evaluate parents' needs.
- Accommodate families' work schedule.
- Use technology to link parents to classrooms.
- Make school visits easier.
- Establish a home-school coordinator.

- Promote family learning.
- Give parents a voice in school decisions.

Our close association with James Vopat's Parent Project, begun in Milwaukee, Wisconsin, has helped us understand the importance and power of in-depth workshops that let parents set the agenda for concerns to be explored (Vopat 1994, 1998). These workshops are carefully designed to help parents feel welcomed and comfortable at the school and to provide information on particular issues the parents themselves decide are important. Best practice classroom strategies are employed, both to help parents share ideas and backgrounds and to acquaint them with the good teaching approaches being instituted in the school. Parents, together with teachers, write and/or talk about their own experiences with school, read relevant good literature that illuminates school and family issues, and discuss their reading in literature circles.

One variation on this program that Best Practice High School parents have enjoyed is the parent book club. In this simple structure, volunteer parents join in book discussion groups based on the Literature Circles model being used in their children's classrooms (Daniels 1994). The parents select from an array of current and interesting adult titles, keep personal reading logs, and meet Saturday mornings to share their responses to the books they have read. The parents testify that this experience has helped them "fall in love with reading"—some for the first time, and some others rediscovering the lost joy of books. The activity puts parents directly in touch with what their children are experiencing in the classroom and prepares them to help kids with Lit Circle homework, reading logs, and presentations. Such activities build a powerful base of comfort, understanding, and commitment that can then be focused on practical efforts to improve the school. And, of course, they demonstrate best practice teaching that is going on in its classrooms.

In his recent book on the Parent Project, *More Than Bake Sales*, Jim Vopat makes very clear the essential combination of purposeful curricular concerns and community building that is needed in working with parents, just as much as with students:

- *leadership* that helps ensure parent involvement actually happens
- *sharing* that gives everyone involved a voice
- *new information* about aspects of the school
- *home activities* that extend the parent workshops into the community, whether through supporting students' learning directly or pursuing special projects

- *firsthand experience* that demonstrates for parents the kinds of learning the school is promoting for the students

- *a supportive atmosphere* including food, child care, and other elements that help parents feel welcomed

- *book reading* that involves parents in powerful, shared reflective experiences

- *journals* in which parents record family experiences, photos, and art that help celebrate family and connect with their children

- *fun*, which builds trust, and shared, energized experience

- *children at the center*, that is, focusing on furthering students' education

- *flexibility* to adjust to the issues and concerns that parents bring up. (Vopat 1998, 26–27)

At Best Practice High School, parent involvement has been challenging because our families are scattered throughout the city, making it difficult for many to attend meetings. Nevertheless a number of activities are essential for us. First, like every other Chicago public school, we have a Local School Council, comprised of six parents, two community members, two teachers, the principal, and one student. This is a legal governing body, elected at most schools, but appointed at newer small schools like ours. The council chooses the principal, evaluates her performance, and decides whether to renew her contract. It votes on policy matters, approves discretionary budget items, and reviews and approves the school improvement plan. While some Chicagoans may question the efficacy of the Local School Councils, their continued operation represents a remarkable step in community involvement for a big-city school system.

Through a parent-program grant from the Chicago Annenberg Challenge, obtained by one of our partners, Business and Professional People in the Public Interest, parent consultant Mark Rodriguez organizes programs each year, based on parents' interests. One series focused on Best Practice curriculum, starting with an overview and featuring a different subject area at each session. A four-session conflict resolution program included parents from a number of the feeder schools in the neighborhood. And for another series, visiting speakers discussed financial planning for college, how to complete application forms, and other college issues. Best Practice parents come to our five-day summer residential Walloon Institute to learn about innovative curriculum and exchange ideas with parents and teachers from other schools around the country. Midyear and at the end of the school year, Mark holds evaluation and goal-setting sessions for parents to discuss how school is going for their kids, how they liked this year's parent program, and workshops they'd like for the future. Gradually, the program is building a base of involved parents, though much more is needed to fully involve our parents in the school.

SCHOOL NETWORKS

It's a time-honored tradition that teachers go into their classrooms, close the door, practice their own brand of instruction, and share very little with comrades. There are many understandable reasons for this. Some fear low performance evaluations from their principals. In many schools, just as in other organizations, administrators may not know how to build a supportive and trusting community. And new curriculum is often mandated without meaningful involvement of the teachers, resulting in understandable resistance by the people who must make it work. In a school building where each adult is intensely occupied in her own separate room, one of the easiest ways to retain a modicum of autonomy is to say little, while quietly doing things one's own way.

We've talked elsewhere in this book about creating community and giving voice to teachers in their own buildings. But an additional strategy for deprivatizing the classroom is to organize school networks to bring teachers (and parents and administrators) together in groups and to one another's buildings.

At the Center for City Schools, we've learned some tricks to help such activities go well. While local conferences and meetings have been effective, by far our most successful large-scale program for connecting teachers with one another has been our five-day residential retreat, the Walloon Institute. Using grant funds and state Chapter I moneys, our network schools send groups of Chicago teachers, administrators, and parents to northern Michigan for an intensive week of workshops, planning time, and—dare we mention the word—fun. Some schools put their whole staff on a bus and send them up together. We've added a kids' program to make it easier for parents to attend, and the kids add a wonderful touch, reminding us daily about why we're there.

The Institute program, developed and guided each year by coauthor Harvey Daniels, includes presentations by nationally known education experts and children's literature authors, daily sessions with a continuity group, and workshops on special topics that participants request. Since the Institute welcomes educators from throughout the country, Chicagoans rub elbows with people from other cities, suburbs, and rural areas, so they learn about the challenges and successes at schools in other places. And they return home not only informed and refreshed, but with larger perspectives on the possibilities in their own buildings.

Another valuable networking strategy has been cross-building visits. Because teaching is a complex activity, highly dependent on small organizational moves and communication strategies that make it work smoothly, teachers are highly appreciative of the rare opportunities for them to see good classrooms in action. Our observation visits at Best Practice High School are carefully structured two-day programs. As we described in Chapter 11, these visits combine observation, one-on-one discussion between observers and observed teachers, and workshop time for the visiting educators to reflect on what they've seen, and what they'll bring back to their own classrooms.

Our next step in networking, now under way, is to bring together a group of high schools, three in the city and three in the suburbs, one small but the others ranging from medium to large. Some of these schools boast highly developed innovations in curriculum, scheduling, and structural features, while others are just starting on a new path. All are learning from one another and comparing their various solutions to common problems. While Best Practice High School has designed a schoolwide schedule with time periods that vary from day to day, Addison Trail, in the suburbs, has developed a teaming structure that allows for flexible time use during the half-day grouping of periods when each team works with its students. Best Practice teachers can learn from Sullivan High School faculty how to conduct student portfolio demonstrations. Several schools are at work planning new freshman year programs. Teachers in all of the schools are learning about ways to make their classrooms more active and engaging. While the day-to-day life of a teacher is focused on the intense demands of helping all their kids learn, it's also tremendously encouraging for each one to know how others are working toward the same goals.

UNIVERSITY SUPPORT

We'll conclude by describing one more kind of partnership, namely, our own school-university connection, which has provided many of the stories and strategies for this book. The key to this relationship is that it must be as reciprocal as possible, not some arrangement for university gurus to hand down wisdom from above or to exploit the school for research projects. Creating a meaningful relationship involves an extended process of building trust, discovering each party's strengths, points of view, and sensitivities. Perhaps we can provide a picture of what one partnership looks like—not because it's ideal, but to describe many of the realities that such a process must address.

As the school was being planned, we three university partners took a very large role, simply because the teachers preparing to take positions at the school were themselves busy teaching and, being the highly devoted teachers they were, had little time for outside projects. We, however, were extremely fortunate that our dean, now provost, Linda Tafel, with her foresight and commitment to progressive education in public schools, assigned significant proportions of our time to this work. We were the proposal writers, the real-estate agents searching for the right location, political lobbyists, budget planners, and haunters of committee meetings.

Then, the day school began, students arrived and the teachers began addressing the overwhelming task of working with classrooms of overactive ninth graders (mercifully, we began just with one grade level and added a new entering class each year). They also had to create from scratch every policy, practice, and structure needed to run a high school. We've described how we university people stood by, wondering how we could now help, and questioning why all our idealistic plans and images weren't immediately bursting into full bloom. It took a full year to find longer-term roles that were meaningful and that didn't leave us as mere ivory-tower dreamers with time on our hands.

Gradually, this worked itself out. Most obvious has been our role as staff developers, retreat planners, and grant writers, which we described in Chapter 11. But we also learned to simply be present as equal partners, joining in at faculty meetings, helping to interview new teacher candidates, participating in policy decision making. We've pitched in on particular projects and programs, especially when the faculty did not have time to initiate them alone. Steve worked with Sonja Kosanovic to develop and then guide the peer mediation program. Marilyn helped Shelley Freeman, our first internship coordinator, to conduct the job fair for students to learn about business and organization positions available for their internships. Harvey worked with lead teacher Tom Daniels to order computer equipment for the lab and classrooms and, later, to develop students' digital portfolios. All three of us helped with some of the first integrated inquiry projects conducted with the entire freshman class.

In some ways, we have been useful because we are outsiders, particularly in facilitating communication—between staff and the principal, between people serving different functions in the school, and between those experiencing conflicts. We think of ourselves, too, as keepers of the vision at Best Practice, not only by articulating goals and principles with the teachers, but by speaking and writing about what it takes to make high school education meaningful and effective—as we are now trying to do in this book. However, we are repeatedly reminded of how much this task really depends on the teachers, as they find creative ways to enact the student-centered concepts we believe in.

For example, when the teachers encountered great frustration with the initial integrated learning units that they tried in the first year of the school, it was they who began to invent effective solutions for the problems. A central issue was that when students had lots of choice in subject matter for their first research projects, many simply bogged down, obtaining very little information as the unit dragged on with no visible result. One solution teachers developed was to design smaller projects, with choices provided at key points but not throughout every step. The first such unit they dubbed the Island Nations project, combining work in social studies, English, and art. Peter Thomas, the geography teacher, taught concepts about the relationship between geographical features and the social structures developed in various cultural groups. The students worked in groups to imagine their own islands with particular geographic features. Then in English they invented documents to reflect the life of societies that might live on such islands. In art they created representations of their island geographies in the form of sewn rugs and plaster topographic maps. Student choice focused primarily in their imaginative writings, island maps, and visual designs.

In a further development, for the Isms project described earlier in this book, the sophomore teachers reorganized so that each one, whatever his or her normal teaching role, spent a week teaching background on one type of social discrimination—discrimination by race, age, gender, sexual orientation, and so on. This provided students with a base of prior knowledge so that they could make informed and committed choices about what to investigate next and how to express their learning. Thus, the teachers taught us how a creative design could integrate many elements—offering student choice and giving needed instruction; providing historical information and connecting with present real-world issues; using whole-class, individual, and small-group work.

In a variety of other ways, the teachers are equals in our relationship. It is they, far more than we, who can speak with complete credibility to teachers from other schools about the challenges involved in making best practice come alive in an urban high school. They give presentations at conferences. They welcome education students to their classrooms for clinical observation and student teaching. And, of course, they share their insights for publications like this one. They help us understand how every choice we make involves a trade-off and a balance between competing needs for kids' learning and overall growth. And they continue to teach us about the tremendous challenges they face and the courage and creativity it takes to build an effective, student-centered high school program for ordinary kids within any large city bureaucracy.

Finally, as partners we learn every day from the students. Experiences at our internships show us how kids who act loud and silly in the school hallways can turn into dignified citizens when they have a responsible role to play. Students working earnestly in small groups in physics lab show us how we can use their intense need for social interaction as a tool for learning. Kids busy in the computer lab for hours after school show us how desperately they prefer the nurturing atmosphere of the building over hanging out in their neighborhoods. Students interviewing our new teacher candidates show us how they long for active, meaningful roles in their community. Even our most reluctant students keep us honest, reminding us just how challenging but important it is to help a teenager with a history of failure and anger to begin believing in himself or herself and to work hard for a future.

FINDING YOUR NEXT STEPS

Gather: Make a list of people or groups in your community who might be interested in helping your high school to change and improve—not just by contributing money or computers, or ceremonially "adopting" the school, but by getting involved with significant change. Invite some of these people to tour your school. Introduce them to administrators, teachers, students. Help them get to know the school and the good people in it. In a discussion after the tour, ask your potential partners what positive things they recall from their own high school experience. And what negative things do they recall? These questions help get noneducators away from stereotyped or mechanistic images of what school should be. Then share with them some of the ways they might help—whether through school-to-work internships, involvement with a curriculum improvement effort, or funding for a special project.

Read and Plan: Obtain copies of *The Parent Project* or *More Than Bake Sales*, both by James Vopat, and invite a small group of teachers, administrators, and parents to read and discuss one of these books or selections from it. After the discussion, invite the group to plan a workshop series for involving parents more integrally in the school. Ask the parents what their greatest concerns and questions are about the school and their children. Plan to use the most effective avenue of communication to invite parents to an initial workshop. It may be through neighborhood flyers, announcements at local church services, or a neighborhood walk, as was used at Roosevelt High School in Dallas. Consider starting the series with an initial program featuring an inviting theme such as Family Album Night, in which families bring family photos to mount and describe in albums you provide. Schedule it when the most parents are likely to attend. Provide child care for younger siblings. Include teachers and administrators in the program.

Interview: If you wish to create a university partnership, schedule a meeting of university and school people to introduce themselves to one another. Use a structured format in which each group tells about themselves, and the other group asks questions and then discusses their own thoughts and reactions before the agenda moves on. Ask each group to explain what they have to offer and what they hope to gain. As school and university move toward working together, representatives from each should visit the other—university people to learn the assets and needs at the school, and school people to learn and evaluate the approach in other public school projects the university has conducted.

Chapter 13
Graduation Day

I didn't go to a high school—I created one.

—Carlton Jackson

On June 5, 2000, in the auditorium at Chicago's Field Museum, just down the corridor from the famous gallery of dinosaur skeletons, the very first class from Best Practice High School graduated. Ninety-seven seniors, our precious pioneers, walked across the stage and received their diplomas. In the audience were about a thousand beaming mothers and fathers, aunts and uncles, grandparents, siblings, and even a few babies of BPHS seniors, cradled in the arms of proud relatives as their mothers walked across the stage. In a student-planned and student-hosted ceremony, the seniors looked back on four years in their newborn school, gave some thanks, poked some fun, sang some beautiful songs, and made their farewells.

There was a lot of Kleenex used that afternoon, much of it by a staff of thirty educators who couldn't believe that this day had so suddenly arrived. We felt a nearly overwhelming pride at seeing these young people, who had literally grown up before our eyes, striding across the stage and into adulthood with such assurance and confidence. Who were these grown-ups, dressed with such exquisite care, their heads held so high? We had always joked that if Best Practice didn't work out as a school, we could always turn it into a modeling agency. But today, as they paraded by, each with his or her own special style and look and walk, they looked more beautiful than ever.

We felt the sadness of realizing that these faces would be gone from our halls next year. We'd worked hard to provide a safe and strong base for these kids, but what about us? These kids were our anchor, too. What were we going to do without them?

We also relived the loss of our lead teacher and founder, Tom Daniels, gone since October, now offered a beautiful tribute by Alex Chaparro and Itanzia Wilcox. We grieved and smiled as Kathy Daniels spoke of her husband and their extraordinary partnership.

And then there was the music—thank God for the music. The sweet sound of Phyllis Curtwright's amazing choir, belting it out, covering every genre of music from fugue to gospel with the audience singing and clapping along.

Afterward, there was a crush in the lobby. Hugs. Handshakes. Bouquets of flowers. Introductions of families. Bursts of laughter. Posing for photographs. Video cameras rolling. The energy and cheer of these brand-new graduates from their brand-new school echoed off the walls of the old museum. A guard strolled by, investigating the din, took a cool look as if to say, "What are they so happy about?" and then walked on.

Gradually parents started scooping up the toddlers, gathering coats, assembling family members, and saying their good-byes. Trooping out into the bright June sun, they headed off to ninety-three different family celebrations in neighborhoods all over the city. They returned, kids and parents, to their homes, to the same kitchen tables where four years ago they sat in front of a brochure for a brand-new school with a funny name, and for some reason, said yes.

This book is dedicated to Tom Daniels, the founding co-lead teacher of Best Practice High School, a longtime colleague and dear friend. When Tom passed away in October 1999, the *Chicago Tribune* wrote:

Long before he co-founded an innovative public high school in Chicago that would become a model for educators nationwide, Thomas Daniels was known for his unfailing commitment to the philosophy that, given the right support, every child can excel. "Way before it was a cliché, he was absolutely devoted to bringing out the best in every single child," said Chicago Public Schools Chief Education Officer, Cozetter Buckney, a colleague of Mr. Daniels for more than a decade at Austin High School. "He was amazing in that way."

He spent nearly four decades as a progressive educator in Chicago Public Schools, including the past four years as a lead teacher at Best Practice High School, which he helped design and establish.

During his career, Mr. Daniels grew increasingly committed to the values of small schools and individual attention, colleagues and friends said. In 1995, he and his wife, Kathy, also an educator, combined these principles when the Chicago Public Schools embarked on an initiative to foster small-scale learning environments. Backed by a coalition of institutions, the Danielses led the effort to found Best Practice High School as an alternative to conventional schools. Their work paid off in 1996 when the school enrolled its first class.

Mr. Daniels also was a senior fellow of the Illinois Writing Project, in which he and his wife led scores of teacher workshops to help educators improve their schools. In addition, he published several articles about teaching, language, and school reform. Earlier this year, he received the Enterprise Development foundation's Achievement Award for his longtime service to public education.

Before starting Best Practice, Mr. Daniels taught English at Austin, Mather, and Farragut High Schools for more than 30 years. A graduate of Amundsen High School, Mr. Daniels received a bachelor's degree from Northwestern University and a master's degree from the Adler Institute.

The five of us—Tom, Kathy, Steve, Marilyn, and Smokey—worked together for several decades in several combinations; some of our relationships trace back to the 1960s. We've studied together, led workshops, written articles, created a writing project, prowled New York, had backyard barbecues, drafted grant proposals, started a new school, fought and made up, watched each other's children grow, and faced Tom's illness and death.

Now, as the four of us carry on the work, Tom's contribution will be more indirect, but no less powerful. His voice is always strong in our ears. Over and over again, he said three things we will try not to forget as we grow the school he envisioned:

We are a work in progress.
This is the hardest work we have ever done.
We are in this for the long haul.

Works Cited

Aber, J. L., J. L. Brown, and C. C. Henrich. 1999. *Teaching Conflict Resolution: An Effective School-Based Approach to Violence.* New York: National Center for Children in Poverty.

Allen, J., and K. Gonzalez. 1997. *There's Room for Me Here.* York, Maine: Stenhouse.

Apple, M. W. 1993. *Official Knowledge: Democratic Education in a Conservative Age.* New York and London: Routledge.

Atwell, N. 1998. *In the Middle: New Understandings About Writing, Reading and Learning.* Portsmouth, N.H.: Boynton-Cook Heinemann.

Ayers, W., M. Klonsky, and G. Lyon, eds. 2000. *A Simple Justice: The Challenge of Small Schools.* New York: Teachers College Press.

Ballen, J., and O. Moles. 1995. *Strong Families, Strong Schools: Building Community Partnerships for Learning.* Diane Publishing Co.

Barth, R. 1990. *Improving Schools from Within.* San Francisco: Jossey-Bass.

Barton, P. E., and R. J. Coley. 1992. *America's Smallest School: The Family.* Princeton, N.J.: Educational Testing Service.

Beane, J. A. 1991. "The Middle School: The Natural Home of Integrated Curriculum." *Educational Leadership* (October) 49(2): 9–13.

———. 1995a. *Toward a Coherent Curriculum.* Yearbook of the Association for Supervision and Curriculum Development. Alexandria, Va.: Association for Supervision and Curriculum Development.

———. 1995b. "Curriculum Integration and the Disciplines of Knowledge." *Phi Delta Kappan* 76: 616–22.

———. 1997. *Curriculum Integration: Designing the Core of Democratic Education.* New York: Teachers College Press.

Bigelow, B. 1994. "Getting off the Track: Stories from the Untracked Classroom." In *Rethinking Our Classrooms: Teaching for Equity and Justice.* Milwaukee, Wis.: Rethinking Schools.

Black, P. 2000. Speech given at the Principal Investigators for Local Systemic Change, annual meeting of the National Science Foundation, Washington, D.C., January.

Braddock, J. H., and R. E. Slavin. 1993. "Why Ability Grouping Must End: Achieving Excellence and Equity in American Education." *Journal of Intergroup Relations* 10(1): 51–64.

Brodhagen, B. 1995. "The Situation Made Us Special." In *Democratic Schools*, ed. M. W. Apple and J. Beane. Alexandria, Va.: Association for Supervision and Curriculum Development.

Callahan, R. 1962. *Education and the Cult of Efficiency*. Chicago: University of Chicago Press.

Chang, I. 1997. *The Rape of Nanking: The Forgotten Holocaust of World War II*. New York: Basic Books.

Coalition of Essential Schools. 1995a. "A Big School Divides to Go for High Quality Work." *Performance* (January): 17.

———. 1995b. "A Big School Takes the Team Approach." *Performance* (April): 20.

Commeyras, M., K. Sherrill, and K. Wuenker. 1996. "Trusting Students' Questions About Literature: Stories Across Contexts." In *Lively Discussions*, ed. Linda Gambrel and Janet Almasi. Newark, Del.: International Reading Association.

Crain, R. L., et al. 1997. *The Effects of Magnet Education on High Schools and Their Graduates*. Berkeley, Calif.: National Center on Research in Vocational Education.

Daniels, H. 1994. *Literature Circles: Voice and Choice in the Student-Centered Classroom*. York, Maine: Stenhouse.

Daniels, H., and M. Bizar. 1998. *Methods That Matter: Six Structures for Best Practice Classrooms*. York, Maine: Stenhouse.

Daniels, H., S. Zemelman, and M. Bizar. 1999. "Whole Language Works: Sixty Years of Research." *Educational Leadership* 57(2): 32–37.

Darling-Hammond, L. 1996. *What Matters Most: Teaching for America's Future*. New York: National Commission on Teaching and America's Future.

———. 1999. *Teacher Quality and Student Achievement: A Review of State Policy Evidence*. Center for the Study of Teaching and Policy.

Darling-Hammond, L., J. Ancess, and B. Falk. 1995. *Authentic Assessment in Action: Studies of Schools and Students at Work*. Series on school reform. New York: Teachers College Press.

Dauber, S. L., and J. L. Epstein. 1993. "Parents' Attitudes and Practices of Involvement in Inner-City Elementary and Middle Schools." In *Families and*

Schools in a Pluralistic Society, ed. N. Chavkin, 53–72. Albany: State University of New York Press.

Dewey, J. 1938, 1963. *Experience and Education*. New York: Macmillan.

Doda, Nancy. 1991. "Who's Afraid of Homebase?" *Instructor* (Fall): 24–42.

Dorning, M. 2000. "FBI Primer for Schools Lists Signs of Danger." *Chicago Tribune*, September 7, 14.

Dreeben, R. 1968. *On What Is Learned in School*. Reading, Mass.: Addison-Wesley Publishing Co.

Elam, S. M., C. R. Lowell, and A. M. Gallup. 1994. "The 26th Annual Phi Delta Kappa/Gallup Poll of the Public's Attitudes Toward the Public Schools." *Phi Delta Kappan* (September) 75(1).

"Empowering Students: Essential Schools' Missing Link." 1994. *Horace* (September).

Epstein, A. W. 1999. "A New Way to Teach Science Backward!" *Scientific American Explorations* (summer).

Erb, T., and N. Doda. 1989. *Team Organization: Promise, Practices and Possibilities*. Washington D.C.: National Education Association.

Ferrara, J. 1996. *Peer Mediation: Finding a Way to Care*. York, Maine: Stenhouse.

Fisher, P. J. L., C. Blachowicz, and J. Smith. 1991. "Vocabulary Learning in Literature Discussion Groups." In *Learner Factors/Teacher Factors: Issues in Literacy Research and Instruction*, ed. J. Zutell and S. McCormick, 201–9. Chicago: National Reading Conference.

Frank, A. 1993. *Anne Frank: Diary of a Young Girl*. New York: Bantam Books.

Fulwiler, T. 1987. *The Journal Book*. Portsmouth, N.H.: Heinemann.

Funkhouser, J. E., and M. Gonzales. 1997. *Family Involvement in Children's Education: Successful Local Approaches*. Washington, D.C.: Office of Educational Research and Improvement.

Garbarino, J. 1999. *Lost Boys: Why Our Sons Turn Violent and How We Can Save Them*. New York: Free Press.

Garcia, K. 1994. *Building Alliances in Urban Education: Community Partnerships*. Tempe, Ariz.: Education Policy Studies Laboratory, Arizona State University.

Gardner, Howard. 1993. *Frames of Mind: The Theory of Multiple Intelligences*. 10th ed. New York: Basic Books.

Glasser, W. 1986. *Control Theory in the Classroom*. New York: Perennial Library.

———. 1998. *Choice Theory: A New Psychology of Personal Freedom*. New York: HarperCollins.

Hallinan, M., ed. 1994. *Restructuring Schools: Promising Practices and Policies*. New York: Plenum Press.

Harvey, S., and A. Goudvis. 1999. *Strategies That Work: Teaching Comprehension to Enhance Understanding*. York, Maine: Stenhouse.

Hill, B. C., and C. Ruptic. 1994. *Practical Aspects of Authentic Assessment*. Norwood, Mass.: Christopher Gordon.

Hill, P. T., and M. B. Celio. 1998. *Fixing Urban Schools*. Washington, D.C.: Brookings Institution Press.

Hill, P. T., G. E. Foster, and T. Gendler. 1990. *High Schools with Character*. Santa Monica, Calif.: Rand Corp.

Hirsch, E. D. 1996. *The Schools We Need and Why We Don't Have Them*. New York: Doubleday.

Holloway, J. H. 2000. "The Promise and Pitfalls of Site-Based Management." *Educational Leadership* 57(7): 81–82.

Hoover, H. D., and G. B. Bray. 1995. "The Research and Development Phase: Can a Performance Assessment Be Cost-Effective?" Paper presented at the annual meeting of the American Educational Research Association, San Francisco, Calif.

Huxley, A. 1989. *Brave New World*. New York: Harper & Row.

Hyde, A., and M. Bizar. 1989. *Thinking in Context: Teaching Cognitive Processes Across the Elementary School Curriculum*. New York: Longman.

Jackson, P. 1968. *Life in Classrooms*. New York: Holt, Rinehart & Winston.

Johnson, D., R. Johnson, and E. Holubec. 1991. *Cooperation in the Classroom*. Edina, Minn.: Interaction Book Co.

Klonsky, M. 1995. *Small Schools: The Numbers Tell a Story. A Review of the Research and Current Experiences*. Chicago: University of Illinois.

Kohn, A. 1993. "Choices for Children: Why and How to Let Students Decide." *Phi Delta Kappan* 75(1): 23–34.

Kozol, J. 1991. *Savage Inequalities: Children in America's Schools*. New York: Crown Publishers.

Krynock, K., and L. Robb. 1999. "Problem Solved: How to Coach Cognition." *Educational Leadership* 57(3).

Kubota, Carole. 1993. *Education-Business Partnerships: Scientific Work Experience Programs*. Columbus, Ohio: ERIC/CSMEE.

Ladson-Billings, G. 1994. *Successful Teachers of African American Children*. San Francisco, Calif.: Jossey-Bass.

LeBlanc, A. N. 1999. "The Troubled Life of Boys." *New York Times*, 22 August.

Lee, L. E., and M. Zimmerman. 1999. "Passion, Action, and a New Vision for Student Voice: Learnings from the Manitoba School Improvement Program Inc." Manitoba School Improvement Program Inc. On website at www.sunvalley.ca/msip.

Lee, V. E., A. S. Bryk, and J. B. Smith. 1993. "The Organization of Effective Secondary Schools." *Review of Research in Education* 19: 171–267.

———, and J. B. Smith. 1995. "Effects of High School Restructuring and Size on Early Gains in Achievement and Engagement." *Sociology of Education* 68(October): 241–70.

———, J. B. Smith, T. E. Perry, and M. A. Smiley. 1999. *Social Support, Academic Press, and Student Achievement: A View from the Middle Grades in Chicago.* Chicago: Consortium on Chicago School Research.

Leroux, C. 2000. "On the Cutting Edge." *Chicago Tribune*, 27 January.

Lester, N., and C. Onore. 1990. *Learning Change.* Portsmouth, N.H.: Boynton/Cook.

Livingston, C. 1992. *Teachers as Leaders: Evolving Roles.* Washington, D.C.: National Education Association.

MacIver, D. J., S. B. Plank, and R. Balfance. "Working Together to Become Proficient Readers: Early Impact of the Talent Development Middle School's Student Team Literature Program." Baltimore: Center for Research on the Education of Students Placed at Risk. Report 15 (August).

Meier, D. 1995. "Small Schools, Big Results." *American School Board Journal* 182(7): 37–40.

———. 1996. *The Power of Their Ideas: Lessons for America from a Small School in Harlem.* Boston: Beacon Press.

Mosco, M. 2000. "How Albany Failed English." *New York Times*, 5 February.

Nabhan, G., and S. Trimble. 1994. *The Geography of Childhood.* Boston: Beacon Press.

National Association of Secondary School Principals. 1996. *Breaking Ranks.* Reston, Va.: National Association of Secondary School Principals.

National Center for Research in Vocational Education. "Fairdale High School Magnet Career Academy." On website at ncrve.berkeley.edu/abstracts.

National Commission on Excellence in Education. 1983. *A Nation at Risk: The Imperative for Educational Reform.* Washington, D.C.: U.S. Department of Education.

National Commission on Time in Education. 1994. *Prisoners of Time.* Washington, D.C.: Goals 2000.

National Educational Technology Standards for Students: Connecting Curriculum and Technology. Eugene, Ore.: International Society for Technology in Education.

National Middle School Association. "NMSA Research Summary #9: Advisory Programs." Website document.

National Resource Center for Youth Mediation. 1995. *Student Mediation in Secondary Schools, Training and Implementation Guide.* Albuquerque, N. Mex.: New Mexico Center for Dispute Resolution.

Newmann, F. 1995. *Successful School Restructuring.* Madison, Wis.: Center on Organization and Restructuring of Schools.

Newmann, F., G. Lopez, and A. Bryk. 1998. *The Quality of Intellectual Work in Chicago Schools: A Baseline Report.* Chicago: Consortium on Chicago School Research.

Newmann, F. M., A. S. Bryk, and J. Nagaoka. 2000. "Authentic Intellectual Work and Stardardized Tests: Conflict or Coexistence?" Consortium on Chicago School Research.

Noble, A. J., S. Deemer, and B. Davis. 1996. "School-Based Management." Policy brief. Newark, Del.: Delaware Education Research and Development Center.

North Central Regional Educational Laboratory. 1995. "Critical Issue: Transferring Decisionmaking to Local Schools: Site-Based Management." Website report at www.ncrel.org/sdrs/areas/issues/environment/go/go100.htm.

Oakes, J., with T. Ormseth, R. Bell, and P. Camp. 1990. *Multiplying Inequalities: The Effects of Race, Social Class, and Tracking on Opportunities to Learn Mathematics and Sciences.* Santa Monica, Calif.: Rand Corp.

Partee, G. 1997. "High School Reform and Systemic Districtwide Reform in Boston, Massachusetts." Washington, D.C.: American Youth Policy Forum. Website report.

Perie, M., and D. Baker. 1997. *Job Satisfaction Among America's Teachers: Effects of Workplace Conditions, Background Characteristics, and Teacher Compensation.* Washington, D.C.: National Center for Education Statistics.

Peter D. Hart Research Associates, Inc. 1994. *Internal AFT Survey of Elementary and Secondary School Teachers' Views on School Reform.*

Philips, J. 1998. "Students as Responsible Resources." Bay Area, Calif.: Partners in School Innovation. On website at www.partnersinschools.org.

Porter, C., and J. Cleland. 1995. *The Portfolio as a Learning Strategy.* Portsmouth, N.H.: Boynton/Cook.

Preston, R. 1995. *The Hot Zone*. New York: Anchor Books.

Raphael, T., and S. McMahon. 1997. *The Book Club Connection: Literacy Learning and Classroom Talk*. New York: Teachers College Press.

Raywid, M. 1995. *The SubSchools/Small Schools Movement—Taking Stock*. Madison, Wis.: Center on Organization and Restructuring of Schools.

Resnick, M. D., et al. 1997. "Protecting Adolescents from Harm: Findings from the National Longitudinal Study of Adolescent Health." *JAMA* 278(10): 823–32.

Rhodes, S. 2000. "Getting Testy." *Chicago Magazine* (February) 49(2): 41–43.

Richards, Cindy. 2000. "Annenberg Looks for Lessons as Program Winds Down." *Catalyst* 11(6): 1, 5–7.

Rogers, C., and H. J. Freiberg. 1994. *Freedom to Learn*. New York: Macmillan.

Rubin, B. M., and J. Graham. 2000. "School Provides Unique Antidote for Depression," *Chicago Tribune*, 9 April, 1, 15.

Rush, P. 1999. "A City Site Classroom." *Educational Leadership* 57(3): 63–66.

Sarason, S. B. 1982. *The Culture of the School and the Problem of Change*. 2d ed. Boston: Allyn & Bacon.

Schoenstein, R. 1990. Interview.

Seceda, W. 1992. "Race, Ethnicity, Social Class, Language and Achievement." In *Handbook of Research on Mathematics Teaching and Learning*, ed. D. Grows. Reston, Va.: National Council of Teachers of Mathematics.

Sharan, Y., and S. Sharan. 1992. *Expanding Cooperative Learning Through Group Investigation*. New York: Teachers College Press.

Sizer, T. R. 1992. *Horace's School: Redesigning the American High School*. Boston: Houghton Mifflin.

———. 1994. *Horace's Compromise: The Dilemma of the American High School*. Boston: Houghton Mifflin.

———. 1996. *Horace's Hope: What Works for the American High School*. Boston: Houghton Mifflin.

Slavin, R. 1991. "Synthesis of Research on Cooperative Learning." *Educational Leadership* 48: 71–82.

Smith, K. 1993. "Becoming the Guide on the Side." *Educational Leadership* 51(2): 35–37.

" 'So Now What?' Managing the Change Process." 1993. *Horace*, January.

Stern, D. 1997. "The Continuing Promise of Work-Based Learning." *Centerfocus* 18: 1–6, Berkeley, Calif.: National Center for Research in Vocational Education.

Stern, D., J. R. Stone, C. Hopkins, M. McMillion, and R. Crain. 1994. *School-Based Enterprise: Productive Learning in American High Schools*. San Francisco: Jossey-Bass.

Stevens, R., and R. Slavin. 1995. "Effects of a Cooperative Learning Approach in Reading and Writing on Academically Handicapped and Non-Handicapped Students." *Elementary School Journal* 95: 241–62.

Stone, J. R. 1995. "Cooperative Vocational Education in the Urban School: Towards a Systems Approach." *Education and Urban Society* 27(3): 328–52.

U.S. Labor Department. 1990. *The Secretary's Commission on Achieving the Necessary Skills (SCANS)*.

Van Slyck, M., and M. Stern. 1992. "Conflict Resolution in Educational Settings." In *Community Mediation: A Handbook for Practitioners and Researchers*, ed. G. Duffy, J. Grosch, and P. Olczak, 257–74. New York: Guilford Press.

Visher, M. G., D. Emanuel, and P. Teitelbaum. 1999. *Key High School Reform Strategies: An Overview of Research Findings*. Berkeley, Calif.: New American High Schools.

Visher, M., D. Lauen, and J. Haimson. 1999. *School-to-Work in the 1990s: A Look at Programs and Practices in American High Schools*. Washington, D.C.: U.S. Department of Education.

Vopat, J. 1994. *The Parent Project: A Workshop Approach to Parent Involvement*. York, Maine: Stenhouse.

———. 1998. *More Than Bake Sales: The Resource Guide for Family Involvement in Education*. York, Maine: Stenhouse.

Vygotsky, L. S. 1962. *Thought and Language*. Cambridge, Mass.: MIT Press.

Wang, C., and T. Owens. 1995. *The Boeing Company Applied Academics Project Evaluation: Year Four*. Portland, Ore.: Northwest Regional Educational Laboratory.

Wasley, P. A. 1991. *Teachers Who Lead: The Rhetoric of Reform and the Realities of Practice*. New York: Teachers College Press.

Wheelock, A. 1992. *Crossing the Tracks: How "Untracking" Can Save America's Schools*. New York: New Press.

Wheelock, A., and L. Lynne. 1997. "Making Detracking Work." *Harvard Education Letter* 13 (1). On website at www.hugse1.harvard.edu.

Wilhelm, J. 1995. *You Gotta BE the Book*. New York: Teachers College Press.

Witten, P. 1996. *Sketching Stories, Stretching Minds*. Portsmouth, N.H.: Heinemann.

Wood, G. 1992. *Schools That Work*. New York: Dutton.

———. 1998. *A Time to Learn*. New York: Plume.

Zemelman, S., H. Daniels, and A. Hyde. 1998. *Best Practice: New Standards for Teaching and Learning in America's Schools*. Portsmouth, N.H.: Heinemann.

Zemelman, S., P. Bearden, Y. Simmons, and P. Leki. 1999. *History Comes Home: Family Stories Across the Curriculum*. York, Maine: Stenhouse.

Index